REMEMBERING MICHIO

Michio Kushi (1926-2014)

Special Commemorative Edition
Published by Kushi Institute

Compiled and Edited
by Edward Esko and Alex Jack

REMEMBERING MICHIO
Special Commemorative Edition
Individual Essays Copyright © 2015 by the Contributors
Printed with Permission of the Contributors
ISBN: 1508852146
ISBN-13: 978-1508852148

All rights reserved. Printed in the United States of America. No portion of this book may be used or reproduced in any manner whatsoever, including digital, without written permission except in the case of brief quotations embodied in critical articles or reviews.

For further information on mail-order sales, wholesale or retail discounts, distribution, translations, and foreign rights, please contact the publishers:

Kushi Institute
198 Leland Road
Becket, Mass. 01223
(413) 623-5741
www.KushiInstitute.org

Introduction

Michio Kushi's unswerving devotion to One Peaceful World served as the North Star for the generation that came of age during the height of the nuclear arms race, the spread of chemical farming and fast food, and the medicalization of society. He and his wife Aveline introduced natural, organic foods to the modern era and taught that a balanced diet centered on whole cereal grains and other predominantly plant quality foods was the key to recovering our physical health, moral compass, and spiritual orientation. They enabled us to become our own best physicians and healers.

Michio touched and transformed the lives of countless people. Over his long, eventful life, he played many roles—son, brother, husband, father, friend, businessman, teacher, counselor, author, prophet, and spiritual guide. Whether we met him once, or enjoyed a relationship over many years, our encounters with Michio were one of the most treasured experiences of our lives.

The tributes in this book are often funny and amusing, at times perplexed and wondering, frequently wise and enlightening, but always sincere and heartfelt. They mirror the love and gratitude of the worldwide macrobiotic community that he inspired and led over the last half century.

In these pages, we glimpse Michio's many sides, as members of his family, teachers and students, counseling clients, and associates share their memories, reflections, and anecdotes. The most indelible portrait we glimpse, of course, is of Michio in the lecture room, drawing spirals on the blackboard, explaining the hitherto unexplainable, and like the commander of the *Starship Enterprise* suddenly transporting the entire class to a higher octave at warp speed with his spiritual teachings. Also familiar to many readers will be snapshots of what it was like getting personal guidance from Michio in a counseling session, unexpectedly in a classroom, or a private scolding. Off center stage, too, we glimpse life growing up in the Kushi family, living in the Kushi House, and occasional bingeing with Michio after the last class or consultation of the day. Then, most mysteriously, there are the many private moments in which Michio reveals a person's past relationships, current family situation, or future destiny that no one could possibly know.

And throughout the epic landscape of these cherished memories appear Aveline, his devoted helpmate and the heart and soul of the early American macrobiotic community; George Ohsawa, his mentor and guide; Shizuko Yamamoto, who came to New York and popularized Shiatsu; John Denver, the singer and a staunch supporter of macrobiotic education; and many other artists, scientists, physicians, healers, chefs, and natural foods pioneers who became an integral part of the movement. Midori, whom he married after Aveline passed away and helped him navigate his later years, also appears in some chronicles.

Naturally, the supporting cast also includes the many delicious, healthful foods the Kushis introduced to modern society, especially brown rice, miso, tofu, tempeh, daikon, leafy greens, nori, wakame, kombu, sea salt, gomashio, pickles, bancha twig tea, kanten, amasake, and dozens of others. As in a Noh drama, a Greek chorus, or a Shakespearean play, as Michio and Aveline taught, they are the true behind-the-scenes actors in the unfolding drama of our lives.

Together this collection forms an intimate, compelling portrait of the early days of macrobiotics in America. We share the excitement and enthusiasm of dozens of Michio's earliest students as they discover the power of food, yin and yang, and the Order of the

Universe. With the Kushis, many of them went on to start, or later staff, Erewhon, East West Foundation, *East West Journal*, Sanae and Seventh Inn restaurants, Kushi Institute, and other Boston-based macrobiotic organizations that changed the way America eats and heals. Their coming-of-age stories are intensely personal, self-reflective, and above all joyful and life-changing. From Boston, students of the Kushis spiraled across the country and around the world to start natural foods companies, restaurants, educational centers, and holistic health care practices that have shaped today's global culture.

We are grateful to all the contributors for sharing their stories and reflections. At Kushi Institute, we will continue to gather and collect memories, articles, and teachings of this remarkable man. Please send your material to Kushi Institute, 198 Leland Rd., Becket MA 01223, or email them to mlprograms@kushiinstitute. For information on the Kushi Institute and how you can help preserve Michio's teachings for future generations, please see the end of the volume.

One of the best ways to remember Michio is to embody universal principles and practices in our daily lives and become a bright, shining example of the macrobiotic way. We can also preserve his legacy and continue the dream by supporting and participating in macrobiotic education, helping to create sustainable agriculture and food practices in our local communities, and joining together with love and gratitude to create a world of enduring health and peace.

Alex Jack
Executive Director
Kushi Institute

Edward Esko
Associate Director
Kushi Institute

Becket, Massachusetts
Summer Solstice
June 21, 2015

Contributors

Cathy Albanese 8
Carlos Aponte 12
Andrea Beaman 16
Jan Belleme 19
John Belleme 21
David Briscoe 24
Simon Brown 25
Bob Carr 28
Martha C. Cottrell, M.D. 31
Mina Dobic 34
Christian Elwell 38
Edward Esko 41
Wendy Esko 50
Bernard Faber 53
Alice Fava 54
Olaf Fischer 60
Drusilla Graham 63
Virginia M. Harper 68
Rod House 69
Naomi Ichikawa 71
Alex Jack* 73
Gale Jack 83
Phil Jannetta 85
Woody Johnson 92

Sachi Kato 93
Bill Kaufman 97
Kit Kitatani 98
Ron Koetzsch 100
Susan Krieger 103
Dennis Kucinich* 106
Gabriele Kushi 110
Hisao Kushi* 113
Lawrence Hauro Kushi* 116
Norio Kushi 119
Phiya Kushi 121
Sean, Lianna, and
   Angelica Kushi 138
Janet Lacey 142
Carol Louro 143
Judy MacKenney 146
Larry MacKenney 149
Bob Mattson 155
Mitsuko Mikami 158
Tom Monte 160
Rich Myers 168
Gideon Nelissen* 171
Wieke Nelissen (with
   Horriah Nelissen)* 172

Mayumi Niimi Nishimura 176
Patricio Garcia de Parades 180
Zlatko Pejic   189
Christina Pirello   195
Jessica Porter   201
Michael Potter*   203
Sandy Pukel   206
Arthur H. Robbins   209
Evan Root*   218
Michael Rossoff   222
Naoki Sakaguchi   227
David Sergel   230
Rudy Shur   234
Kezia Snyder   237
Bill Spear   239
Jane and Lino Stanchich   243
Sanae Suzuki   246
Bill Tara   250
Eric Utne*   254
Chico Varatojo*   259
Denny Waxman   263
Melanie Brown Waxman 268
Ken Williamson   271
Toyufumi Yoshida*   276
Bettina Zumdick   278

*Originally presented at the memorial service for Michio at the Arlington Street Church in Boston on January 31, 2015. In some cases, the talks have been revised for this volume.

The Kushi Institute   280
One Peaceful World Day   282
About the Contributors   284
Michio Kushi   294

Remembering Michio
Cathy Albanese

Way back when, in 1986 while I lived in Yellow Springs, Ohio, I began to practice macrobiotics. I bought strange new products like miso and seaweed, attended cooking classes with enthusiasm, heard lectures from Kushi Institute teachers who visited, and even, I think, saw a small black-and-white photo of Michio Kushi himself on a wall poster. But I didn't think much about the sources of my new knowledge, and to me Michio, if he came to mind at all, was a kind of Ancient of Days. I wasn't sure whether he was alive or had departed, and his existence hovered in my mental space like a genial but vague and ghostly presence.

That all changed the next year when I moved to Santa Barbara and joined the local macrobiotic potluck group. There I met Elise McConnell, daughter of the founders of McConnell's Ice Cream, who not surprisingly raised her on their product. Elise at the time appeared healthy, and she was bubbly and lots of fun. She had traveled extensively in Europe and was intensively interested in macrobiotics. So when she discovered that Michio Kushi was speaking and consulting in France while she was there, she signed up to see him. She told the story of being ushered from an eerily quiet waiting room, with people who appeared to be very sick, into a consultation room where a group of very serious men were sitting at a long table with Michio in the center. Before the waiting-room experience, she had no idea that, generally, people with serious disease conditions saw Michio, and she had come because she was curious and wanted to learn. Michio looked straight at her in a few moments of discerning silence, and then he spoke firmly and declaratively — and not without a little humor. "So! You have been eating lots of ice cream!" Elise was bowled over, and — hearing the story — so was I. Now, after my almost two years of macrobiotic practice, Michio assumed stature as a living teacher and one with a near-clairvoyant ability to see.

As I grew in my macrobiotic commitments, I began attending Summer Conferences and appearing at macrobiotic events in my area or my family's on the East Coast. I ended up having three private consultations with Michio — not for serious disease but for the chronic digestive difficulties that plagued me. In the first, I remember beginning the conversation with Michio by telling him that my Western astrological chart had shown clearly that the doctors would never figure out what was wrong with me. Michio laughed and laughed, announcing that he was no doctor and that the chart was therefore nonoperational. In the second, he gave me the thrill of my life by looking at my ears and facial physiognomy and admiring a balance that he perceived. (I felt like Ms. Macro America and practically floated out of the room.) In the third, on the West Coast, the late Cecile Levin was my scribe. Michio told me to eat tangerines (they are located, in East Asian medicine, in the stomach/spleen/pancreas transformation). Cecile interrupted and, with West Coast chauvinism and orange trees growing all around us, suggested oranges instead. Michio did not blink an eye and stuck firmly with his recommendation. "No," he said, for oranges, and thumbs up for tangerines.

The time that stands out the most for me, though, did not happen as part of an individual consultation but in a group consultation in the summer of 1988. I had been practicing macrobiotics for two years, and for the second of those years had been using Celtic sea salt regularly. I had noticed that when I sat up in bed to read a novel in the evening, I would feel a pain on my right side that was strong enough to make me want to lie quickly down. "The big A," I would mutter to myself, because arthritis ran through our family. Now, at Summer Conference, after a Shiatsu treatment in which my therapist hit the kidney point on the sole of my foot and I hit the ceiling, I was seeing Michio in a group because my therapist had announced a kidney stone. When Michio came around to me as part of the consultation and I asked him whether I had a stone, he said that, indeed, I had one. But he acted as if I had a little cold. This was something straightforward and simple, his attitude and bearing conveyed, and I could easily get myself better. So with a daikon-heavy diet plan, no more Celtic sea salt, and a commitment to ginger compresses, I went home feeling empowered and ready. I had no previous knowledge of kidney stones, and in these pre-Google days no curiosity about finding out. So I didn't know I was supposed to feel lots of pain. I just knew that Michio seemed to think that this was a small matter and I could fix it. And I did! I passed the stone easily in a matter of months, astounding the people to whom I told the tale. It was only afterwards that I began to hear horror stories about kidney stones and all the pain and hospital interventions I was supposed to experience. Silently, I thanked Michio again and again for the knowledge and the confidence that he had passed on to me—a gift beyond my ability to measure.

By the 1990s, I began a slow progression through the Kushi Institute "levels," interrupted over and over again by the demands of my university career. Only in recent years, with a semi-retired status, did the progression become swifter. Through it, I had my final encounter with Michio. In March-April of 2014, our Level IV group traveled from Becket to the Brookline Marriott for a class with him. I remember the long hotel tables in the small room in which we sat and Michio at a table in front of us with a large white paper roll on an easel by his side. He began without the easel and his characteristic drawings that would follow. Instead, in deep earnest, he lectured us on the meaning and mission of Level IV training. The first three levels, he said, were for personal and family health needs, but now, in Level IV, what was most important, was the *social*. We weren't doing this for our immediate families or ourselves anymore. We had a job to do out there in the world to spark people to take control of their lives and their food and to find their path out of the sorrowful lifestyle jungle dominated by the Standard American Diet. He seemed to think that we could do that, and once again the sense of empowerment was so strongly there. We had the knowledge, and we had the ability—rational *and* intuitive—to assist others.

In typical Michio fashion, he followed the charismatic message with an exercise in which we all participated. We paired off and looked across the room at one another—a giver and a sender in each pair. We sent thoughts and feelings to our partner, and the partner reported back what he or she felt. The experience was a powerful reminder that yes, thoughts were things, and they—with their related feeling components—could affect the lives of others. The lesson stood. We needed to think with our hearts and spread to those who came to us the same sense of *their* competence and *their* power to change their life situation through careful macrobiotic practice that had been offered to us.

With all of this, remembering Michio is for me an exercise in remembering the way he gave each one of us the power to take control of our own lives and shape it into a vehicle for the fulfillment of our fondest dreams and hopes. Thank you, Michio. I shall never forget—and never forget to be grateful. The imagined Ancient of Days whom I conjured in 1986 has become a true Ancient of Days. Michio hinted at that during our class, telling us that he might leave us sometime in the not-too-distant future but that he would be there in the stratosphere watching and cajoling us to be our best macrobiotic selves. I surely hope that he is!

Remembering Michio
Carlos Aponte

July 1972 was all Michio, all the time. We attended lectures at his home on Boylston Street (Route 9), near the Brookline reservoir, morning, afternoon, and night, seven days a week for four weeks. Intensive does not adequately capture what we experienced. Three times a day, as we sat on the floor of his living room, Michio would lead the way showing us the connections between a flower in a pot and the materializing energy of the expanding universe. It was almost as trippy as getting high.

In those days, the focus on food had not yet become dominant. He would weave in and out of ancient and future worlds, the origins of life and humanity on this planet, male and female relations, parenting, cooperative endeavors, healing, acupuncture, organic and natural agriculture, massage, home remedies, physical diagnosis, and so much more. We took notes till we ran out of pencils. One by one, he "read" us, in group therapy style interactions, seeing spirits surrounding one person, and the relative birth influences of mother and father in another. We never tired and could not get enough of it. He even told me it was schizophrenic of me to categorize his emphasis on Northern Hemisphere civilizations as "Northern" people bias toward Southern Hemisphere people. Took me a while to figure that one out.

After that, I left Boston to start college. Three years later we were back, my partner, child and me, working at Boston City Hospital, and participating in every seminar I could attend. Once, I dreamed that Michio was flying in his backyard and I was flying with him, holding on to his shoulders. When I shared this, he laughed and said it was a true dream. Wow. Extra points for the unconscious! Another time I arranged a meeting at the Seventh Inn restaurant between Michio and Dr. John Shen, my teacher of Traditional Chinese Medicine and acupuncture in New York City. Both were masters in their own domains and leery about the meeting. They didn't say more than a half-dozen words, but just checked each other out from the corners of their eyes. Afterwards, Michio shared that he didn't think Dr. Shen could teach cosmology. "I knew that!" I said. Just wanted to hook you guys up, like potential partners. But it was not to be. Each built vast networks of healing in their own dream style.

I didn't see Michio again for thirty-five years until his 80th birthday at the Kushi Institute (K.I.) in Becket, Mass. Two marriages, four children and three professions later, I was studying, working and recuperating there, doing a midlife tune up and update, after decades teaching, practicing, and spreading the principles and practice of balanced living, mostly on my own, while I made my way through the yellow brick road of work, money, and office politics. Along the way, I had opened and run the first macrobiotic restaurant in Puerto Rico, had a healing and teaching practice in New York and Puerto Rico, taught courses, helped a few people, and most importantly, was privileged to bring four wonderful human beings into this world, helping to raise them conscious of their innate goodness and balanced in their ways in the world.

I cried like a baby, with sobs and all, when Michio said goodbye to us at his birthday party. Felt like I'd never see him again after he had helped me find myself and realize my true human potential. Saw him just a couple of times again during the last few years at the annual Summer Conferences or at the K.I. During my work at the K.I., I stumbled across a storage room in the main house with hundreds of videotapes and thousands of audiotapes.

To my surprise and astonishment, the videos were mostly of Michio, in lectures on every topic, but especially of the Spiritual Development Series he had mostly done at the K.I. in the 1990s. Much of this material was not transcribed nor published. To help preserve this material for future generations, I began, in my spare time, to organize and classify these, creating inventory sheets in excel, placing tapes and their inventory in new containers. All of the paper cartons were by now coming apart from the elements and time. Even the rubber bands were coming apart.

All in all, and with the help of some volunteers, we catalogued over 900 VHS videotapes of Michio, either original and/or copies, along with another 100 or so, of Aveline cooking and other macrobiotic teachers lecturing. In addition, there were hundreds, if not thousands, of audiotapes of Michio, senior macrobiotic teachers, and many guest lecturers, that we did not get to classify and repackage, for lack of time, as I left the K.I. for further adventures elsewhere.

With the publication of anecdotes of "Life with Michio," such as those described in these pages, in a soon to be published collection, it is our deepest desire and dream that these Michio videos be digitalized forthwith, at the earliest possible moment, before the chemicals in the tapes start degrading and/or they start splitting. Once digitized, there are many options and avenues available to the worldwide macrobiotic community who have an interest in preserving these fantastic videos of *Michio in his prime*; funny, energized, dealing with (us) hippies and post hippie children, as well as all manner of folk from our hometown, planet earth.

We have provided the Kushi Institute with outlines of the potential that exists for getting this material out of the boxes and into the minds, ears, and eyes of humanity. Seeing and hearing Michio in motion, talking, moving, drawing, laughing, questioning, pushing and pulling, is a human experience with a unique master teacher and evolved human being (with all our imperfections), that we who had the privilege of experiencing, owe to our brothers and sisters. Current and future generations deserve to fly the friendly skies of the Milky Way with Michio *sensei*, round trip as we did. Let's pool our resources: educators, investors, project managers, archivists, graphic artists, video and audio editors, focus groups, trainers and practitioners alike; we can all make this happen, from the simple to the sublime.

At a minimum, we can place all the original tapes online for free access by anyone wanting to do research, or just listen, watch, and learn, from every and any computer and cellphone on the planet. For free. In addition, we can edit them, with senior macrobiotic teachers alongside experienced video and online education design specialists, to create whole courses in the specific topic areas he addressed. These can be provided for a minimum cost plus fee basis online, and even sold in a non-copyable format. In this category, the most important course and/or curricula is the Spiritual Development Training Series, as it is an area that Michio clearly found important enough to bring to us, in volume and repeatedly, but yet did not publish. *So now is the time, dear friends.* Let us place Michio in the virtual world where future generations can enjoy "Surfing the Zuvuya" with him, as the Maya shaman would say.

Remembering Michio
Andrea Beaman

On my journey to health and wellness, I've had the opportunity to study with many great teachers.

One of my favorites was Michio Kushi.

Michio pioneered the Macrobiotic movement in America and founded the Kushi Institute in Massachusetts.

It was there, at the Kushi Institute, that I received firsthand guidance from the master of macrobiotics himself.

He taught us about the Order of the Universe, the connection between the quality of our food and the quality of our health, and the importance of striving to create One Peaceful World.

One day during our studies, we had a Q&A with Michio and I got the opportunity to ask him about flax oil.

I had been reading a lot of information about flax and I started incorporating it into my diet while I was living at the Kushi Institute.

I said, "Michio, what do you think about flax oil for a healing diet."

He slowly shook his head and said, "No flax oil."

"Why no flax? I've been reading so many good things about it." He shook his head and wagged his index finger at me, "No flax oil."

"But, what about the essential fatty acids? Everyone in the health and wellness communities is recommending it."

He softly gazed at me, "No, flax oil." And, then he slow-motion karate chopped the air as if cutting off anymore of my questions. "Awwww c'mon, Michio! That's not a good answer."

He sighed, "Tell me… what is your Chinese Astrological sign?"

"Monkey," I said.

"Ahhhhhhhhh...that makes perfect sense."

"What makes sense?"

"My sign is Tiger. I am the old Tiger sleeping underneath the tree, and you are the monkey throwing coconuts onto my head."

Besides his wealth of universal knowledge, one of the things I loved most about Michio was his light spiritedness and great sense of humor.

He was correct, by the way, on a "healing" diet flax and other refined oils can be hard for the liver to process.

Many years later, I attended an Integrative Nutrition conference in New York City. The audience was filled with health coaches on a mission to save the world from bad eating habits.

Who walks onto the stage but my old teacher, Michio. He shared with the students his standard lecture about food and the importance of adopting a macrobiotic diet and lifestyle.

At the end of his talk, he asked the audience one simple question. "Why do you think you are here on the earth?"

The students in the auditorium began shouting out their answers.

"To teach everyone about eating organic!"

Michio shook his head no.

"To make the world a better place!"

He shook his head no again.

"To save the earth!"

He wagged his index finger and shook his head, no.

"To stop cancer and disease!"

He shook his head no, yet again.

"To make a difference in the world."

That was my answer and I was sure it was correct!

Michio shook his head no and then karate chopped the air.

He softened his gaze, looked at all the eager students, and simply said, "No…You came here to the earth to play with your friends."

The master teacher strikes again! And, the older I get, the more I understand the truth behind his wise statement.

Yes, we are here on the earth to play with our friends.

Thank you, Michio, for playing with us.

Rest in peace, Tiger.

Remembering Michio
Jan Belleme

My spiral into macrobiotics began in the winter of 1976, when a college friend invited me to a symposium on the nature of energy at Boston College. I went along for something to do, knowing nothing about any of the speakers except Peter Tompkins, co-author of *The Secret Life of Plants*. Little did I know that the decision to go would change the rest of my life. I was impressed with several presentations, but after five or ten minutes of Michio Kushi's talk on the Evolution of Consciousness, I was knocked completely out of my orbit. Although I could not confirm the profound ideas he conveyed from any personal experience, it struck me as pure truth, and I wanted more!

Shortly after that, I discovered that some of Mr. Kushi's students were giving classes at the University of Massachusetts in Amherst, where I was finishing my degree. I took cooking classes, a wild foods foraging class with Ken Burns, and spiritual practices with Sherman Goldman. Two or three times that winter and spring, I drove to Boston for a weekend seminar with Michio, and then decided to move into one of the study houses.

Sherman introduced me to a Zen monk named Genro who ran a study house in Brookline, and he said I could move in at the beginning of September. In August, I learned that Genro had to close the house, and I had nowhere to go. That was one of those moments you look back on later and realize that what you thought was a disaster turned out to be perfect. Call it fate, destiny, whatever you like—it was meant to be. Ken Burns was up in Amherst again, so I asked him if he knew of anyplace I could move into. There was an opening in his and Ann's house, so I moved in on September 1 to continue my macrobiotic studies. About a week after arriving, a handsome, olive-skinned guy named John, who I had heard was off on a motorcycle trip, showed up for dinner in white cotton yoga clothes looking like John the Baptist. I couldn't have been sure of it at the time, but the immediate attraction and interest I felt foreshadowed another major shift in my life trajectory.

Over the next months, I studied Shiatsu massage, cooking, wild foods, macrobiotic philosophy, and had the opportunity to transcribe many of Michio's lectures for his publications. John and I became close friends during that fall and winter. When we found ourselves with plans to go on individual macro adventures in different directions that June, we realized we didn't want to be apart for long, and we've been sharing our adventures ever since.

I'm forever grateful to Michio for providing the opportunity to profoundly change the course of my life. Because of his charismatic personality, deep knowledge, and relentless devotion to teaching macrobiotics, I met my adventurous, witty, and loving life partner and we've had two wonderful, healthy sons. In his tribute John mentions a bit about the various books, articles, and macrobiotic businesses we have had the good fortune to write and build, all of which stem from Michio's influence. All of those ventures have been very rewarding, but as a mother, I am even more grateful for the fact that we had been taught how to keep our children healthy through diet and natural remedies. While other parents were running back and forth to the doctor and giving their children one round of antibiotics after another to deal with ear infections, bronchitis, and other illnesses, thanks to Michio and his macrobiotic teachings, like many other macrobiotic parents, we were able to use home remedies to quickly relieve our boys' occasional fevers, colds, or earaches. What a blessing!

Remembering Michio
John Belleme

In college I read an article in a highly regarded journal that said due to genetic engineering, organ transplants, and other technological medical advances, children being born at the time (1967) may never actually die. I was euphoric and had to be part of this exciting, life-saving research. From that moment I focused all my energy on becoming a medical researcher. I wanted to make my contribution to immortality.

About the spring of 1975, I was working in a hospital doing cutting edge research on applying chemotherapy directly to heated glioblastomas, one of the deadliest forms of brain cancer. My responsibility was to scrub up and go into the operating room to get tumor tissue from the neurosurgeon to prepare for examination with a powerful electron microscope. I would prepare pictures of tumor cells to see what effect our new treatment had on tumor cell death. Our purpose was to kill most of the tumor, and then go back into the patient's brain a few days later and remove the rest of the living cancer. After about eighteen months of this grueling procedure, we had not prolonged the life of one patient. I was despondent. Maybe my children were not going to live forever. Depression is one way the universe tells us that it is time for a change in our attitude and values.

About that time I came across some of Michio Kushi's writings. Michio's synthesis of traditional folklore, Taoism, Eastern medicine, metaphysics, cosmology, modern nutrition. and spiritual practices gave me a cause and reason for everything from a mole on my nose to the expanding universe. According to Michio, health and happiness were the result of a way of life. What a revelation! I had no idea. What an extraordinary relief to make some sense out of the confusion and hopelessness I was feeling. Maybe we would live forever. Just not in this body.

Within days my life had changed forever. I had a purpose. After reading Michio's writings, I knew that we are all connected and my sense of isolation lifted. I was living in South Florida at the time and happened to wander into the Oak Feed Store, the Mecca for macrobiotics in Florida. I struck up a relationship with local macrobiotic guru Sandy Pukel. After working for Sandy at the store for several months, he suggested that to learn more about macrobiotics I needed to go to Boston, live in a macrobiotic study house, and study with Michio and Aveline Kushi. So I hopped on my Triumph motorcycle and blasted off to Boston to move in with macrobiotic teachers Ken and Ann Burns. Turns out it was a great place to learn macrobiotic cooking and philosophy, but Ken had a little Samurai fever, so he kept the house around 45 degrees in the middle of a Boston winter, a bit chilly for a guy from Miami.

Michio lived right down the street and lectured at the Burns house often. Ed and Wendy Esko and Stephen and Tamara Uprichard lived directly across the street. The Garvey house was nearby. I was living in a macrobiotic vortex and was completely involved with the rapidly growing macrobiotic community.

After a few months my son John came to stay with me. Ann Burns got him interested in food and he went on to graduate from the Culinary Institute of America. John has become a south Florida icon of culinary fusion, which stems from his experience as a 12-year old in the Burns house.

But the best was still to come. I had moved into the Burns house in the spring of 1976. My macrobiotic journey has been often exciting, sometimes stressful but never boring. I have much to be grateful for, but what I am most grateful for is that Michio set in motion an extraordinary set of events that caused me to meet Jan, the love of my life, and from that union came Justin and Mike, two sons that have brought a deep and profound joy to my life and in many respects have been my teachers.

Although I would not trade my macrobiotic experience for anything, there were a few times when my journey was less than serene. Michio was always looking at the big picture. He had a macro-cosmological view. But this sometimes caused him to pay less attention to details. In 1979 he sent Jan and I to Japan to do a one year miso-making apprenticeship. Michio said that a well-known Japanese macrobiotic businessman would meet us at the Tokyo airport and he would take us to the miso shop where we would study. Well, the man showed up and asked a question that totally freaked us out! "Where am I taking you?" he asked. I was in a panic. It seemed that the communication between Michio and this man was less than precise. We had flown half way around the world and did not know where we were going. After a very stressful few weeks, things worked out and the result is Miso Master Miso (The American Miso Company), one of the largest traditional miso shops in the world.

I don't want to suggest that Michio is like a Biblical figure, but like great thinkers of the past, Michio had many disciples, who in turn went out and influenced the health of the world by teaching and starting numerous companies. Everything that has happened seems to lead back to an opportunity Michio created by his teachings. Michio and his writing and lectures have been responsible for all the books and articles Jan and I wrote and all the businesses Sandy Pukel and I started, not to mention the endeavors of countless other students. The ripple effect seems endless. Yes, maybe Michio will live forever — not in the flesh, but in the influence he had on countless others.

Remembering Michio
David Briscoe

It was that time when I was alone with him around 1986, driving in Springfield, Missouri, when he was there to lecture at the Holistic Medical Association's convention, that sticks with me now.

I asked him how he does it, how he deals with so many people, with so many problems, so many demands, all the time, day and night, and non-stop.

Michio looked surprised by my question. "As soon as I turn away, as soon as I finish meeting or talking with someone, my mind is empty again," he said.

An empty mind. Not a vacant mind. There is a difference. Through all the days since he gave me that little treasure, alone with me in the car some thirty years ago, I have been learning again and again about "empty mind" in all aspects of life. Thank you, Michio.

Remembering Michio
Simon Brown

In 1995 I organized a spiritual seminar for Michio in an old English stately home, called Gaunt's House. The seminar was a mixture of chanting, meditation, exercise, discussion, and fasting. On the second day Michio asked me if we could go into the local town, Wimborne Minster.

I had hired a builder's style white van, to bring food and cooking equipment to the Spiritual Seminar. We climbed into the van and drove off. Michio was dressed in a smart white shirt, with a dark waistcoat and suit jacket. Below, he wore green corduroys. To me it seemed a complete mismatch. That morning I had taken some photographs of Michio and Aveline for future publicity. I was still slightly irritated with myself for not having the courage to ask if he had some other trousers.

When we arrived, the small traditional English town looked dead. I drove around a couple of times but the only building that looked like there was life inside was a dark hotel. I think Michio had become used to the U.S. style of cafes being open all day, so it was a disappointment. We parked and wandered in. Michio wanted something to eat. We were told the kitchen was closed. In the end we negotiated to have some smoked salmon sandwiches in brown bread along with coffees.

We sat on dark maroon velvet seats around a mahogany table in an empty saloon. There was a strong smell of beeswax. During the next hour I experience some of the most stimulating conversations of my life. We discussed infinity, the world of illusions, matter interaction with energy whilst drifting carelessly through the universe. Every now and then Michio would bring an esoteric observation down to a very practical detail. The basic message, I got, was that we are all here to play freely. Yes, it all may be a self-constructed illusion, but at the same time we can be real, in terms of how we eat, treat others and act. Where many people might have found the paradoxes that developed out of our discourse confusing or irritating, Michio found them amusing. He accepted the contradictions in a way that became quite life changing for me. If it is all play and illusions why get upset with someone else's illusions?

I had previously known Michio since 1982 when I met him at a macrobiotic camp in the Poconos. Since, I hosted many seminars in London, spending a lot of time with Michio on his visits. Somehow, in that moment, eating our sandwiches, and talking I felt I saw a whole new side to Michio. Looking back it was his mental flexibility and ability to explore a subject in many different ways, without getting attached to any. Perhaps the coffee and beeswax contributed?

I always considered Michio to be a highly intellectual, academic man. He was obviously clever and able to take a diverse set of thoughts and connect them in a way that created new and profound realizations. I suspect that because of that Michio attracted a group of interesting, intelligent, and imaginative students. In that sense his greatest legacy is the people he has left behind and the intelligent conversations they are still having.

Out of all my times with Michio, there was a spark of magic in the hotel interaction that has stayed with me in incredible detail, even though twenty years have passed. Some of his words feel imprinted in my mind.

Once we finished we climbed back into the van. After all the mental exercise my mind was exhausted and I soon became lost. We had about ten minutes before Michio was due to start his next lecture. I encountered that horrible sinking feeling where the roads were looking distinctly unfamiliar and none of the signs were remotely helpful. Perspiration was forming across my forehead.

Michio must have realized something was wrong and gently offered directions at each turn until we arrived safely and just on time at Gaunt's House.

Remembering Michio
Bob Carr

One day I was driving Michio to a lecture in Montreal. He had a small spiral (yes, "spiral," as Michio always could find spirals in everything) notebook with him. We got to the venue and went for a cup of coffee, then to the lecture hall. Michio asked, "Do you have my notebook?" I said, "No, it must be in the car." So I ran back to get it. I was somewhat worried, as I never lock my car. There was the notebook, on the front seat, lying open for anyone to see.
I picked it up and glanced through it to make sure I had the right thing. Inside were small, very orderly outlines of most of the lectures I had heard Michio give over the last twenty years I had known him. Neat, concise and very orderly, like Michio. I would have loved to have that notebook, which was half in English and half in Japanese; however, I was extremely glad that no one had taken it…that would have been a loss to Michio and the rest of humanity (assuming Michio was really human and not a friendly alien). I returned the notebook and Michio said "Thank you" and probably thought nothing of the instance.

Another day, back in Cleveland, Michio was doing nonstop consultations. My secretary at the time had a consultation with him, and I was the scribe, taking notes on whatever he said so she could listen attentively. As my secretary came in the door, Michio looked up and said, "Hi, Diane, you and your husband used to go out for pizza every Thursday, right?" Her jaw dropped, as did mine; that he could know something nobody could know without knowing her before, which he didn't. He did this type of thing with many of the clients, letting them know he knew stuff about them from another orbit. What a way to make a connection!

When living at a Kushi study house in Boston in the early 1970s, I would attend Michio's morning and afternoon lectures in his nearby house. His kids were running around, sometimes in the middle of his living room, where he had a large blackboard and twenty or more students. One day the topic was diagnosis, and Michio said that with refinement, you can diagnose, you can see, someone's ancestors, how they were developing in the womb, their early growth, as well as their present condition. He said you could even see, without previously knowing, what they had for their last meal. The next day, as we entered the room for the morning lecture, Michio told each student what they had for breakfast. One person had oatmeal, one had miso soup, and another had toast with tahini. One student, who later was to become a well know macrobiotic teacher came in the door and Michio said "Hmm, you had eggs for breakfast and coffee," all of which was verified by each student. With the last person to come in, Michio said something different. "Ah so, breakfast OK, but last night you had two beers...Miller Light!" Amazing, he even named the brand. No one could believe his or her ears, but it was often hard to comprehend how Michio knew what he knew.

Along those lines, talking of studying diagnosis with Michio, he would often bring up a student to illustrate a point or show what he saw in us. Once he asked me and another fellow to come up to the front of the class and said, "Look, both of these boys ate eggs while growing up. But one of them ate fried eggs and one of them scrambled eggs. Which one was which?" And all the students either guessed or could see and correctly identified who ate what. I was the scrambled egg. Michio was able to transmit an understanding and discernment to his students in amazing ways.

One day in the classroom with Michio, the discussion was about the Bible. We were talking about Cain and Abel, the one husbanded animals and the other grew grains. The story goes that Cain, the crop grower slew his brother, Abel, who raised animals. I mentioned to Michio that that seemed weird, that the more vegetarian oriented son of Adam and Eve would be so fierce, rather than the one dealing with (and maybe eating) animals. Michio said, "True, it was the other way around...Abel slew Cain." I said that that is how I would have imagined it to be, but what happened? Michio responded that the story was written down by scribes, who were more like copy machines than truly intellectual historians, and one of the early scribes made a typo, reversing the names, and all the following scribes continued copying the mistake. I said "Amazing! How did you know that?" to which Michio said "I was there." I was speechless at his response and still think about what that means in a larger sense. It's about how to tap into Being There.

Remembering Michio
Martha C. Cottrell, MD

My first meeting with Michio was intense—at least as far as I was concerned. I received a call from his son Larry saying that his father would like to meet with me to discuss a research project with Boston University for which they needed a physician with a macrobiotic background. At that stage I had attended lectures at the Macrobiotic Center in Manhattan and I had heard Michio speak, but never really had any one-on-one contact with him. I had signed a petition to take a stand against a bill introduced in Congress by Florida Senator Claude Pepper, which would make it a felony for any physician to promote "wholistic medicine." Having experienced the reversal of my own "chronic" diseases by studying macrobiotics and changing my diet and lifestyle, I was incensed by this, and not only signed the petition, but wrote on the petition that as a physician who had been helped and was in the process of changing my approach to the way I practiced medicine, I would be more than happy to help in any way I could to oppose this attempt.

Subsequently, I received a phone call from Neil Stapleman, a macrobiotic counselor in Manhattan, who engaged me in a very in-depth conversation for over an hour! I felt that I had been "grilled," and I understood why. Was I being used by the powers that be as a setup to entrap others? It was very interesting, and I had no idea that that conversation would change my life!

Shortly after that call from Neil, Michio's son called saying that his father would like to meet with me. I was flabbergasted!!! Of course I would be honored to meet with him! On the date set I went to the address given to me in Manhattan, where Michio was giving consultations. I was met by Michio's son, Larry. Larry graciously informed me that his father was running late, which, as I learned later through the years of working with Michio, was not unusual! Larry asked that I please go down to the restaurant on the first level and wait there for his father. So down I went with great anticipation. After finding a booth that faced the entrance, I sat and waited for Michio's appearance. In he came. I was immediately impressed with his energy and his smile. "Sit down. Sit down," he said to me for I had risen out of great respect for him and bowed before him as one ought to do before a great teacher. "Sit down. Sit down." He then called the waiter over and asked, "What will you have to drink?" Being a lifelong coffee drinker, but having been around macrobiotic counselors who emphasized tea, and being in the presence of THE Teacher/Counselor of All, I timidly said, "Tea for me, please." Michio quickly responded, "Tea for the doctor, coffee for me!"

I laugh even today as I write this loving memory of the man who changed my life, enriched my life beyond my wildest dreams, and who I came to love, respect, and admire. He was the most remarkable human being I have ever known. In that same meeting, as Michio explained to me the research program with AIDs, I listened intently and at the same time thought to myself, "I would give anything to study with this man." When Michio finished discussing the project he asked if I would be available to be a part of the study. Immediately I responded with "It would be an honor, sir." He looked into my eyes for what seemed like an eternity and then said very softly, "Dr. Cottrell, would you like to study with me?" My heart skipped a beat. I caught my breath and I said, "Sir, there is nothing I would like more!" He smiled and said, "Good. It is done."

Thus began the greatest journey of my life, and it continues to this day! Humbly and thankfully, I thank the powers that be that brought our paths together. He changed me forever as he has many, many people around the world, and those of us he changed have also planted seeds of change through our studying with him. His life, his dedication to bring about One Peaceful World, and the tens of thousands of those he has taught, will continue to bear fruit, assuring that Michio's Dream will live on way beyond his physical life as well as our own.

Thank you, Michio!

Remembering Michio
Mina Dobic

I first met Michio Kushi some thirty years ago in Boston, Massachusetts. I flew in to see him for my first macrobiotic consultation two weeks after major surgery in my home country, some 4,500 miles away.

After being diagnosed at the age of 45 with a Stage IV ovarian cancer with metastasis to the liver, bones, and lymph system, I was given by the western medical experts no more than two months to live. With two beautiful growing children and my husband, the love of my life, I simply couldn't see the sickness being the end of my beautiful life. One afternoon, in our newly built house, sitting around the dining room table, we made a decision to stick together and fight as a family to beat cancer whatever it took, and that also meant wherever we had to go. And so, with my family's love under my broken wings, the journey of hope and my full recovery began. I had a consultation with Michio two weeks later.

Fast-forward a year of practicing macrobiotics, I was cancer free celebrating Chinese New Year with Michio and Aveline Kushi at the Kushi Institute in Boston. My incurable illness was cured! You can read in detail about my recovery in my book, *My Beautiful Life*.

Less then a year after my recovery, the entire family; my husband Bosko, my son Srdjan and my daughter Jelena, left the comfort of our brand new home in Serbia and arrived at the Kushi House in Brookline with four suitcases. That's all we had to our names. We left everything behind; family, close friends and everything we owned to learn more about macrobiotics and share the knowledge back home with people who may need it. And so our friendship with Michio began.

At our arrival at the Kushi House, we met Michio in the downstairs library. He just happened to be back from a trip. He casually invited us a few months before at the lecture in Belgrade to come and study at the Kushi Institute. Michio said this essentially to everyone he met: "Please come to Boston to study macrobiotics." But unlike most people, we took it and ran with it and so needless to say he was a little surprised to have the entire family standing in his house. For us, however, it was the only way to ensure we would study with the best macrobiotic teacher in the world. Michio, the way he was, understood. We sat down and quickly came up with a plan. I realize now it wasn't easy for him to take responsibility for the whole family. But we had only one goal, and it was to study macrobiotics. And that was simply enough.

My husband and my daughter were given an opportunity to live and study at the Kushi Institute in Becket, but when it came down to my 16 year old son, Srdjan, something interesting happened. Michio asked Srdjan, what he would like to do. There was dead silence in the room. We were, 4,000 miles from home, with no back up plan, in a foreign country and now our brilliant, but still adolescent son was given an opportunity to start making decisions about his own life. Srdjan looked at us in awe and excitement and quickly answered, "I would like to stay here and study macrobiotics in Boston." Michio then looked at Bosko and me, and said, "Is it okay with you?" And that was that! Srdjan completed his macrobiotic studies at the Kushi Institute in Boston, a year later. He then joined us in Becket where I was studying to become what I am today; a macrobiotic teacher and counselor.

During our time at the Kushi Institute in Becket, my husband Bosko would often drive Michio to the General Store, the only grocery store in town, which also was a gas station, a video rental store, and a coffee shop, all under the same roof. Michio and Bosko would sit together, sip coffee, eat some peanuts while enjoying each other's company in silence. Some fifty cups of coffee down the road, Bosko finally asked Michio, "Mr. Kushi, every time we come here you order coffee, sip it slowly and don't say a word. You must have a lot on your mind." After reflecting for a minute, Michio answered, "I like to take time to observe people. One can learn much just by watching and listening." We now live in Los Angeles, walking distance to a popular outing called The Grove. Almost every week, you can find Bosko, now sipping his tea, watching people, observing faces, taking it all in, in silence.

Michio was also known for his incredible insight. I remember after my surgery one of the side effects was discharging clear liquid for which I actually had to wear adult diapers. I would have to change them up to 30 times on some days. This went on for about a year. Finally, I decided the next time I saw Michio I was going to ask if he knew how long the discharge would last. His visits to Becket were busy with lectures, consultations, and meetings, but he always found the time to say hello to me and I'd hear his upbeat voice from down the hall, "Hello. How are you? That's great!" And he would always put me in a good mood. So when he arrived the next time, I asked if I could talk to him privately for a few minutes. "Of course," he replied. After sharing my problem with him, Michio simply answered, "One more week." First I didn't understand if he was serious and if that was simply it. He smiled and repeated, "One more week. Okay." And that was it. To this day I am not sure if his knowledge of Oriental diagnosis gave away what was going to happen or maybe it was simply that I needed someone's approval to complete my healing, and to me, Michio's words were always encouraging. They were medicine. Sure enough, a week later I was diaper free!

Our time together with Michio and at the Kushi Institute gave us a powerful compass we needed to navigate through life in health, happiness, and with joy, and we are still sailing together as a family. We miss you Michio! We will never forget how you helped us get to where we are today and you'll be with us every tomorrow.

Ten years after leaving the Kushi Institute to start my practice I wrote a book *My Beautiful Life* in which I share in more detail our family's story and experiences with Michio.

Remembering Michio
Christian Elwell

The first time I experienced Michio Kushi was on my twenty-eighth birthday at the Noh Center in Boston, four days after Christmas, in 1974. The previous year, seeking meaning in life after my father had recently died of cancer at the age of fifty-one, I myself became seriously ill with hepatitis while on a spiritual quest in India. At the time, not knowing anything about illness or disease, I thought it was the end of my life. I realized that for all my education, I had not a clue how to live, how to take care of this precious gift of life in human form. If only I could live, I thought, I would return to the land of my birth in New England and grow raspberries.

While traveling back from India, I met friends at the Findhorn Community in Scotland, who declared I must see Michio Kushi upon my return to Boston. I had become fascinated with the teachings of the Shivapuri Baba who had lived to the age of 134. His primary teaching was *Right Life;* that to achieve the highest goals of human striving—in his language, "to see God"—one needed a persevering strength and devotion, which could be gained only through the practice of Right Life; that each individual must find right life for himself or herself according to the various conditions of climate and culture within which one lived.

So, when finally I made my way to the Noh Center, *Right Life* was my mantra. I wanted to live right life. That evening, as if designed by the Order of the Universe itself, Michio's entire talk was just that: Michio outlined the foundations for right life, now, of course, through the language and cosmology of macrobiotics. My narrow-minded view of Right Life opened into an ever-expanding view of *Great Life*. Although there were perhaps twenty people sitting on the floor at the Noh Center that evening, I felt as though Michio was speaking directly to me.

Not only that, but the little room of the Noh Center itself gave way to imagined space. Suddenly, we were sitting under a palm tree in some ancient land before our teacher, who was instilling the depths of our souls with primordial teachings about what it means to be and become human, and how we must orient ourselves to Life on Earth.

This, then, was my first and life changing experience of Michio Kushi. It was a transcendent experience yet grounded in fundamental, "how to" tools for actual living, how to eat, how to cook, yes! And encoded within these practical arts, how to orient oneself, to cherish the simple pleasures and participate in the powerful dreams of Life itself, to unite with its awesome beauty. Michio gave us permission to walk again barefoot on the dew-born grass, to laugh again and trust in the face of ugly and mean appearances, with full confidence in the magnificent Order of the Universe. He opened *Great Life* for us in a kind of communal clairvoyance, punctuated by the endearing cadence of his unique and unforgettable way of speaking English.

A few weeks after that, I met Michio directly for the first time. He was giving a seminar on Oriental medicine at a conference room, somewhere in the upper stories of the Boston Park Plaza Hotel. During one of the breaks I headed for the elevator down to street level to get outside for a walk. When I entered the elevator, there inside was Michio standing alone as the elevator doors closed behind me. OMG! No place to hide! At the time, I was still struggling with bouts of fatigue from the hepatitis, spiritually disoriented after my father's death, and feeling culturally out of place, with great uncertainty even as to my name. I felt like a dissolute and lost soul.

But as the elevator went down to earth, I felt no critical judgment coming from Michio. He welcomed me to the seminar and then asked my name. "Christian," I said with a mixture of self-doubt, embarrassment, and shame; for the name carries so much historical baggage and untold mystery at the same time. With the kindest smile, with sincerity and warmth, Michio said in his simultaneously enigmatic and prevailing positive manner, forever reassuring, "Ah so, *Christian*. That is very good name!"

As did many others, I experienced the transformative magic of Michio's shining presence. For so many of us who felt lost and unbelonging, Michio realigned us with our pre-natal dreams; he remembered us to paths of meaning and purpose, finding joy and devotion to our common humanity.

That was his work, his gift.

The last time I saw Michio was about two years before his death. Outwardly frail and worn, he shook my hand with such strength that it took me by surprise. His voice came deep in low-pitched tones, as he firmly said, "Thank you very much for your hard work!" while vigorously shaking my hand. That was another great gift that Michio practiced and modeled, and continued giving to all of us: endless gratitude!

Thank you, Michio!

Remembering Michio
Edward Esko

The year 2014 was deeply challenging. On July 26, our family lost our beloved father, grandfather, and great-grandfather, Edward Esko, Sr. Ed Sr. passed away peacefully in Philadelphia at age ninety surrounded by his loving family. Ed Sr. was the hidden supporter of the Esko family's macrobiotic dream. Because of him, and my mother Elizabeth (Liz), now eighty-seven, our efforts on behalf of macrobiotic education became possible. We owe my parents gratitude beyond measure.

Then, on December 28, we lost our friend, counselor, mentor, and teacher, Michio Kushi, who passed away peacefully in Boston at age eighty-eight surrounded by his loving family.

My relationship with Michio goes back more than forty-years. It began in 1971 when I went to his lecture at the Friends Meeting House in Philadelphia. Michio's lecture was a life-altering event, more profound than witnessing JFK's motorcade as a ten-year-old or watching the Beatles' first appearance on the Ed Sullivan Show.

I had started macrobiotics the year before with Diet Number Seven and copies of *You Are All Sanpaku* and *Zen Macrobiotics*. My first attempts were somewhat crude and even comical. I tried cooking brown rice in Liz's kitchen, with moderate success. I chewed each mouthful fifty times or more, counting every bite. I stopped meat, sugar, and dairy cold turkey. The tipping point came when I attempted to roast bancha tea in Liz's skillet. Not knowing what I was doing, I turned the flame too high. Soon the twigs started burning and smoke filled Liz's kitchen. I'll never forget what happened next.

Ed Sr. appeared with hands on hips and a stern look on his face. He resembled Ward Cleaver when Ward would admonish his son Theodore (the Beaver) on the popular 1960s sitcom, *Leave It to Beaver*. He said something like, "We tolerated the Rolling Stones. We tolerated Woodstock. (Don't forget, we were just coming out of the Sixties.) We tolerated your slacking in your studies in college…but …we're NOT going to tolerate THIS!" Ed Sr., a veteran of the U.S. Army Air Corps in the Second World War, was an executive at RCA, the Radio Corporation of America, at that time owner of the National Broadcasting Company (NBC.) He was one of the first computer programmers in the U.S. and worked for a time at RCA headquarters at 30 Rockefeller Center in New York. He wasn't about to put up with any hippie dippy shenanigans.

Although my first reaction was to break out laughing, at that point I knew it was time to leave. I packed my sack of organic brown rice, my container of tamari soy sauce, my books, some sea salt, and bancha tea and set out on my journey in search of enlightenment. My first stop was the house in the Germantown section of Philadelphia, which several members of my rock band were renting, including my brother Jeffery. (Jeffery and I had led several popular rock bands in the late Sixties and early Seventies. In 1968, we appeared on nationwide television with Stevie Wonder and B.B. King.) I continued with my practice and study of Diet Number Seven and my readings on Buddhism, Zen, Taoism, and Yoga philosophy. Diet Number Seven was essentially a fasting regime. It couldn't be sustained for more than a week or ten days. From that jumping off point, I adopted a more broad and flexible macrobiotic diet, which I continue to enjoy to this day.

The first stage of my relationship with Michio was clearly that of junior to senior. Michio and I were both born in the Year of the Tiger, Michio in 1926 and me in 1950. For Tiger Year persons, there is a clear ranking according to seniority. Young Tigers respect older Tigers and older Tigers tolerate and often mentor young Tigers. The older Tiger often establishes a territory or orbit to which the junior Tiger is cautiously admitted, and to which, if the relationship is to continue, over time, the junior Tiger must prove commitment and establish bonds of loyalty and trust. For me, Michio's orbit was the Boston macrobiotic community, which in the early 1970s encompassed the Erewhon warehouse on Farnsworth Street, the Erewhon retail store on Newbury Street, the Seventh Inn and Sanae restaurants on Park Square and Newbury Street, Tao Books, the *East West Journal*, the network of study houses in Brookline and Cambridge, and, most importantly, Michio's twice or thrice weekly lectures.

I have never felt more hopeful and excited about the future than I did on that clear sunny day in September of 1972 when I stepped off the train at South Station. With the first whiff of the salt air of the Massachusetts Bay, I knew I was embarking on the adventure of a lifetime. I moved into a macrobiotic study house in Cambridge and began attending Michio's lectures. I enjoyed shopping at Erewhon, eating delicious gourmet meals and snacks at Sanae (named after Lima Ohsawa) and Seventh Inn, enjoying well-prepared meals at the study house (meals were enjoyed communally usually at long low tables with buffet style dishes in the center and everyone sitting on cushions on the hardwood floors), browsing the New Age and spiritual books at Tao, and reading my favorite magazine, *The Order of the Universe*, which featured essays based on Michio's lectures. I started writing articles that were published in *East West Journal* and, in far off California, in *The Macrobiotic*, edited by Michio's colleague, Herman Aihara.

When combined with the vibrant Boston macrobiotic community, composed mostly of young healthy twenty-something's seeking knowledge and spirituality, these activities made me feel that I was in heaven. I felt totally connected and plugged in. My social life became more active: dances and parties were often held in the Boston study houses, which were actually rented mansions with many bedrooms, spacious kitchens, and huge dining and living rooms. My level of idealism at the possibility of changing the world through macrobiotics had never been higher.
My relationship with Michio evolved fairly quickly to the second stage, that of a junior associate working together with a senior asso-

ciate toward a shared dream and vision. Michio invited me to move into the Kushi family study house in 1973 at 440 Boylston Street, a huge roomy mansion located on Route 9 in Brookline, to assist with projects and activities. Back then, Aveline would cook on a daily basis, so I had the opportunity to experience macrobiotic food, including perfectly cooked brown rice, at its best. Together with serving as a chauffer (Aveline drove but Michio didn't) my first assignment was to edit the East West Foundation's first annual report titled *One Peaceful World.* Soon, Michio invited me to serve as Vice-President of the East West Foundation. Michio was the President of the non-profit organization he had founded.

Meanwhile, in July I visited Liz and Ed Sr. in Philadelphia for my cousin's wedding. It was there that I met Wendy, who later became my wife and mother of our eight children. Wendy moved to a study house in Boston in the autumn, and soon we were engaged and in the following year married, with the blessing and support of the Kushis.

The Kushis had returned from their first visit to Japan and outside the U.S. the day before the wedding. Even though they were suffering from jetlag, they joyfully presided over the wedding. Coincidentally they had brought back an antique Japanese wedding kimono that had been the property of the Kushi family and insisted that Wendy wear it for the ceremony. Wendy also studied cooking with Aveline and joined the East West Foundation as accountant and bookkeeper, a role she continued to play for a number of years.

One evening, Michio, Wendy, and I went to a movie in Watertown. It was titled something like, *The Seventh Voyage of Sinbad.* It was a Grade B movie that chronicled Sinbad's mythical adventures sailing the ocean and fighting monsters and eventually realizing peace and freedom. In one scene, Sinbad and the Princess were battling the giant one-eyed Cyclops. Michio was enjoying popcorn and was especially intrigued by that particular episode. The sequence ended with Sinbad and the Princess shooting a spear into the single eye of the Cyclops, eventually bringing him down. When the sequence ended, Michio leaned over to me and said, "Ah…Sinbad and Princess are Ed and Wendy. Cyclops is delusion of modern science." What endlessly fun, provocative, and nonstop study!

Michio and Aveline had moved into 62 Buckminster Road, the giant stone mansion in Brookline that used to be a Catholic girls school, not far from 440 Boylston. The classrooms had been converted into bedrooms and still had blackboards attached to the walls. Buckminster Road soon became the epicenter of planetary macrobiotic activities, meetings, projects, and developments. Our first son, Eric, was born in October 1974 at home at 440 Boylston with the assistance of a traditional doctor and midwife. When we brought the new baby to Buckminster Road for the first time, Michio took one look and said, "Ah, the lost Atlantian (from the mythical continent of Atlantis) has finally returned."

Many initiatives were launched in those years. I would commute daily from Brookline to the East West Foundation (EWF) office at 359 Boylston Street in downtown Boston, just off the Arlington Street Church, Ritz Carlton, and Boston Common. The day would often start with a morning walk down Route 9 to Michio's favorite morning coffee shop, Sealy's on Cypress Street. Over black coffee, we would review events and discuss future plans. Then I would jump on the Green Line for downtown and Michio would return to his office at Buckminster Road. For evening coffee, Michio's favorite spot was Mister Donut (now Dunkin Donuts) about a mile from 62 Buckminster East on Route 9. I remember the pleasant hike down Route 9 in summer and the bracing trek through snow, ice, and highway traffic in winter.

After working late into the night, Michio's favorite after hours coffee spot was the International House of Pancakes. He would ask, "Do you have the guts to go to Pancake House?" Of course we said yes. Standard fare at "Pancake House" was hot black coffee, buckwheat pancakes dry (without butter or syrup), and sometimes dry rye toast. Rather than syrup, Michio would actually sprinkle *salt* on the pancakes! It was Spartan fare at its best. After such a yang-contracting snack fueled by caffeine, coupled with the free exchange of ideas and plans, we were totally fired up and ready to challenge the food industry, modern medicine and science, and change the world.

The EWF office in downtown Boston was on the second floor. It was tiny, slightly larger than a closet. It was attached to a large open room that we used for Michio's lectures. The space was actually known as the "Noh Center." It had been the space where Aveline had set up a stage for her study and practice of Noh drama, considered to be the most refined and spiritual form of theater and performance in Japan, usually reserved for the Imperial Court. She invited one of the top Noh masters from Japan and arranged classes and performances.

Once the Noh phase ended, Michio and the EWF inherited the downtown space. Michio's early lectures at the Noh Center took place at a small blackboard propped atop cinder blocks. The EWF eventually purchased a high school blackboard. Michio's lectures were incredible. The depth and breadth of his topics was unparalleled. His blackboard writing, drawings, and graphics were perfect works of art. The Noh Center in downtown Boston was packed three or four nights a week with students eager to study with Michio.

I would work at the downtown office during the day and stay after hours to prepare the room for Michio's evening lectures. This is where some real time training occurred. From time to time Michio would call, usually around four or five in the afternoon. He would say, "Ed, I'm tied up with some urgent business. Can you cover the first half-hour of the lecture until I arrive?" I would have to face a packed house of students who had come to see Michio. I improvised and did my best to hold the fort until Michio arrived. This happened several times until on one occasion, the five o'clock call came in and Michio said, "Ed, I'm tied up, and won't be able to make it, can you cover THE ENTIRE LECTURE?"

When eight o'clock rolled around, fifty or sixty students filed in to the Noh Center. They had each paid five dollars for the lecture. Once they were settled, I walked to the front of the room and announced that Michio would not be coming and that I would be covering the lecture. Almost immediately, half the audience got up and left. That took all egos out of the process and represented feet to the fire training at its best. Michio had the habit of throwing his students into the ocean and consistently saying, "swim."

Thanks to Michio, Aveline, and Shizuko

Everyone owes Shizuko Yamamoto a tremendous debt of gratitude. A student of George Ohsawa and contemporary of the Kushis, Shizuko passed away recently in Japan at age ninety. Her bright, positive energy and wonderful sense of humor were a joy to be around. Her teaching of macrobiotics and Shiatsu was always brilliant and fun. Our family especially owes her unending thanks.

The year was 1974, in the month of July. Wendy and I were helping Michio and Aveline with the East West Foundation. We had arranged a weekend seminar in New York City, where Shizuko lived and practiced, and had driven down from Boston. Michio and Aveline sat in the back seat, together with Sally April, who was letting us use her new Audi sedan. Wendy sat in the front passenger seat. She was six months' pregnant. I was the driver.

On the drive down we enjoyed the luxury and power of the new Audi. The weekend event went smoothly, with the usual fun and excitement of Manhattan restaurants and nightlife. When Sunday rolled around, it was time to head back to Boston. After leisurely morning coffee on a sparkling summer morning, Wendy and I met up with the Kushis at Shizuko's apartment. I was eager to get on the road. I was and still am intimidated by the drive in and out of New York City, even in broad daylight. My worry was that as the afternoon wore on we wouldn't set out until dark.

Well, as it turned out, things dragged on and that is exactly what happened. With some trepidation I pulled out of the parking garage. The seating arrangements were the same as they were coming down. Michio, Aveline, and Sally were in the back seat, and Wendy was in the front passenger seat. We left the Upper West Side around 9 PM. Somehow I managed to get onto FDR Drive in an attempt to reach route 278 and 95 North through the Bronx and up into New England. While crossing the bridge from Manhattan, I made a wrong turn. We wound up on Randall's Island, then a deserted patch of wasteland far below the bridge and highway. Randall's Island was poorly lit. It was almost pitch black. The Kushis were sleeping in the backseat. Wendy was half asleep beside me. Not knowing where I was going, I started searching desperately for the way back to the highway. Then out of nowhere, a car appeared sideways in front of me. Bam! I hit the car directly on its left front fender. Sally's brand new Audi was totaled. I was in complete shock and panic.

As a result of the impact, Michio, Aveline, and Sally were thrown forward into the front seats. Fortunately no one was injured. Because they were sleeping they were relaxed and able to absorb the impact without trauma. The problem however was with Wendy's pregnancy. She herself was not injured but the shock and impact caused the baby to drop. Realizing that *there was a very real danger that we could lose our first child*, my panic escalated beyond the immediate to the existential and total.

As if things could get any worse, the car we hit contained four very tough looking young males. They were understandably upset. Fortunately they were unhurt. However, they were gesturing threateningly and swearing profusely as they exited their car and surrounded ours. I wasn't sure where this was going, or whether we would face the possibility of violence. The situation was rapidly deteriorating. I don't know how I did it but somehow I managed to hold the local guys at bay until the police arrived.

Events happened fast and remain a blur, but somehow we managed to make our way back up to the tollbooth on the busy bridge. This was before cell phones so we had to explain, over the roar of traffic, to the toll collectors that we urgently needed to call friends for help. We put an urgent call through to Shizuko. She told us to wait and that she would contact Japanese friends who had a car and who would come and pick us up. Finally there was a glimmer of hope.

Waiting uncertainly at the tollbooth that summer night with the glaring lights, heat, nonstop noise, and exhaust was like being in hell, especially with my escalating panic about Wendy. Fortunately, Michio and Aveline remained remarkably calm and that helped me from going completely insane. After thirty minutes of sheer agony, a car pulled up. It was our Japanese angels. We quickly got in and headed back to Shiuko's apartment.

Shizuko immediately diagnosed Wendy's condition. She had Wendy lie down on cushions and asked her to breathe calmly and deeply in order to relax. Then she started to gently massage Wendy's abdomen. She began at the lower abdomen and gently pushed upward. It was apparent that she was trying to reposition the baby to a secure position up in the uterus. She repeated this procedure for about a half hour until she turned to all of us, smiled, and said, "It's going to be OK. Baby back to normal. Wendy needs to rest."

Following all of the intensity, uncertainty, and sheer panic of the evening, I felt the most incredible feelings of joy, relief, and gratitude. *Shizuko had saved our family*. Even now, forty years later, whenever I try to recount the story, it is impossible for me to do so without choking up. My gratitude to Shizuko is boundless, limitless, and eternal.

Michio, Aveline, and Sally returned the next day on the Amtrak train. Wendy and I followed a day or so later. Fortunately no one had been hurt and so we continued with business as usual. Sally's insurance paid for the car and our son Eric was born in October.

Thank you Michio, Aveline, and Shizuko…from the bottom of my heart.

Remembering Michio
Wendy Esko

I met Michio Kushi in August 1973 when I attended a spiritual development seminar he was giving in New York City hosted by Shizuko Yamamoto's East West Center. The topic wasn't particularly exciting to me at the time, but it was an opportunity to meet the teacher who I had heard so much about while living at Denny and Judy Waxman's study house in Philadelphia.

Needlessly to say, I was not disappointed by his refreshing view of spirituality. His simplicity of expression, practical application in daily life, plus his unique sense of humor captured my inner child; my sense of wonder and excitement had returned after so many years being lost. I can honestly say that this encounter was life changing.

One prayer that I have kept close to my heart, and one that Michio said often in the many spiritual development classes he gave was, "When we see the sun and moon, the sky and stars, mountains and rivers, seas and forests, fields and valleys, birds and animals, and all the wonders of nature, let us remember that we have come with them all from the infinite universe. Let us be thankful for our environment on earth and live in harmony with all that surrounds us." When I read this prayer, I can still picture myself sitting in that very first class with eyes closed, listing to this most moving prayer, with chills running down my spine. I had found happiness, a sense of oneness. Hearing Michio teach that body, mind, and spirit were one, and that something as simple as the food we choose to eat was the key to health, happiness, and world peace filled me with inspiration. It gave me a whole new outlook on and purpose in life.

I moved to Boston the following month, living in one of the Kushi study houses, and began attending Michio's lectures at the Noh Center in downtown Boston. Every lecture was more interesting than the last. We learned to apply the principles of yin and yang in our studies, which included countless topics. I can honestly say that those lectures were the most useful classes I ever attended.

Eventually I began working for the Kushis helping organize seminars together with Ed and others. In 1974, Michio was giving a series of lectures in New York. Quite a few Boston students decided to drive down or take the train, including Ed and I. After the seminar ended Michio and Aveline were scheduled to take the train back to Boston, but at the last minute Michio decided to ride with Ed, me, and another friend. I was about six months' pregnant with our first child at the time. We got in the car and started driving toward the expressway. I hadn't put my seat belt on yet. Michio said, "Wendy, put your seat belt on." Everyone looked at him and again very sternly he said, "Wendy, put your seat belt on right now." It was such a shock to hear him speak so forcefully, that I immediately put the belt on. Within just a few minutes a carload of intoxicated teenagers pulled in front of us just before we entered the expressway. Boom! We hit them on the left front fender. Fortunately, they were unhurt. Ed's head hit the windshield and shattered it, but possibly because he is so hardheaded, he was unhurt.

Having put the seat belt on at the time I did quite possibly saved my life and the life of our unborn son, Eric. Aveline slept through the whole event and woke up asking what happened. Michio later explained to us that during the seminar he had a vision of one of his students being in a car accident, but he couldn't figure out who it was. We later learned that he figured out that it was Ed and I. I am eternally grateful for his loving, caring, selfless decision to ride with us, which he believed helped protect us from greater harm. I am also grateful to Shizuko Yamamoto for the massage she performed that helped keep the baby securely in place.

While the above act is a clear example of his selfless nature, I have watched Michio give of himself tirelessly; helping thousands upon thousands of people discover health and happiness. In doing so he has helped raise humanity's consciousness. We are now experiencing a major shift in the dietary choices of humanity, a shift toward healthier lifestyles, a revolt against GMOs and industrial agriculture, and a shift of the medical profession to finally recognize the importance of quality food. As I see all of these changes happening, I can't help but think of how Michio started this all in motion and how he has yet to get the credit he deserves for his role. Hopefully, the groundwork that Michio has laid and shared with so many will lead to the fulfillment of his ultimate dream — One Peaceful World.

I am deeply grateful to Michio and Aveline for having touched my life and family, and for their precious friendship, and teachings that will continue to guide me through life.

Remembering Michio
Bernard Faber

I send you my heartfelt condolences regarding Michio's passing. He was a truly outstanding teacher, a pioneer of the natural foods movement and a Bodhisattva of medicine.

The first time I saw him lecturing was at a seminar in Amsterdam in the early Seventies. At that time I felt he was coming from outer space to rescue us. Well maybe he was...But the dream of One Peaceful World and the macrobiotic teaching of sustaining health through natural foods are so very humane and may well be the only hope for our civilization. The scope of his teachings went far beyond my imagination. His ability of opening up our limited minds was incredible.

I feel humble and very grateful for his teachings.

Remembering Michio
Alice Fava

I was shocked and deeply saddened to hear of Michio Kushi's passing on December 28, 2014 in his eighty-eighth year. Next to my own parents, Michio Kushi has had the biggest influence in my life. I would like to express my heartfelt condolences to his sons and their families and Midori. And special thanks to Midori for taking such good care of Michio!

I feel very blessed to have studied with Michio over the years. He was a great man, inspiring, full of enthusiasm and endless energy. I don't know anyone who could keep up with him. I never heard him utter an unkind word. He never tired of teaching even though it must have been exasperating to repeat the same things over and over. After the Fukushima disaster, he said that many friends (old timers by now) were asking him how to protect against radiation. He seemed surprised to be asked and said that everyone should know by now: miso soup, brown rice, sea vegetables, cooked greens, umeboshi, etc. I thought I sensed a bit of despair in his voice, that we were still asking these kind of questions after all these years!

I would like to express my gratitude to Michio for dedicating his life to nourish my dream. I didn't even know I had a dream until I came across first, George Ohsawa, and then Michio's teachings. I can never repay my gratitude but I will do my best to keep his teachings alive through our efforts at the Macrobiotic Centre of Toronto.

I last saw Michio in March of last year. I travelled from the Kushi Institute to Framingham, Mass. with other Level 3 students for a private session with Michio. I had not seen Michio since the 2012 Summer Conference. This time, when Michio entered the room, I was overcome with emotion and the overwhelming feeling that this was the last time I would be in his physical presence. It was difficult for me to maintain my composure throughout the hour-long talk. So I focused on writing down every word he said, verbatim. Here is his message, in his unique style of English, from that day:

> Everyone, in order to develop yourself and what you'd like to do or accomplish for that purpose:
>
> 1. Always be open minded and listen to people, nature, and;
>
> 2. Observe people, nature, and universal movement;
>
> 3. Do not speak much, please be careful; when people speak, listen first and speak afterwards;
>
> 4. Surround yourself with a clean and orderly desk, papers, closet etc., clean and orderly; handbag very messy inside but looking nice on the outside, don't do;
>
> 5. Clothing: Should not be luxurious but neat and orderly and fitting your type; some of our friends wear cotton clothing, like a wrapped up Roman toga; the mind (sic) is off and not normal to society; fitting to your style; quality on skin to be cotton; outer garment, some mix OK;
>
> 6. Should be able to cook, very important, regardless man or woman; even old time counselors, especially males, cannot cook; some can cook but not everyone; you are not counselor, because, unless you can cook, you don't know what kind of dishes you recommend, what type of taste, miso, vegetables etc.; in order to help that sick person get better; unless you can cook, you are not a counselor;

7. Teaching: Purpose is to make people healthy and well; so teachers must also know how to cook; especially if married, you cook, sometimes sharing, sometimes changing, but both can cook and eat together. Marriage: eat same type of food together; family—eat the same type of food together; if eat same type of food, then we are family, same blood, same thinking, same action; our purpose is to make healthy, peaceful minded persons developing spiritually throughout the world and sharing healthy good food and changing our blood and having similar type of thinking; not concerned about color, religion, nationality etc.; we are concerned about people's blood, cells, whole body and whole way of thinking; we are concerned about quality of human being. Good quality people with good quality blood are very, very few; also, among political leaders, quality of blood not good; whatever you do, quality of food should be good; then intuition and thinking will become clear.

NEXT: Try to visit famous, leading persons, people in the world who are influencing society—choose yourself the person and ask, "I'd like to see you if you have time—ten minutes if you have time etc. In that way, up to thirty years old, I met many famous people. I wrote letters and asked for their thoughts and advice. Constantly learning is needed; as you grow, comes good common sense, wisdom, and judgment coming quite automatically, naturally comes out your love for people; other people and me are one and the same; brotherhood/sisterhood naturally arise.

WHAT IS LOVE? Many people get love and desire mixed up; man and woman love is desire; Jesus said, "The highest love is to die for that person," we are all one. Here is my version of Jesus' saying:

> *For One or for Them*
> *I become Food*
> *Nourishing Their Life and Dream…*
> *And Die*

1. Mother's love;

2. WWII: Soldiers who dedicated their lives to their country and died thought their death would help their country and their people. "I don't mind to die."

WAYS OF SEEING: In the old days when I taught in Brookline, we were seeing only one dimension but there are many different ways of seeing: front and back, top and bottom, inside to outside, and left and right; all different ways of seeing and ways of understanding; also, when we see people, we tend to see only one way, not comprehensively, so we can't understand the whole person; we are prejudiced and discriminating and misjudging all the time; we are doing this because we don't see everything.

Michio then spoke at length about heaven's force and earth's force, left and right, front and back, and facial diagnosis:

Today, out of the many directions, let's study right and left as examples.

When we are living on this planet the forces of yin and yang distinguish everything. Yin and yang are not left and right. They are earth's force going out and heaven's force coming in. Must understand left and right also. Heaven's force is the universe's force. It is yang or contractive. On the other hand, earth's force is yin, or expansive. Which side of the body is yin force going up, and which side is yang force going down? By that we understand left and right. Saying hello with right hand is yin force, pressing down with the left hand is yang force.

THE FACE: Right side of face, yin force, mother; left side of face, yang force, father. Mother more yin force right side, father more yang force left side. Right side, more mother's heritage, left side, more father's heritage

PALMISTRY: Right side, mother's heritage. Left side, father's heritage. There are three main lines on palm. The lifeline shows digestion, and then there are the circulation and nervous system lines. Very similar on both hands yet different.

THE FACE: Morning the right side is brighter, more emotion, and inspiration, right side of the brain is more active. Towards evening, the left side of the brain is more active; the left side of the face is brighter and more theoretical, analytical, and down to earth. So, in the morning, the right side is brighter and in the afternoon the left side is brighter. Front and back are also different: in the morning the front is more active, in the evening, the back is more active.

The right and left sides of the face are not the same; very different father and mother, if the sides of the face are very different, parents may have separated. Look for features twisted in one direction, differences in the eyes, eyebrows. If very different, chances are the parents separated. If slight difference, everyone has slight differences. When talking and one side of the face is more active, parents very different one from the other. It shows the parents not eating together, very easy to separate.

If take too much yin, left side get more sick, right side discharges more yin. Yang food harms left side but causes more trouble on the right side. In the morning, more symptoms appear on the right side. Later in the day, they appear on the left side.

You can see the home in the chin. If the chin is swollen, too much humidity in the house. If the forehead is clear, property OK but if darkness, pimples etc., property has troubles.

Brother's condition, left side of the face. Sister, right side.

Michio finished his talk by saying:

Discover by thinking, by observing. Eighty-eight years old now but I know nothing but I can think, speculate, imagine, but I don't know anything; really study, discern secret of universe, it's endless; learn from other people, but you discover for yourself; I learned many things from teachers, grade school and up;

but more and more discovered myself and learned that way for sixty years and became able to teach, advise, suggest etc. Life is continuous study; endlessly seek the secrets of the universe; have wonderful adventures; make discoveries for many people's happiness;

Learn also the difference between left and right!

Farewell Michio...Please know that you are well loved and please continue to have fun!

Remembering Michio
Olaf Fischer

One of the biggest challenges running the Kushi Institute (K.I.) was having enough financial resources to meet our financial obligations. Michio and I met twice monthly to go over finances and discuss ways to raise money through programs and fundraising.

At one time when the K.I. was particularly stressed financially and I was getting frustrated trying to get my point across to Michio that I needed him to do a consultation for a longtime supporter that he had been refusing to do for some reason, he leaned over to me put his hand on my arm and said: "Olaf, I really appreciate all you do for the K.I., but you are focusing too much on the bottom line. The bottom line is not important. What is important is that we help people. The K.I. does create new macrobiotic teachers and leaders but what is most important is that we help as many people as possible. Don't worry so much about money it will show up in time." And he was right. We were able to raise the funds needed from a source totally unexpected.

On another occasion we were sitting in Dunkin' Donuts at 1:30 a.m. in the morning talking about macrobiotic philosophy and the future of macrobiotics. He ordered coffee for him and tea for me. I asked what would happen to the macrobiotic movement after he passed away. At that time he was in his late seventies. Who would be his successor? What would happen to the K.I.? He looked at me for a long time and then said there would never be another Michio, just like there would never be another Olaf. He felt that if the macrobiotic movement as it started with Ohsawa and continued with him was coming to an end it would take on another form and new leaders would emerge.

I was scribing for Michio in one of his consultations. The client was a woman in her late forties and she was in the late stages of breast cancer. She's gone through the conventional system, radiation, double mastectomy, chemotherapy, and the works. The doctors told her that she only had a few months, maybe a year. Michio did the consultation, very compassionate, one of the best I've seen him do. At the end of the consultation she asked him if there was really hope and if everything was going to be OK? He looked at her for some time with that look of compassion and knowing in his eyes that I've seen so many times. Then he said putting his hand on her arm and said, "Don't worry there is always hope and whatever will happen everything will be OK." At that moment we all knew that the consultation was all about helping her having the best life possible for what was left of it and have a peaceful death. The client started crying but told Michio that she understood and thanked him for being honest. After the consultation I asked Michio just to make sure I understood it right if what he meant that everything was going to be OK even though she was going to die soon and he said: "On a higher level of consciousness everything is always OK. I could see that on a higher level she already had made the decision to leave this life but still needed to accept it in her mind. The consultation was just another step towards that acceptance. Death was just another stepping stone and not a big deal really. We just make it that way because we don't understand it and are afraid of it."

I worked closely with Michio Kushi for over ten years running the K.I. and there were times when I was frustrated and ready to let it all go. However, Michio was a great teacher and mentor to me, and I feel his passing was a great loss to all of us. I might not have always agreed with all of his decisions and everything he did, but there is no denying that Michio and Aveline were a powerful force in starting the alternative health food movement and through their teachings helped thousands of people worldwide live a happier and healthier life. With his passing an era has ended.

Remembering Michio
Drusilla Graham

After many years of studying with Michio and Aveline , it was on a One Peaceful World Tour of Japan that I began to truly appreciate and understand the spirit of macrobiotics. Without Michio's encouragement, for which I am so grateful now, I might have stayed home. How unfortunate that would have been. The insights and understanding gained went far beyond the concepts he was teaching because there one was able to experience them.

"Man is a reflection of his environment." Being in the one that nurtured and helped to formulate Michio Kushi was extremely helpful in understanding his teachings. In America our education is more conceptual, reductionist, and materialistic, based on getting ahead, doing things for self-motive and/or profit, and ultimately creating separation. Michio explained that in Japan the focus of education is very different. For centuries they have placed the highest value on the nurturance of humility and gratitude, respect for others, and never forgetting to honor one's ancestors. The emphasis is on developing one's judgment, beyond just sensory and sentimental levels to a more all-embracing holistic orientation. This is at the heart of macrobiotics. On this particular trip to Japan we visited the villages of both Aveline and Michio. It was here, outside the big cities, where we experienced these time-honored traditions, making it possible to appreciate in this light Michio's dream in teaching macrobiotics.

Aveline's home is in the mountain village of Yokota. In the village next to Aveline's several of us were privileged to spend a night in the homes of friends and family. Myself and another woman were paired to stay with a local farmer whose specialty was Camilla oil — very delicate oil used both cosmetically and medicinally. The reception we received in his home and throughout the village made us feel like family being welcomed home after a long absence. Everyone we met expressed genuine delight and gracious hospitality in hosting us, often showering us not only with physical gifts but even the more precious gifts of constant attention to our comfort and ease of adaptability by explaining customs, helpful expressions, and how routine matters are addressed. There was no question that our hosts had spent days and great effort in preparation, evidence of the honor they felt our visit to be. Before departing on the tour Michio had suggested we bring some small gifts to reciprocate the hospitality we would receive, but we were unprepared for the extent of, not only individual kindness, but also the villagers' endeavors collectively to welcome us.

At the home where we stayed a private room was created by sliding shoji screens, sectioning it off from the rest of the house. Here homemade futons were laid on tatami mats, spread with beautiful natural bedding, so fresh and simple. Kimonos made by the woman of the house were presented to us as gifts along with Camilla oil and home-grown dried shitake mushrooms. After our introduction and communication through body language and pocket translators, our hosts escorted us into the village where we joined others from our tour staying in the same village (maybe six of us total), to a reception at the office of the highest official, the superintendent of schools! This gives you some idea of the prominent place education is given in Japan. In his office a tea ceremony was offered and a translator provided so he could tell us about his village and invite us the next day to visit a local school.

He explained the next event on our agenda would be to visit a community center where a macrobiotic meal was being prepared. This turned out to be not a meal but a banquet of delicious and simply prepared locally grown food in a beautiful setting in the mountains. After our long travels, the food and endeavors put forth were true *mana* to our tired bodies and revived us to continue on to yet another planned event where the locals had arranged an evening of skits, song, and dance. In the Japanese spirit of all-inclusiveness, the microphone was eventually passed to us. So swept up in the revelry of our reception, we gladly put together some songs despite the fact that we were not all American. Amateurishly but happily we sang for our hosts, which delighted them to no end. We concluded with a Japanese-tourist dance menagerie. It is hard to describe the bonding and appreciation we were all feeling at this point; they so happy to host us and we so appreciative of such a warm and spirited welcome. Without the constraints that talking can impose on such a gathering, we were free to communicate not unlike children who play freely through just movement and song. Such a happy and unique evening!

The next day this outpouring of hospitality was continued when schoolchildren prepared a special program for us. Upon entering the school, the first impression was how neatly the children's shoes were arranged before each of their "cubbies;" they wore slippers inside school. We observed a classroom and proceeded to the auditorium where rows of cotton mats were laid horizontally across the floor for each class (instead of chairs). The children filed in quietly, taking their place along side each other, with no talking or squirming. Then each class upon being called stood up in unison and proceeded in an orderly fashion to the stage where they began their performance.

Michio and Aveline explained the emphasis put on education by telling us that when a child enters school, the most important teaching is behavior and relationships: how to treat family, friends, and ancestors. Children are guided and instructed in this study for many years. For example, they are taught when a teacher enters a room, everyone respectfully stands and when asking a question one likewise does the same. At the table, an elder is always given the best position and everyone stands until this person is seated. An older person or parent has more experience therefore one is always respectful and takes care of them, grateful for the opportunity to reciprocate for the nurturance one was given as a child. Additionally and importantly, children are taught how to cook and eat, and to be modest and humble, always expressing gratitude, even for difficulties. They are taught to be quick, precise, and prepared to answer any challenge, distinguishing them by an ability to establish order everywhere.

Later, rejoining the rest of our group, we proceeded to a rice field that had been left unplanted so we could participate in a traditional rice planting. We removed our shoes, rolled up our pants, and stepped into the muddy water, guided by the villagers, as a musician dressed in traditional garb, beat a drum, providing a cadence to our planting. Afterwards, many villages came together for a picnic in a field adjoining the rice paddy, a reenactment of the common practice of a grand celebration after all the rice has been planted. The wide assortment of food was mostly rice-based, all prepared in imaginative ways. It was such an incredible endeavor and took enormous planning on their part to envelop us in this way in their culture and traditions. Even though again we didn't speak the same language we all communicated in the spirit of appreciation and enjoyment.

Other highlights of the trip were visits to the Kumano Shrine, Michio's ancestral shrine where we viewed the statue of the Ya Kushi Nyorai Buddha, a symbol of the universal spirit of healing and salvation, which is designated a National Treasure of Japan. We also visited Michio's family temple, Dai Taiji, which has been continuously maintained for over 1400 years and where we participated in a ceremony honoring ancestors.

This trip gave one a glimpse of the Japanese culture and the spirit in which Michio grew up, the one he brought to macrobiotics. In planning the One Peaceful World Tours, of which there were several, he made it possible for those fortunate enough to go to experience a way of life so very different from that in the West. Michio never tired of finding new ways to educate, or he might prefer to say, play. This trip was one that anchored his teachings in the mind of our cellular bodies by being immersed in a culture that still retained a practical application of the order of the universe.

And having Michio as our guide and translator was invaluable because of his in depth understanding of the Order of the Universe and the history of Japan.

Michio interestingly pointed out that the volcanic soil that created the island of Japan is highly energized. When there, one feels this in breathing the air, walking in the mountains, feeling the energy emanating from waterfalls, bathing in the mineral baths, eating the food, being surrounded by the intention of thousands of temples and shrines, and being in a culture where almost everyone is an artisan carrying on century-old family crafts and traditions, from making tofu and miso to forging cutlery to developing textiles and so much more. Hardly noticeable but equally energizing and influencing is the ancient language of Japanese that as Michio explained, uses the word "Ki" hundreds of times a day. How apparent the powerful influence of one's environment.

Thank you, Michio, your passion for life enlightened and enlivened us to the wonders of this special part of the world. There is no question that it deepened our understanding of the possibility, with perseverance to the principles and spirit of macrobiotics, of creating harmony and peace

Michio's prayers are many. This one comes to mind in appreciating his endeavors to bring the West to meet the East:

> We have all come from One Infinity
> We all are living within One Infinity
> We shall all return to One Infinity
> We are on the endless journey of life, appearing and disappearing
> We all are brothers and sisters manifested from One Infinity
> Let us love each other,
> Let us support each other
> Let us help each other and
> Let us realize our endless dream of One Healthy, Peaceful World.

Remembering Michio
Virginia M. Harper

My heart is filled with gratitude for a man that dedicated his life to his calling — a calling so big as to include World Peace gained through personal peace. He dedicated his life to teaching health, spiritual development and living in harmony with all of nature and humankind. His teachings paved the road for personal inner awareness. It was through the teachings of Michio and his wife Aveline that I was able to regain my health. Their mission to spread macrobiotic philosophy began here in the United States in 1949 and although it was before my time, it gained momentum and credibility as a healthy natural lifestyle that helps all who choose to embrace it. It is through this base of knowledge that my life continues to be full. Surrounded by my precious children, I say thank you Michio for your generosity of time, knowledge, and love that has allowed me to live fully! Your spirit lives on in all of us whose lives you influenced. Your teachings are now respected in the medical, alternative, and scientific worlds. These teachings will also live on as we continue to share. And, the love you embraced us with is now embracing you and your family. Well done, dear teacher, well done.

Remembering Michio
Rod House

I first met Michio in August 1965. It happened at a most interesting time. I was thirty-one years old. I met Michio after many years of searching for answers to life and my place in it.

I grew up in Philadelphia. The year 1965 was a time of spiritual change. I felt a great need for a wider way. I needed a change in my lifestyle, something that would help me with my work. My friends suggested an environmental move. They took me on a month-long trip from Philadelphia to Boston. Along the way they talked about a unique technique called macrobiotics and of a great teacher in Boston. Along the way they directed me to Vermont to visit a Hindu ashram there in the hills. I met Nina Katana, director of the ashram. She was an artist and teacher of the healing arts.

Nina was a friend of Michio's.

After showing me the layout of the ashram, she took me to a room colored with rice paper light, with fresh breezes wafting through. She sat me down on a futon pillow and tatami mat. She served me a bowl of miso soup and a cup of bancha tea.

Nina showed me some selections from George Ohsawa's book *Zen Macrobiotics*. When the time to go arrived, she handed me a piece of paper with Michio's name, phone number, and address in Brighton, Mass. She then said, "You should meet this man!" As we were leaving she handed me a fresh plum and said, "It's a hot day and long trip, bite into the plum and suck out the juice. It will slake your thirst."

I arrived in Brighton and knocked on the Kushis' door. The door opened and a petite doll-like woman [Aveline] appeared. "What can I do for you?" she asked. I explained how I got there. She then nodded here head saying, "One minute please." Then Michio appeared. Looking me up and down he said, "Can I help you?" As I attempted to tell him of my journey, he swiftly moved his hand to the right side of my chest; then to the left, and then to the middle, saying, "You have pain here, here, there!" I thought, "Either this man is a wizard, or he knows something I should know." He said to me, "What is it you want to do?" I said, "I want to study with you." He placed his hand on my shoulder, inviting me into his living room. We sat and talked for one or two hours or so. It was like a condensed seminar on the unique principle and its application to all things past, present, and future in very simple light. I felt the release of old ways and rigid convictions dissolve.

He asked me to stay and study more. I explained to him that I needed to return to Philadelphia to settle affairs. We agreed to keep in touch by phone and mail. I started a small study group and began inviting Michio, Shizuko Yamamoto, and other macrobiotic teachers to do periodic seminars. I finished my Bachelors and Masters Degrees in two years. Then, in 1970, I left Philadelphia for Massachusetts. It was truly amazing how quickly the macrobiotic lifestyle can improve all things.

Day by day, I could see the relationship of all things in this life we live. Now, in retrospect, I recall this memory of our first meeting as though it was always happening, even before we met, as though past, present, future are continuously ongoing.

Three days after Michio's Memorial, I awoke in a dream. In a total landscape filled with life energy, Michio appeared. He waved his hand, wishing us well, sending his spirit to us to continue the work we have yet to do, smiling with that enigmatic smile of his.

Remembering Michio
Naomi Ichikawa

I graduated from the Kushi Institute in Becket in the summer of 2010. After returning to Tokyo I attended an advanced class with Michio at the Kushi Institute of Japan (KIJ.) Michio's lecture was energetic and inspiring. One thing in particular made a deep impression on me. Michio told us that unfortunately we were having wars between countries, but that in reality, national boundaries don't exist. If we see our planet from the universe, there are no national borders. We are actually one. Why are we fighting with our family and friends?

I was astonished at Michio's message. It became obvious that national boundaries are manmade and artificial and that a diet of animal food leads people to become aggressive and easy to fight with each other.

When I was a student at the K.I., my classmates came from all over the world. They were from Israel, China, Japan, Kuwait, Australia, Korea, Trinidad, and throughout the U.S. What a wonderful experience! We shared food, studies, and friendship. Our group was very harmonious. We experienced One Peaceful World.

Michio also said that macrobiotics was the way to erase artificial boundaries. I agree totally. After hearing his lecture I decided I would teach macrobiotics as the way toward One Peaceful World. I feel endless gratitude toward Michio and Aveline for showing us the way to a peaceful and happy future.

Remembering Michio
Alex Jack

Michio Kushi touched the lives of tens of thousands of individuals and families—often one by one—with his personal advice and guidance, as well as his lectures, seminars, and conferences. He transformed millions with Erewhon, his pioneer natural and organic foods company, and with his books, videos, and cassettes. He influenced billions with the breakthrough scientific and medical studies he inspired at Harvard Medical School, the Framingham Heart Study, and other medical centers that led to new national and international dietary guidelines and the transition toward a predominantly plant-based diet. He changed the way America and the modern world eats and heals. He set the direction for realizing humanity's eternal dream of one healthy, peaceful world.

As a catalyst for calm, steady, orderly change, Michio's impact on our era is boundless. He and his devoted wife Aveline trained a generation of whole foods teachers, chefs, and food producers. They taught a generation of healers, physicians, and other health care practitioners how to diagnose, prevent, and relieve chronic and acute disease naturally without harmful drugs, surgery, and scans. They inspired the first prison projects to rehabilitate offenders with diet. Their students brought together warring Christians, Muslims, and Jews in the Middle East. They introduced nondenominational spiritual training practices that led to union with God, the universal spirit, or what Michio called One Infinity.

With endless gratitude, the macrobiotic community paid farewell over the New Year's holidays to its longtime leader; inspiring teacher, counselor, and author; beloved husband, father, and grandfather; and unsurpassed cultural bearer and spiritual guide.

Like Moses, Buddha, Jesus, Muhammad, Gandhi, Martin Luther King, and other great teachers of life, Michio was not always understood or appreciated in his lifetime. Like them, he had personal flaws and deficiencies. But in the unfolding spiral of history, Michio will be remembered as one of humanity's greatest prophets, healers, and spiritual teachers.

It has been a privilege to have known and worked with him closely for many years, as a student and teacher, editor and author, and as employee and manager of several organizations Aveline and he founded.

Among the many memorable experiences that stand out, one of the most enlightening took place at his home on Bucky Road in Brookline about 25 years ago. We were working together on a chapter for a book in the family dining room one night late. Because of his busy counseling schedule, we often wouldn't start work on writing projects until after midnight.

On this occasion, I finally got up the courage to ask him: "What is the essence of macrobiotics?" I wanted to know the central teaching or practice. Was it a principle or a technique, or both? George Ohsawa often wrote, "Principle without practice is useless. Practice without principle is dangerous."

Over the years, in classes and conversations, Michio had always penetrated to the heart of things. He would often say, "You don't need to know yin and yang." "Brown rice is wonderful, but not necessary," implying there were of course many other whole grains and healthy foods. Clearly, not all cultures and civilizations thrived on rice. Nor were they superior to those that did not.

I also remembered him admonishing us, "Never forget the spiral. You can forget everything else. The logarithmic spiral is the form that mirrors our universe, our human form and structure, and our evolving lives." Perhaps it was proper chewing or keeping a calm, clear mind and spirit. Maintaining an open mind, or what traditionally is known as non-credo ("do not believe") was also on my short list of most important qualities. This tenant, a favorite of Ohsawa's, was embodied by such diverse personalities as Socrates, Doubting Thomas (Jesus's skeptical disciple), and Harry Truman, the plain-speaking president from Missouri, the "Show-Me State."

Without a moment's hesitation, Michio glanced up from the text he was reviewing and said evenly: "Love thy parents."

I was stunned. "Honor thy father and thy mother" was, of course, a time-honored concept, the fifth of the Ten Commandments. But coming from him it was totally unexpected.

My initial reaction was that his response was a not-too-subtle personal warning to me to put my own relationship with my parents in order. Clearly not, I quickly realized with great relief. I had wonderful, loving parents, and except for the usual childhood mischief (such as running up to the pulpit and sitting in the minister's high back chair at the Unitarian Church in Evanston, Il where my dad was the minister), I was rarely rebuked or disciplined. On the contrary, I was always nurtured and supported throughout my formative years through college, graduate school, and my early adulthood as a journalist in Vietnam and following my father and serving as a civil rights and peace activist.

Both my parents then were still alive, and I enjoyed excellent relations with each. The only two things that upset my father in recent memory was first when I was thrown out of Boston University School of Theology for organizing a sanctuary in the chapel for an American G.I. who refused to fight in Vietnam. Thousands of students rallied in round the clock support to protect him from the authorities and virtually closed down the university for a week. Eventually, after a week of nationwide antiwar publicity, the FBI raided the chapel and whisked the soldier away. My dad supported the protest. But after I was expelled from seminary, I lost interest in becoming a minister and following in his footsteps and that of my grandfather.

The second thing that upset my father was devoting my life to macrobiotics. He didn't understand what it was all about and used to say that he hadn't raised his son to be a cook and write about food. Reflecting the conventional view of that era (shared ironically by the early macho macrobiotic community) was that cooking was woman's work. As for writing books with Michio, he advised me to "get a real job" as an editor with a solvent magazine or book publisher. Except for these disappointments, my father was always very supportive, and he remained my hero for the rest of his life. Throughout his life he had devoted his whole being to human rights and peace, participating in the first sit-in and freedom ride against segregation in the 1940s, befriending Albert Schweitzer in Africa (about the same time Ohsawa was there), and becoming an intimate of Martin Luther King to whom he helped introduce Gandhian principles of nonviolence. My father took me on my first trip to Japan as a child and later to Europe, China, and around the world. Michio really admired my dad (who was also one of the original World Federalists like he was) and spoke highly of him.

If not my own parents, to whom was Michio referring when he said, "Love thy parents"? Next I wondered if he was implying I was not filial enough to him and Aveline. They served as surrogate parents for a generation of macrobiotic students and teachers, including most of my closest friends and associates. I was eternally grateful for the love and friendship of both Kushis. But because my own parents were so kind, compassionate, and encouraging, I never looked at Michio or Aveline as my parents.

I didn't engage Michio in conversation about what he meant by "love thy parents." I was so surprised I remained speechless. Michio returned to glancing at a draft of the chapter we were working on and quickly changed the topic.

Of course, his words echoed in my mind for many years. About twenty years later, I finally realized what I think he meant. I was teaching at Rosas, the contemporary dance company, in Brussels where I had been invited to teach by Anne Teresa de Keersmacher, the director. Anne Teresa had founded the company and PARTS, a dance school, which once served as the national dance company of Belgium. She was a world-renowned dancer and after changing her diet introduced a macrobiotic lunch program at her school. Anne Teresa gave a stellar performance at Michio's 80th birthday party in Amsterdam where I was then living. She used the I Ching, Nine Star Ki, yin and yang, and other principles of macrobiotic philosophy in her compositions and choreography.

Preparing my lectures on macrobiotics and sacred dance, I discovered that all traditional societies had rituals of growing up to mark the transition from childhood to adulthood. Of course, they differed from culture to culture. Most involved dance and musical rites of some kind, or other practice such as a vision quest in the wilderness. The essence of the experience was that the children, usually in their early teens though sometimes older, were initiated into becoming adult members of the community. They learned through dance, song, and myth that their birth mother and father were no longer responsible for them as they had been during their childhood. Now their true parents were heaven and earth — sky and soil, sun and moon, or other yin/yang polarity — and from now on their divine father and mother would be responsible for all their needs — physical, emotional, mental, and spiritual. Of course, they would still live with their families after the ceremony and in many cases continue to do so as part of an extended family. But an axis shift had taken place in their consciousness. They graduated from the horizontal relationship they enjoyed with their earthly parents and family to a direct vertical relationship with heaven and earth's forces.

Sadly, today in modern society we have almost no rituals or ceremonies to mark the stages of life. Most young people don't know when childhood ends and adulthood begins. Is it when they are old enough to vote? Drink and smoke? Have sex? Be drafted or resist going into the army? Get a job? In my own case, I remember referring to my peers as kids, as well as cats and chicks) until well into our late twenties! This lack of order and identity lay at the root of so much restlessness, uncertainty, and suffering today, as young people don't know what is expected or them and float through life without direction or a dream.

In the final analysis, I feel that these multiple levels of meaning were conveyed by Michio to me in that one injunction, "Love thy parents." Please self-reflect, he seemed to be telling me, on who are your true parents and honor them. It is actually the same as Jesus's response in the Gospel of Matthew when he is asked, "Teacher, what is the greatest commandment?" He replied, "You shall love the Lord your God with all thy heart." God in this case means the spirit of heaven and earth. And indeed, in Hebrew, "Lord" and "God" are not identical. Lord (*Elohim*) means Divine Mercy, while God (*Adonai*) means Divine Justice. Compassion and righteousness are equivalent to yin and yang, or earth and heaven — exactly the same meaning as love thy universal parents.

Indeed, a decade later, I went on after that midnight satori to write with Michio *The Gospel of Peace: Jesus's Teachings of Eternal Truth*. This book, a collection of once heretical sayings of Jesus that came to light in 1945 (three months after the end of World War II and my birth) are now widely acknowledged by Judaism, Protestantism, and Catholicism as the earliest, most authentic teachings of Jesus. Michio used it as his main text in Spiritual Development Training Seminars at Becket for ten years. I agreed with him that it was the most profound macrobiotic teachings ever composed. Though totally enigmatic to scholars, lay readers, and all of us students, Michio would explain clearly and simply, after hours of fruitless discussion among us, what each saying meant. We were all astonished and felt that the only way he could unlock the meaning of this gospel was if he had lived it! Michio shrugged off any such speculation on our part, but amusingly noted that he was related to Jesus in a previous lifetime!

One other classic story about Michio comes to mind and one I love to tell students in my classes. Michio is renowned for his unparalleled intuition about food quality. From one taste, he can discern not only every ingredient in a food but also each step of cooking or food processing, including the climate and environment in which the crop originated! (Today there are still a few old farmers who can tell from one sip of a glass of milk what individual cow it comes from.) In Michio's case, his diagnosis of food was similar to that of people. From a glance, he could tell you everything about them, including their diet and health history, as well as their family heritage going back seven generations.

The first time I managed the K.I. in the late 1980s, we had a staff dinner on Friday evenings in the then small staff dining room behind the kitchen in the Main House. One evening, Michio was still counseling and joined us late after we had almost finished eating. The dinner featured cod (or some other white-meat fish), and we were all relaxing after a long, rewarding but tiring week.

When Michio arrived and sat down to join us, we immediately made him a plate, including a generous helping of cod. We had a congenial conversation while he ate, but soon noticed that he hadn't touched the fish. "Aren't you going to try the delicious cod?" someone asked. "It's really fresh." Michio smiled and said simply, "It's not good." What, we all thought! It was nicely cooked, balanced with ginger, lemon, and daikon, and very delicious. Again, we remonstrated with him that we all enjoyed the fish and he should have some to replenish his energy.

Without saying a word, Michio stood up and went to the radiator where Marbles, the nearly blind calico cat was sleeping by the windowsill. Marbles was the last survivor from the former Franciscan monastery that occupied the property for many years. Michio gently picked up Marbles, set him on the floor, and took the fish from his own plate and put it on a saucer in front of the cat. Marbles bent down, smelled the fish, and turning up its nose and tail, proceeded to walk away and resume its nap by the radiator.

We were all left speechless. Even old Marbles, the blind antique cat wouldn't touch the fish and had better intuition than all of us senior teachers and expert cooks combined! He hadn't lost his marbles after all. We had! Without another word, Michio resumed his place and finished his meal. No one said a word. No one had to. Michio — the 2 Soil Tiger, a kindly big cat at heart — had gently proved his point. Our ignorance was infinite! With that one wordless gesture, he showed us how much more there was to learn. Truly, Michio was an amazing teacher of life.

The last time I saw Michio was in Boston several weeks before he died. Edward Esko and I had gone in to see him in early December and report on K.I. business and activities, as we did once or twice a month. He had fallen that morning and bruised his side. I had been very concerned since the August Summer Conference for his health and well being. Michio had gone to Japan to teach in July and followed it up with a rigorous two-week teaching and counseling schedule in Becket. He looked more fatigued than ever. Just prior to our final meeting he had returned to Japan in late autumn for several more weeks of intense teaching and meetings. He was in the dangerous *An Ken Satsu* (Dark Killing Sword) position for the month in Nine Star Ki cosmology. I had expressed my concern about his traveling, but he never listened to advice about his personal safety. On his return, he was so exhausted we cancelled his lecture at Thanksgiving — the anniversary of his arrival in America in San Francisco in 1949.

Two substantive things took place at that last meeting. First we reported to him on the success of the Breast Cancer Seminar at the K.I. and how two researchers, one from Tufts University and the other from Johns Hopkins Medical School, attended and approached us offering to organize the first randomized, controlled clinical trial of the macrobiotic approach to cancer. This was the gold standard of medical testing and could lead to a paradigm shift in cancer treatment with diet. Michio was thrilled, as if it proved successful would fulfill a forty-year dream that he and Aveline had of demonstrating the efficacy of a macrobiotic way of eating in relieving this disease. Since the first Cancer & Diet conference at Pine Manor College in Brookline that the Kushis sponsored in 1976 this had been a cherished dream.

Second, we reported that the dietary guidelines for Ebola he dictated a few weeks earlier had been emailed to 200 medical centers, government agencies, and relief organizations and posted on the K.I. website. He took satisfaction that macrobiotic recommendations (the only ones on the Internet addressing the subject), including an analysis of the origin, cause, and treatment of this deadly epidemic, had been made available to the medical profession and the general public. Deeply concerned about the emergence of novel pandemics, he predicted that there would be one greater scourge heralding the end of modern civilization and the rise of a new era of humankind based on macrobiotic, holistic, and spiritually oriented principles. The three challenges he listed were nuclear weapons and energy, AIDS, and Ebola and similar viral outbreaks. His litany reminded me of the Four Horsemen of the Apocalypse, an image in the Book of Revelation he used to lecture about. Macrobiotics he predicted, held the key to passing safely through this time and the start of a bright new era as Polaris, the pole star, reached its zenith in the early 21st century and started to sink in the northern sky.

In publishing the Ebola recommendations, he insisted that we include our names as co-authors. "In the future many scientists and physicians will call or come to the Kushi Institute and turn to you." In retrospect, it was the closest thing to goodbye that Michio said to us, and I was startled me because it implied he would not be with us much longer.

Michio's death made me reflect on my father's last days. He came down with pancreatic cancer, as had Michio (though in Michio's case, he did not tell us). At my encouragement, my father came to Becket and enrolled in the Way to Health program for a week and had a consultation with Michio. In one poignant moment, my father thanked me for all my help. "You know, what you are doing with diet and cooking is truly wonderful," he confided. "I'm very proud of you." That was the last meaningful conversation we had, and I was very grateful he had finally recognized and acknowledged the primacy of diet and cooking. My father changed his way of eating and ate as best he could and followed my remedies, but he was unable to recover and died peacefully a couple months later. My sister and I were at his bedside, as Michio's wife and four children were at his.

These are just a few remembrances of Michio — our heavenly teacher — as one era ends and a new one begins. He inspired us to discover our heavenly father and earthly mother. He guided us to love all of our parents, earthly and divine, and he influenced us to become better parents and sons and daughters ourselves. In the words of I Corinthians, "Love never fails. But where there are prophecies, they will cease; where there are tongues, they will be stilled; where there is knowledge, it will pass away. For we know in part and we prophesy in part, but when completeness comes, what is in part disappears . . . .. And now these three remain: faith, hope and love. But the greatest of these is love."

Like Moses, Jesus, Lincoln, Gandhi, and Martin Luther King, Michio did not overcome his final challenge. He suffered a sudden health crisis brought on by too much speaking, counseling, and traveling during the last year of his life, as he went the extra mile to spread his message of enduring health and peace. In a talk to the Levels students last spring, Michio shared a poem that he had composed about Jesus sacrificing his life for humanity:

> *For One or for Them*
> *I become Food*
> *Nourishing Their Life and Dream...*
> *And Die*

In retrospect, Michio's last poem was prophetic about his own destiny. Though he failed to cross the river Jordan himself, he led the modern era through the Wilderness to the Promised Land. He passed the torch on to us and the next generation to lead modern society safely through the Spiral of History into the New Era of Humanity. He was truly a man of the age and a man for the ages.

Farewell, dear Michio. May your spirit ascend peacefully into the world of light on the wings of our prayers and thoughts. May you become one with the universal spirit of love. May we be forever One.

Remembering Michio
Gale Jack

I first met Michio and Aveline when they gave a seminar at the Today Church in Dallas in early 1979 then came to Brookline in 1980 for a five-week study while my young son and I stayed in a nearby study house. Later I completed Level II in Brookline while staying with Alex.

In early March, 1988, after we married, Alex and I moved to Becket where he took over as director of the Institute there and I took over as bookkeeper and Alex's assistant in that — as a Licensed Professional Counselor, I was a natural to listen to all of the daily complaints of the students and staff and offer a condensed version to Alex in cases where listening and sympathizing wasn't enough to resolve the problem.

When the Kushi Institute moved their classes to Becket, I was there. When Michio began his Spiritual Seminars, I was there. When the six Level 4 seminars in which Michio was the main teacher took place, I was there. At some point during those years I became aware that Michio and I were clairvoyantly connected — largely through his ability to read my mind.

Once during a consultation, a visitor asked Michio what the people depicted in Michelangelo's drawings in the Sistine Chapel were eating. Michio was temporarily stumped so I visualized the people and the chapel in my mind for less than a minute and then he quickly answered her.

So it was no surprise to me that when I sat across from him in the One Peaceful World building in Becket last August and could see signs of his upcoming death — the hollow cheeks and dark aura that I had seen in my sister before she died — signs that he had taught us to recognize — that he knew my thinking. He responded, "Yes, one day I will die…and whatever happens, I want you to continue teaching macrobiotics and setting an example for others."

I had talked with friends about Michio's condition as well — given that more yin individuals die in years with more upward, yin energy, often when they're in a position that is opposite their own energy in the 9 Star Ki calendar. So it was with great sadness, but no surprise, when we learned that Michio had passed away. I should say that he left his physical body because every time I visit Becket, he'll be there. Every time I reach for one of his books, he'll be there. Every time I teach a cooking class or serve a macrobiotic meal to my family, he'll be there.

Though my brothers and sisters may leave me, my children may leave me, my grandchildren may leave me, my best friends and longtime partners may leave me, I will never walk alone on this earth because he will be there — his spirit will be there.

Remembering Michio
Phil Jannetta

Someone once said that the mark of a great individual is his or her willingness (and ability) to address the major issues of their time. Michio Kushi personified this definition, and more.

He was a tireless teacher and counselor. By consistently reaching out to the scientific and medical communities, and to governmental agencies, he forged links to both institutional decision makers and the general population.

Michio founded centers for macrobiotic education around the world where students learn the theories and skills to fashion the quality of life they aspire to. He established, and inspired others to start, businesses oriented toward macrobiotics. These enterprises provide the foods, goods, and services that make living a macrobiotic lifestyle so practical and convenient.

Above all else, Michio continually encouraged his students to develop themselves so that, with understanding and skill, we could make a positive and lasting contribution to the world.

Decades before becoming daily topics of public discussion, Michio anticipated the major issues facing our world today, and the trends that loom in our future. More importantly, he taught us how to approach these issues holistically, by tackling their causes — as difficult as that may sometimes seem.

Future generations of individuals and families, communities and societies will consolidate the vision of a peaceful and varied world, based on wisdom and fellowship, that was the focus of Michio's life.

What follows is a personal remembrance. I leave it to others to catalogue the numerous specific achievements that highlight Michio's remarkable work.

Meeting Michio
People are of course attracted to macrobiotics for a variety of reasons. In the wake of the 1960s "cultural revolution," many were drawn by the infinite vision of life, applied on a personal level, that the macrobiotic perspective and philosophy embodies.

My introduction to Michio Kushi (and to macrobiotics) came at the 1976 Summer Conference at Amherst College in Western Mass. Incredibly, Michio lectured two and often three times a day, two hours per class — for ten days! (It was only after I started teaching myself that I realized what a feat of inspiration and stamina this was.)

Like many before me and many after, I was captivated by the vision of the Order of the Universe, of Origin and Destiny and of Meaning and Purpose that Michio presented.

With elegance, good humor, and thoroughness, he addressed the very issues I had been trying to answer for myself. In ten days of lectures, Michio demonstrated the relationship between diet and health, body and mind, individual and family well-being and social harmony. For the first time, I understood that by flexibly fashioning a lifestyle based on natural principles, we promote and direct a lifetime of personal development.

Please Come to Boston
After one of his final lectures, I went up to thank Michio for the insight and inspiration he had given us. He looked at me a moment, and then simply said, "Please come to Boston" — words I would

hear him repeat many times to many individuals in the years to come.

I know now that his was an invitation to come and learn how to change myself from the inside out, and then how to show others to do the same.

Michio's suggestion made little impression until I returned home and realized I lacked the know-how to put into practice all the concepts I had been exposed to. Within weeks I had settled my affairs, packed and moved to Boston. Four days later I had the good fortune to start working at the East West Foundation, the forerunner of the Kushi Institute.

It was a heady time. Michio gave regular weekday evening classes and weekend seminars. He invited such remarkable individuals as Herman and Cornelia Aihara, and Shizuko Yamamoto, as well as teachers from Japan, to share their experiences and insights.

Students from various backgrounds gathered in Boston from around the world. It was a vibrant community, full of high energy and bright hopes for the future. I genuinely felt that I had come home.

Dreams, Large and Small
Embracing a dream large enough to dedicate one's entire life to achieving was a consistent topic of Michio teachings. It reminded me of a grade-school teacher once reciting the ditty: "Aim for the stars and you will reach the moon. Aim for the moon and you will embrace the clouds. But, if you only reach for the clouds, you may never get off the ground."

The symbolism resonated, but I did not know how to make it personal. I had never heard of having a dream for one's life.

Michio linked the concept of an endless dream of well being for all, with the essential nature of self. In doing so, he helped me recognize how such a vision adds direction, momentum and a sense of infinite possibility to life.

Interestingly, soon after I moved to Japan, a new Japanese friend asked me, "What was my dream?" Supposing this was a macrobiotic concept, I was taken aback, until I recalled Michio saying, "Humanity shares a common dream. A peaceful world for all is our deepest intuition."

Truly, we are all dreamers. Our aspirations for personal happiness, I came to realize, are natural expressions of this larger dynamic.

In Japan
In the mid-1980s, I got to see a different side of Michio, when he and Aveline started to visit Japan regularly. My wife and I had by then started the Macrobiotics Tokyo Center in 1982. We now had the good fortune to spend much time with the Kushis, helping them in small ways, and sitting in on meetings with government officials, business leaders, and Japanese macrobiotic teachers—many having studied with George Ohsawa themselves.

We organized Michio's English-language seminars for the ex-pat community and attended his lectures for the Japanese public. With patience and perspective, Michio geared his presentations to the hyper-modern society that was Japan in the 1980s. Its economy was soaring, its traditions disappearing.

Michio reminded the Japanese of the natural principles their traditions embodied, and how these practices were the heart of their society. He explained the reasons behind the customs, and the benefits they bestowed. Importantly, he showed how traditions could and should be updated, in mindful ways, to reflect the circumstances and needs of contemporary Japan.

Many farmers and producers of traditional Japanese foods and other goods, and teachers of traditional arts, experienced resurgence in demand for their products and services, thanks to these efforts.

At the same time, Michio offered a wide view of relationship to help the island-bound Japanese realize they were part of a community of nations—a fact that would soon become undeniable with the advent of the internet, the rise of China and the global economy.

Michio enthusiastically reported on the positive developments being made in Europe and the U.S., and encouraged the Japanese to catch up. I fondly remembered him taking the same approach to motivate his students in Boston. There, he regularly described the progress and achievements unfolding in Europe and Japan.

Miracles

One of my responsibilities at the Kushi Institute in Brookline was to take notes during Michio's consultations. On a revisit, in which a middle-aged man reported much progress, Michio asked how well he had been able to follow the suggestions. It was amazing to me that the man had not been as conscientious as I thought he should have been, and yet experienced remarkable improvements in his health and outlook. Afterwards, I commented to Michio that, despite his less than perfect follow through, the man's recovery was miraculous. Michio replied in his succinct way that "All of life is a miracle."

Yes, I realized. Miracles are all around us, if we have the eyes to see them. Being part of the macrobiotic community made this easy. I regularly witnessed individuals change illness into health, despair into hope, confusion into clarity. On a personal level, I saw how I had been able to consciously and flexibly changed the course of my own life. These indeed are miracles.

Yet, they are merely part of a much larger miracle — of the immense and peaceful transformation in social and institutional, scientific and governmental attitudes towards fundamental issues of health and well being.

As a single example, consider our dramatic shift in attitude towards food over the last fifty years. We have come to value organic farming and natural-production methods, eating whole, seasonal and local, home cooking and family meals. Although it may take another generation to consolidate, we have lived through a revolutionary change in perspective regarding the connection between personal well-being, the food we consume and the environment that produces it.

Spiritual Seminars
I was living in Japan when Michio started offering regular spiritual seminars at the Kushi Institute in Becket, Mass. I made it a point to participate each year. The teachings and practices, beautiful natural setting, and simple eating combined to work extraordinary changes in my fellow participants and myself.

By emphasizing daily practices that enhance body and spirit, Michio helped many gain a new appreciation for their own faith. More have found reliable ways to integrate the metaphysical with the physical.

A Legacy for Humanity
From concepts of holistic health, family and community well being, and spiritual development, Michio helped initiate, guide, and foster the awakening taking place in our collective consciousness. His enduring gift was teaching us how to discover and clarify our own life's dream, and how to broaden our motivation to include the welfare of all.

As the years have passed and I have both witnessed and experienced life's inevitable ups and downs, I have come to see that a peaceful world is not simply a worthy aspiration. Its outline is now actually emerging.

The groundwork is being laid in our expanding perception of fellowship and shared well being, made possible by living in harmony with natural principles. As we gain skill and confidence, the application of these insights will accelerate. In time, humanity will have the chance to consistently make the choices that produce this new era.

At Michio's Memorial Service, held at Boston's Arlington Street Church, Michio's youngest son, Hisao concluded his talk with words to the effect that: "My father was many things, an educator, an author, a businessman. But in the end, he was a dreamer. And I will miss that."

With his dreams, Michio has left us the key to the age of harmony that he dedicated his life to realizing. His students, and the generations of students that follow, will pave the way for the fulfillment of this vision.

Thank you Michio. I owe you much. Wherever you are now, I know you continue to pursue your endless vision.

With much gratitude.

Remembering Michio
Woody Johnson

Memories of Micho! So many! Almost too many! The good times we had together.

I remember studying in Boston with Michio at the old Noh Center on Boylston Street with him in a black three-piece suit, no less. I always saw him in a black three-piece suit. I saw him talk about yin and yang so many times to groups of three to twenty-three people.

Unfortunately I slept through many of his talks. Sorry Michio! Some of it must have stuck though. With the help of my wife Florence, I'm still practicing macrobiotics.

Then there were the great evenings following Michio's lectures at the 1200 Motel on Beacon Street in Brookline. Over great dry whole wheat toast and black coffee and perhaps French fries, we would reflect on the evening's talk and discuss future plans.

And most of all, thank you Michio. I'm still dreaming about future plans.

Remembering Michio
Sachi Kato

"Wa 和 — or Peace — will manifest when we eat brown rice." —
Michio Kushi

"Michio Kushi" — the first time I heard the name was at Inaka, a restaurant in Los Angeles. Back in the day, Inaka was the only macrobiotic restaurant in L.A., and I was waiting tables. It is a small family-owned restaurant that is like an oasis in the life of a big, busy city. Many customers came to dine in this relaxing hideaway, and often we discussed macrobiotic philosophy and the correspondences between food and "yin and yang." At first, I thought it was strange to consider food as energy, but soon I became intrigued by the concept. That is how I was first introduced to macrobiotics. Intellectually, I couldn't understand very well then, but I had a gut feeling there was something to it. This intuition strengthened my interest in macrobiotics and in meeting this *sensei* — Michio Kushi — one day.

Years later, I pursued macrobiotic education. I took the Levels courses at the Kushi Institute of Europe, and soon learned that Michio Kushi was still teaching actively in Japan. I enrolled in Level 3 at the Kushi Institute of Japan in 2010 and looked forward to meeting and studying with him.

I was surprised to find that the lectures in Level 3 — the advance course at the KIJ — were almost all about spirituality. They dealt with such subjects as "Where did we all come from?" and "Where are we going after this life?" Michio presented these questions in many lectures, and we discussed spirituality. He encouraged us to meditate, empty our minds, and purify ourselves. His message was unique, and I strove to grasp everything he taught and not miss a single word. He was often comical, making jokes and telling amusing stories. I was impressed how strong and capable a teacher he was despite his old age.

At the end of the final lecture of Level 3, he gently asked us if we had any questions. The classroom grew silent. Michio said, "OK, since there are no more questions, I will bid you so long. This may be the last occasion I will spend time together with you."

Then a sudden urge arose within in me to venture a question. I raised my hand and asked, "*Sensei*, what is the dream of brown rice?"

Michio had been lecturing about the dream of different foods. He taught us that food was spirit, and that each food had its own unique dream. When we eat certain vegetables, their dreams live within us. Before this talk, it never occurred to me that vegetables have a mind and a dream, or goal, in life. One part of me thought this idea was ridiculous, but another part was intrigued by the subject. It was an eye-opening experience, and I began to see things in a totally different perspective.

"What is the dream of brown rice?" At the very moment I asked Michio the question, strangely, the answer came to me. It was a revelation. A little voice echoed in my heart and whispered "Peace."

I was at a loss for words and tried to grasp what happened at the moment. The sensation was very strong and overwhelming. Then a vision of a brown rice field appeared. The tall brown rice straws were full of grains, bent over with full heads ready for harvest, and blowing in the wind. The golden fields were shining. It was a serene and peaceful scene, totally tranquil, and I could almost hear the sound of the straws touching and making waves. Then the message came to me that the rice grains don't speak a word, but are waiting for us to eat them for the purpose of manifesting their dream of "Peace." The vision was very moving. What an amazing and sacred dream the grains have! They just want us to make the world a peaceful place!

The sensation was so overwhelming that in that split second I burst into tears. Everyone in the classroom must have wondered what happened to me. But Michio remained sitting quietly without speaking.

Then finally I said to Michio, "*Sensei*, I got it. The dream of rice is 'Peace,' isn't it?

Michio didn't reply directly. Instead he quietly asked his wife, Midori, to come to the front of the lecture room and instructed her to write the Japanese word for "Peace" or *Wa* 和.

Michio gently said, "If you look closely at this word *Wa*, it contains two symbols. On the left is 'rice straw' and on the right 'mouth.' This word *Wa* has a profound meaning: By eating rice we can manifest peace."

Until then I never knew that Japanese ideographs have such a deep meaning. My appreciation deepened toward my ancestors who must have understood the concepts to compose those words. This was one of my special moments with Michio *sensei* who taught me the essence of life.

Michio's lecture was clear and very easy to understand. I know now he just wanted us to understand the essence of life and how to live simply and meaningfully. He taught us how to live gracefully and eat well. If we understand more about the dreams of vegetables, rice, and other foods, we can appreciate better nature's gifts.

Michio emphasized eating well as the principal practice of macrobiotics because it enables us to manifest our dreams. He often said to us, "The purpose of life is to play." In my view, this means by eating in a balanced way, we are able to realize our potential and achieve our dreams. That is the ultimate freedom, and our lives become "playful."

Thank you, Michio *sensei*.

Remembering Michio
Bill Kaufman

Michio exponentially expanded my world. The first time I met Michio was at his home where he gave me a complimentary diagnosis. Through facial physiognomy alone, an art he had perfected (and generously taught us) he told me many things that I immediately recognized as true, and nailed exactly where my chronic back pain was and why it was occurring. He said "problem with kidneys, left kidney in particular." I was astonished enough to drop out of a full doctoral fellowship in philosophy and move to Boston. I was studying to become a philosophy professor at the time, but thought, Michio had more practical, and in a philosophical way, true knowledge to teach me than all the philosophy professors I had studied with combined.

Sometimes Michio's ideas seemed a "reach," but he was always thinking, theorizing and seeing new relationships between his observations and his standing and evolving theories.

A beautiful macrobiotic wife and four healthy, smart, successful children (all who had the macrobiotic advantage through inception and gestation) and six grandchildren later, I will always feel grateful for Michio's kindness and generosity. I really doubt if I would have been around to write this now, were it not for Michio Kushi.

Remembering Michio
Kit Kitatani

The mortals, including human beings, must leave this world when the time comes. It gives a tremendous and very sad experience to the people left behind. But we must understand that this transition is nothing but a peaceful step to eternal peace for the person leaving this world. We are sad when we hear about someone passing away but for the person concerned, it should be taken and remembered as a spiritual journey to the spiritual world where we can "be with God" and be peaceful.

When I heard about Mr. Michio Kushi passing away, I was shocked, to be honest, as I had not expected his "sudden departure" from this world. I was not aware, being in Japan and not seeing him often that he was unwell, though my impression was that he had aged a little bit. I expected him to be active much longer to accomplish his dream of building a "Peaceful World." However, now he is gone. I therefore promise to his soul that I will work toward building a peaceful world along the path he established in 1980s, together with the disciples of his and with those who share his vision and philosophy.

Sometime soon after the turn of the century, I had an opportunity to ask him whether he was interested in revising or updating his "One Peaceful World." His answer was simply "No." I took it then that I was expected just to follow his footsteps to build a peaceful world in the manner Mr. Kushi was practicing.

Besides being a great leader to make his followers healthy, physically and spiritually, Mr. Kushi was always a philosopher. Besides, he was one of the most kind-hearted and considerate persons blessed with compassion and love for other people. I have encountered only two persons in my life who have never, never lost his/her temper, and who never talked negatively about other persons. One was my senior colleague in the United Nations, a Mr. K. K. Tsien, and the other was Mr. Kushi. Mr. Kushi was always kind and considerate, never lost his temper or defended his position even when he was attacked in public. In Japan, we call and treat this kind of person as a saint. He will remain in my mind as a model and an excellent leader to follow.

Now that he is gone and he looks at us from the Heaven above, I know that I have his guidance and inspiration anytime I want. I just close my eyes and can be with him to feel the "togetherness" and tranquility. I shall do one thing in my life now, with renewed determination—it is to pursue my mission of building a peaceful World together with those who inherit Mr. Kushi's philosophy and love for other people.

Remembering Michio
Ron Koetzsch

In December 1966, I was a graduate student at Harvard in a PhD program in the History of Religions. My field of concentration was Japanese religion and culture, and I was taking an intensive course in Japanese language. I had become a vegetarian some months before and was eating brown rice (usually mixed with eggs and tomatoes!) almost every day. In retrospect, it is clear that I had prepared myself for something. That something turned out to be my life-changing meeting with Michio Kushi.

I lived at the Center for the Study of World Religions in Cambridge. A friend of one of the other residents was a follower of Kirpal Singh, the Sikh master. Knowing that I was interested in Eastern spirituality and also diet, that friend of a friend mentioned that a Japanese teacher of "Macrobiotics" (a word new to me) was giving lectures each week at the Arlington Street Church in downtown Boston.

So one evening I took the "T" to the Arlington Street Station and found the side door to the church and the small meeting room where the lectures were held in those very early days. Seven or eight people were seated around a long wooden table. Michio stood at the far end of the room in front of a blackboard, dressed in his signature black suit, and lectured for two hours straight. He smoked, and others present also smoked. I don't remember exactly what Michio spoke about that first evening, but, whatever it was, it struck a responsive chord. I made an appointment for a personal consultation.

On January 10, 1967, I went to the Gardner Road house in Brookline to meet with Michio. We sat across from each other in the very large dining room on the second floor of the house. Aveline was nearby in the kitchen with Hisao, still a toddler, cooking dinner. Michio listened intently to my personal concerns and to my broader questions about macrobiotics. He responded compassionately, with insight and humor. What he spoke had the ring of truth and seemed to bring back ancient memories. That conversation began a personal relationship with Michio and his family that changed and vastly enriched my life.

In June of that year, I took a leave of absence from Harvard and moved into the Gardner Road house. For a few months, I was the shopkeeper at Erewhon when it was still in the basement space at 203B Newbury Street. In December 1967, I went to Japan and for my first months there lived with Michio's parents in Hoya-City. When I returned to Boston to continue my graduate work, I again lived with the Kushis, first on Boylston Street, then on Buckminster Road, and also in Becket.

I taught at the Kushi Institute, helped out at the Summer Conferences, and wrote for *East West Journal*.

My relationship with Michio was one of student to teacher. He helped me form a coherent, positive worldview and a practical, healthful way of life. Our relationship was also one of colleague to colleague in that I shared in his lifework of spreading macrobiotics and a consciousness about diet and health.

But there was also the more intimate dimension of almost father to son. I felt from the beginning that I had Michio's unconditional affection, approval, and respect. He was always interested in what I was doing. He always had time for me, even when he was overburdened by his myriad commitments and responsibilities. Throughout my impecunious thesis-writing years, Michio and Aveline allowed me live in their home gratis as one of the family.

Michio was a man who was absolutely committed to a dream, to a vision of "One Peaceful World," of a healthy, happy humanity living in harmony with nature and with each other. He devoted his life to that dream. In the process, he helped change the way our culture thinks about food and health and transformed the lives of thousands and thousands of people. I am sure our feelings of gratitude and love nourish and support him as he continues his journey in the world of spirit.

Remembering Michio
Susan Krieger

In the 1970s I was living in England, learning about and dealing in the European antique business. I was happy with my work yet knew that I needed more fulfillment on a personal and spiritual level.

It had been years since I was introduced to macrobiotics while living in New York City in the '60s, and now in England I was ready to study and practice for my present and future health.

There was an upcoming lecture in London with Michio, and I was determined to go, to see and meet the leader of macrobiotics. He was reputed to be a brilliant visionary, teaching revolutionary insights and solutions for individual health, environmental balance, and world peace based on ancient Asian teachings. The lecture room was very large and full of people eager to hear and see Michio.

When I first saw him speak of macrobiotic medicine I felt I was in the presence of a gifted, compassionate, and creative thinker. After his presentation I spoke with him about my mother's health; he responded, "Don't worry, she can heal this with macrobiotics. Please study and teach her to cook and eat with balance and take care of herself. She will be fine."

Soon thereafter, I went to the Macrobiotic Center in London, which was in a private house where I studied theory and cooking and made new macrobiotic friends. After a few months I courageously opened one of the first vegetarian macrobiotic restaurants in England.

I desired to further my studies with Michio and was asked to visit Brookline where the Kushi Institute of America was located, to do advanced studies with Michio, Mrs. Aveline Kushi (a fantastic cooking teacher and woman) and Shizuko Yamamoto (famous Shiatsu Macrobiotic practitioner.)

Michio and Aveline invited me to teach for them at the Institute. This honored me and eventually I moved to Brookline for years of intense study and practice with the Kushis and Shizuko while teaching courses in Shiatsu, Oriental diagnosis, and other macrobiotic topics. We teachers met with Michio often to review our queries and to hear of his latest insights.

As I observed Michio helping many people recover their health through his teachings and consultations, it was obvious that he had a unique knack for making people feel at ease and instilling hope, diagnosing and communicating with his known charms what they needed to hear to become motivated in their macrobiotic journey of healing and wellness. He was a humble man who inspired worldwide macrobiotic education and the growth and consumption of high quality organic foods. Michio's lesson for us all is that when a venture failed he learned from it and continued manifesting his dreams, writing dozens of books, influencing the Japanese people to return to their traditional way of eating, and supporting the continued success of the Kushi Institute. None surpasses Michio and Aveline's untiring and successful influence of bringing organic whole-grain agriculture and eating to the Western world.

After I moved to New York City Michio asked me to organize consultations and teachings for him. Michio wanted the prestigious hotel to prepare certain dishes for Aveline's health. Synchronicity! The chef had been a student of the Kushis and was honored to cook delicious healing dishes for Aveline.

I can honestly say that my connection and friendship with the

Kushis were and continue to be a powerful force in shaping my life, health, and work.

Deepest respect and love to the memory of ...

Michio, a magician of creating the best for all people and the planet.
Aveline, for her unending love and support of my continuing journey.
Shizuko, a master of healing and Shiatsu, for her patience and love.

Remembering Michio
Dennis Kucinich

I first met Michio Kushi thirty years ago when he and Aveline made an extraordinary presentation about diet and nutrition at a church in the Cleveland area. Their insight about the relationship between physiognomy and health and dietary habits regaled the audience with the consequences of literally becoming what you eat, if you ate a lot of chicken, meat, pork and other animal products. You could see people in the audience squirming in the nakedness of the anthropomorphic implications of appetites, speculating about the diet of the stranger sitting next to them, imagining human beings presenting subtly as barnyard animals. It was a moment of high humor worthy of James Thurber's *A Thurber Carnival*, where animals acquired human traits.

Michio and Aveline had made their point: You are what you eat, so take care, Michio Kushi, perhaps better than anyone in the last century, understood the transformational and the redemptive power of food, its relationship to personal health, environmental integrity, and world peace. His East-West apostolate was a commitment to the transcendent power immanent in every moment, the communion of spirit and matter, yin and yang, which made of the partaking of food a holy sacrament of divine nourishment of the temple of self.

Michio Kushi understood the condition of inner harmony of mind, body, and spirit arrived at through a macrobiotic diet came from a quickening of vibration and light as the substance of food united with the person consuming it. Knowing that what is innermost becomes outermost, Michio Kushi took the theory of the unity of matter to a higher spiritual expression—that of human unity, that we are all one, interdependent, interconnected across infinity of time and space.

The potential for human unity came from each individual taking responsibility for his or her own health, pursuing the diet of a compassionate, non-violent harvest, respecting, preserving all which inhabit the natural world from harm and so achieving the reconciliation with the natural world which the philosopher Thomas Berry said is the great work of our lives.

The great work of Michio Kushi's life was to raise the consciousness of the world about the power of food, the essentiality of dietary choices, the path toward health that strengthens the body and liberates the spirit.

At this moment in human history where the biosphere is threatened by short-sighted agricultural policies which selfishly waste precious water resources, poison the land, befoul the air, pollute gene pools, it is the gentle spirit of Michio Kushi, which can lead us back towards a Garden Eden filled with fruits, vegetables, and grains from the cornucopia of life, where all are fed and all live in harmony, and thus we can turn the myth of the Fall of Man into an At-One-Ment, a celebration of return to Grace, the achievement of Enlightenment —One Peaceful World.

This was the vision of Michio Kushi, now it is his legacy, to be resurrected to help save the planet from destruction with regenerative agriculture, agro-ecological principles, plant-based diets and the abolition of war.

We who were privileged to share a day or blessed to share a lifetime with Michio knew his genius rested upon simplicity of thinking, of personal habit, of living, of eating. His gift for clarity enabled breakthrough thinking, which accelerated evolutionary thought in human health, ushering in new insights into medicine and healing.

Michio Kushi's philosophy and writings helped to make what was once called Alternative Medicine, mainstream. His partnership with Alex Jack produced world-acclaimed texts on disease prevention and the achievement of total health, principles which are now bedrock of integrative medicine.

Michio's message was not simply about the wholeness of food, it was about the wholeness of life: You do not have to suffer, you can live, enjoy a long life, and be happy. For some this may seem cliché, but for Michio Kushi, the attainment of health, happiness and inner peace was in fact the goal of life, as was love, the love of his family, especially his beloved life partner and wife, Aveline.

When Aveline passed, Michio faced a great crisis because his love was no longer with him on his journey. His health suffered. His vital energy waned. Then he met Midori. He was revitalized, summoned back to life. Through Midori he reclaimed his own spark of light and love, which he carried forth to his final days.

In 1999, I had the honor of welcoming Michio and Aveline Kushi to Washington, DC, at the celebration of the acquisition of their collection by the Smithsonian. A few days later, I introduced Michio Kushi to a major committee of the House of Representatives where he testified how a macrobiotic diet could be a powerful therapy for women suffering from certain types of cancer.

He added, joyfully, singing a happy song, every day, like *You Are My Sunshine*, could enhance disease prevention or recovery

Let us take his wisdom, and at this moment call forth the expressive power of his joy. Please join me, if you wish, in singing a few lines from Michio's happy song, *You Are My Sunshine.*

> *You are my sunshine.*
> *My only sunshine,*
> *You make me happy,*
> *When skies are grey.*
> *You'll never know dear,*

How much I love you,
Please don't take
My sunshine away.

Our lives will forever be warmed by the mere thought of you, dear Michio.

We abide in your light and your light abides in us.

Thank you.

Remembering Michio
Gabriele Kushi

It was the spring of 1976, and I was on the road to Amsterdam. My journey to study with the great macrobiotic teachers Michio and Aveline Kushi had begun.

Since 1971, when I was just twenty-one, I had been intrigued by the macrobiotic yin and yang teachings and the corresponding practices of eating. These concepts and foods were new and exciting, and not only in my small hometown in Germany. At the beginning of our macrobiotic study group, there were only nine of us, and we often cooked and ate together. We ordered brown rice, seaweed, and miso from Holland. I was not a cook, and so the task of making my first nori roll from a book was very daunting to me—forget about strawberry shortcake!

The German *East West Foundation (Ost-West Bund),* the macrobiotic food distribution and natural food store *Mother Earth*, and the *East West Publishing Company (Ost West Verlag)* were great ventures that sprang out of these early years. *East West* published Michio and Aveline's books and study materials, which we painstakingly translated during many late nights. Forty years later, in 2015, the *East West Publishing Company* published my book that I co-wrote with Michio Kushi, *The Macrobiotic Kitchen in 10 Easy Steps. Balanced Eating in the 21st Century.*

This first Macrobiotic Conference in Amsterdam was my long-awaited opportunity to study macrobiotics in person. Needless to say, I always sat in the front and gobbled up as much as I could. At one of Michio's lectures, during the yin and yang spiral demonstration (you have probably seen it), he asked who wanted to be his model. Eagerly I raised my hand, and he chose me to come onto stage to sit down on the chair. He said, "Close your eyes, observe. Tell how you feel." First I felt very comfortable, becoming very quiet and in tune with myself. Then something changed abruptly, and I got confused and irritated. Not knowing what he had done and why I felt such a dramatic shift, I thought he was performing magic. He then explained the experiment: "When I hold the nail clipper still, it turns clockwise—yin. This is the energy that is in tune with female energy. When I changed the direction of the pendulum over your head to counterclockwise (yang, the energy that is in tune with male energy), your body got confused." His demonstration about the yin and yang energy movements had a very profound influence on me. Nail clippers (and eventually pendulums, after I became comfortable with my own teachings and my intuition sharpened) became a tool that I used in my counseling sessions for many years to determine which foods would be good for my clients.

Early next morning in Amsterdam, I attended my first cooking class ever, and it was with Aveline and Lima Ohsawa. These two seemingly delicate ladies handled heavy cast iron pots and pans with such grace as they cooked the most delicious-tasting food. The smell of fresh-ground gomasio—how can one ever forget that? At the end of class Aveline asked me to help fill plates to give out samples of the food they had just cooked. I was touched, and felt honored to do this.

Two years later, at age twenty-eight, with a red backpack holding all my possessions, I was on a plane to Boston with a $50 standby return ticket. I never used it. Many exciting macrobiotic things were happening at that time in Boston, including strawberry shortcake at the Seventh Inn. With several other international students, in 1978 I began my macrobiotic studies at the newly opened Kushi Institute. I lived and cooked at the Kushi (Bucky) House for many years and apprenticed counseling with Michio and cooking with Aveline, my beloved macrobiotic teachers. In 1981 Michio and Aveline also became my in-laws, and their son Haruo (Larry) and I are proud parents of our daughter, Angelica.

Remembering Michio
Hisao Kushi

Uhh. Hello!

I am Hisao Kushi. I am the youngest of the boys and it's quite a sight—all of you here. I am, I guess, here to talk about what it was like to be Michio Kushi's son, which, as you can imagine, was quite an adventure. As you can tell from all of these speakers and I am sure all of you have each had your challenges sort of trying to describe what Michio Kushi was like 'cause he sort broke a lot of boundaries in terms of categorization.

So one of the challenges that I had, and I know that my brothers had is, as a kid, when you're in school every year, every couple of years you have to take these standardized tests and, you know, you fill in last name, "Kushi," first name, "Hisao" and one of the questions right there is: *Father's Occupation*. And that is a stumper right there, before you get to the test, that's a problem.

So depending on the year I would pick a different occupation. So, one year I picked "teacher" because that's what he did. Lots of people came to our house, they learned stuff, went out into the world. He would travel around the world, he would give lectures he would...so, I'm like, "teacher"! And of course, that becomes a thing, you know, "So! What does your dad do?" — "He's a teacher!" — "Oh where does he teach?" — "Um, you know, Europe." — "Is he a professor? — "Mm, not really!"

So, another year, because it became difficult to talk about him as a teacher, I wrote, and I remember this specifically, I wrote "author" and remember because I wasn't quite sure how to spell it. But I wrote, "author," but I figured well that would be pretty simple because he writes books. So again, it's one of those things where people would say, "Oh what does your father do?" — "Hey, he's an author! He writes books." — "Oh, great! What kind of books?" — "Well, non-fiction? You know." — "What are some of the books he's written?" — *Your Face Never Lies.*

As I got older, the answer to the question, "What does your father do?" — I started to say, "He's a philosopher." And the thing is if you say, "philosopher," people are like — they don't know what to do with that. "What does your father do?" — "He's a philosopher." — "Okay." You know.

But I think that of the answers was sort of the most accurate because he was a big thinker. He was thinking about the big questions of the day. You know he would think about, "Why do we have five fingers? What is the nature of human violence? How do we raise people's consciousness so that we end human sickness and tragedy?"

One of the things that I remember him telling me as a kid, and he's probably mentioned this to all of you too, he would say, "Make sure that your life's goal, your life's dream, is something that you can't achieve during your lifetime." Right? You know, dream big! Try and get to sort of the fundamental questions and solve those.

And so, and his dream, as we've heard today and as we all knew, was a dream of One Peaceful World, and that was a dream he shared with all of you and with us and allowed us to discover that it was a dream that we shared with him. And not only did he touch your lives, but his life was touched by all of you, and so were all of us in the family. That made all of our lives, including his, much richer. It allowed him to do things the things that he wanted to do and that the world he felt called on him to do.

So, if I were answering that question today on the standardized test, and thank God I don't have to, the real answer, and I think you've heard this throughout the speeches today, is that he was a dreamer in a really simple and profound way. That was what he was at heart, and for us, as his kids, the gift that he gave to us was the permission to dream big and to think about our place in the world and in the universe. That is, I think, something that is unique in our upbringing and that was at the foundation of who we are and how we think about our place in the world.

And so, as a big dreamer and, he was also a man of action, so he could dream big but was constantly full of energy, it is, I can't lie — it's sad to lose that. And so, I think it's up to all of us to tap into those big dreams and to carry those forward in our lives. I love you, Papa.

Remembering Michio
Lawrence Haruo Kushi

Good afternoon and welcome to the celebration of my father, Michio Kushi's life. Thank you for coming here to the Arlington Street Church from all corners of the globe. It's great to see old friends and new ones both and the gathering of family to join us in this celebration this afternoon.

As that song just expressed by John Denver—*What One Man Can Do*—my father can do is dream, and his dream has inspired all of us, I think, to do the best that we can in our own personal lives. I want to thank everybody for being part of our large family. You'll get to meet many of his immediate blood relatives today and this afternoon, but I want everybody to recognize that we consider all of you to be part of our extended family and we're really grateful that you've been able to come here today and be with us and to celebrate and honor the life of my father.

So, just a little bit of words about the Arlington Street Church itself just so you the significance in my parents' life and the macrobiotic community, but way back when, you know, the dawn of the Boston macrobiotic community, my father would come here and actually give lectures. There is a room back behind us that he started in, and in the function room in the basement we held many holiday parties hosted, for example, by Ronald Koetzsch, who is sitting on the side over there, and attended by many people who are here. So it holds that type of significance.

The Back Bay area as well that we're in, right next door at 359 Boylston Street was where the East West Foundation offices were held and classrooms. And then if you walk down Newbury Street at 303b that was where the Erewhon retail store first started before it moved down a couple blocks to 342 Newbury Street. And at 272A was where the Sanae restaurant started, the first macrobiotic restaurant in Boston. So, anyway this whole area holds special significance, and we're glad that you could be here with us today.

So, the John Denver song, as I mentioned and you can see in the program — my father — he [John] performed it several times in the Boston area and he dedicated the song to my father. It was written originally for Buckminster Fuller who was also a good friend of John Denver's, but I think many of the words and the sentiment really expresses the spirit of what my father's life was about.

So thank you and we'll move on to the program. I'll be back up here at the very end.

Remarks at the Conclusion of the Memorial Service following singing of John Lennon's Imagine *with Michio's son Phiya at the piano:*

Thank you once again, everyone, for joining us this afternoon. You're truly a part of our family. Represented on the stage here are all of Michio's sons, children, and grandchildren, and we truly welcome you as part of our family and celebrate this time and this remembrance. Thank you so much everyone who shared here this afternoon. We invite everybody to a reception, which is at the Marriot Copley Place, as you know. It's on the back of your program. It's probably still cold out there, but hopefully you'll enjoy the brisk walk. There will be an opportunity at that time for other people to share their memories and their thoughts, including my other brothers who you just heard from and Phiya's wonderful piano playing, but you'll be able to hear from them as well as everyone else who wants to take the time and opportunity to do so. And so, thank you very much. A handful of us will be available to say, "Thank you" — my uncle, Michio's brother Masao, his wife

Midori, and the immediate sons will join us, join you towards the back of the sanctuary and, obviously, take your time to head over to the Marriot Copley Place. Thank you so much for being here. Thank you so much for everything you've done over the decades to really celebrate and carry the spirit of what my father's life was about. We are all dreamers and we can change the world. Thank you.

Remembering Michio
Norio Kushi

There are three words that come to mind when it comes to my father's passing. I intentionally use the word "passing" instead of death, because the death of my father felt much more like a transition instead of finality associated with the word *death*.

The first word is "magical." In the same way, during the presence of my children's birth, there is a magical feeling; this same feeling was present during the dying of my father. Any differences that may have been there between myself and other family members, whether it is with my father or his wife, as soon as I walked into my father's room, were gone. It all simply dissolved and felt as though it had never been there.

The second word is "beautiful." As I walked into my father's room, he was awake, fully conscious and completely aware of what was happening. My father got to say all that he wanted to say and all that he needed to say. In the end, the only thing that mattered to my father was that there be peace and harmony between all family members, including, of course, his wife Midori. At the moment of my father's passing, Midori was massaging his feet; he was fully awake, peaceful, and happy.

The third word is "gratitude." Also present in the room was this overwhelming feeling of gratitude. I am grateful for my father and mother selflessly providing for me throughout my life. I am grateful for JoAnne and our children for their unconditional love and support. I am grateful for our family, my brothers, sister for their unconditional love and support. I am grateful for all our friends, who are all as intimate as family and live throughout our green planet. Thank you all for sharing in this gift of life.

One more insight that I want to share is the timelessness of birth and death, and that the source of life happening, is not just in the manifest, time-based reality, but simultaneously at a much deeper level beyond the intellect. In the presence of my father, I saw the limitations in assigning the time-based reality of cause and effect to death. The witnessing of the passing is a glimpse into the timeless, a reality void of cause and effect.

Remembering Michio
Phiya Kushi

There are many great lessons and words of wisdom that my father, Michio Kushi, gave me and countless other individuals whose lives he touched through his many lectures, books and private consultations. These select life lessons are ten out of hundreds that impacted and influenced my life for the better one way or another. They affected important life decisions, guided me through challenging times, inspired me to strive to be a better person and to learn to always enjoy life under all circumstances. I share them with you here now in the hopes that they may inspire and be as useful to you as well.

1. Never Sell Your Life — (Always pursue your dream)
This isn't a criticism on prostituting one's self, nor that money is evil but instead is a caution against making a Faust-like bargain of giving your soul to the devil in exchange for untold riches and earthly pleasures. It is a suggestion to never compromise your principles, passion, and dreams for the sake of money or for a cause that you don't believe in. This doesn't mean never getting paid to work or turning down money, but it does mean to never settle for less than doing something that you feel passionate about and would do regardless of the money.

It's fine to earn money and do any kind of work as long as it is part of a much larger plan that serves you and your own personal development and dream. It's also fine to work for a company (or a boss) whose principles you don't agree with as long as it serves your own dream and purpose whatever that may be. In short, work for yourself and pursue your dreams at all times even when you work for others. If you do, you will always have a job that you can never be fired from. Never sell your life.

I first heard my father say these words in one of his lectures when I was a young teenager just beginning to think about getting my first summer job. That summer, I applied to work as a bagger for a local supermarket chain. (This was long before the days of natural and organic supermarkets.) On my first day, a neatly dressed floor manager in a white shirt, dress slacks, and tie gave me a tour and showed me around. Afterward, we sat down and he explained to me about what made this supermarket different from its nearby competitor. He said, "The only difference between the two supermarkets is the service. Everything else is the same. You can buy all the same food there as you can here. So the only thing that can set us apart from our competition is our service including how we dress and take care of our customers." I sat for a moment and thought about what he said and remembered my father's words. I realized that it simply wasn't enough for me to work for a company whose only goal was making a profit by trying to serve their customers better. I believed that quality service should be automatic for all businesses. This supermarket had nothing more to offer and was simply trying to compete with and put the other supermarket down the street out of business. It was a sad and destructive game with no thought on creating a win-win situation. I told the manager, "Thank you, but no thank you," and with that I quit the very day they hired me.

My father's words instilled in me a selfish attitude about the use of my time and whom should benefit from it. I would not allow this body of mine, this life of mine, to be used for things that I did not agree with. I wanted to work for a company that was making a substantial and fundamental positive difference in people's lives. I wanted to work for a place where I could feel proud just by being a part of the company. I set high work standards early in life and have kept them ever since.

For my first job I ended up working for my parent's company, Erewhon, the pioneering importer, manufacturer, distributor, and retailer that launched the natural and organic foods movement. Unlike the supermarket, Erewhon offered unique food products that were natural, wholesome, informative, and educational and were part of a larger vision, philosophy, and goal toward building world peace. Erewhon had a mission that I was proud of and could work for.

Since then, every job I did, every position I accepted, and every company I worked for and managed aligned with my own set of values and principles. These values and principles included never causing anyone any harm, suffering, or unhappiness by:

1. Never selling products that might be dangerous and harmful to others
2. Never do any work that involved weapons, war, or caused any suffering in the world
3. Never working for a company that exploited others
4. Never working for a company that did not put people before profits and encourage a win-win situation for everyone.

While my values and principles may have changed over the years — in fact, they are more stringent now than before — I never compromised them. As a result, I have no regrets for any work I have done in the past and that fact has given me a profound sense of peace and satisfaction in my life for which I attribute to my father's words "never sell my life."

2. Never Complain About Anything — (Take responsibility for your life)

Many years ago my father said, "Never complain about anything unless you, yourself, can come up with a better solution that you, yourself, are willing to implement. Otherwise, you have no right to complain." He never complained about anything, and whenever he had an objection to anything he always had solution. His advice made a lot of sense to me, and I have done my best to follow it ever since.

It should be noted that there are times when complaining has its uses and advantages. For example, it can be useful to complain to persons in a position to make a difference to change unwanted situations for the better. Also, freedom of speech is an important right in the United States, and voicing one's opinion is necessary for social change and responsible political action. Complaining to the right person can make a big difference and is an essential tool in politics today.

However, if we become overly dependent on others to make changes for us, then we risk losing our own strength and power. People who complain aimlessly and constantly to those who can't make a difference become victims of their own doing. Without finding their own solutions and acting upon them they give up their own power to change their own lives. They also lose the respect of those around them.

This lesson, to never complain unless I had my own solution, inspired me to be much more self-reliant by becoming better and faster at solving problems that came my way. It gave me greater responsibility, self-confidence, patience, and creativity. I became better at strategic and long term planning and was able to manage people and run businesses early on in life. I am very grateful to my father for this simple, yet powerful and valuable lesson.

3. Never Criticize Anyone — (Be respectful to everyone always)
Similar to "Never complain about anything" is to never criticize anyone at all. If you have a concern or issue with another person then deal with them directly about it. Otherwise, never criticize them or anyone at all, publicly or privately behind a person's back. Although I don't recall my father expressly saying to never criticize others, he very clearly demonstrated this by his own refusal to criticize anyone.

My father was a very gracious well-mannered gentleman who treated everyone with respect. He always wore three-piece suits as a symbol of his respect for everyone he met. When he was out and about walking in town he would always greet everyone he met with a cheerful smile and a "Good Morning!" He was always charming and would try to lift the spirits of everyone he met. When others challenged him, treated him disrespectfully and tried to publicly discredit and stop him he never complained about or criticized them at all.

I am not as charming or gracious as my father was, yet his example continues to inspire me to never criticize anyone and to always treat everyone with respect regardless of how they treat you.

4. Never Be Angry — (Be calm, tolerant, and compassionate with yourself and everyone else always)

I can count on one hand the number of times I can recall my father getting angry. One of them was in the early 1980s when AIDS was discovered in the gay population in New York City. The media were filled with stories of people blaming homosexuality and of homophobic healthcare workers unwilling to treat the afflicted. My father was outraged and took it upon himself to travel to New York City every month from Boston to give free lectures and cooking classes to AIDS patients. He shook their hands and hugged them. Many of the men in attendance broke down and cried because everyone else was afraid to touch them. The result of his efforts can be found in his book, *AIDS, Macrobiotics and Natural Immunity*. That was one of the rare occasions when my father became angry.

Unlike his macrobiotic mentor, George Ohsawa, who regularly scolded and berated his own students and many others, Michio gained a reputation early on of always being patient and never losing his temper so much so that Ohsawa intentionally tried to provoke and test him with a very nasty accusatory letter. Michio finally lost his temper and wrote back expressing his anger at Ohsawa. Ohsawa replied in jest by congratulating him on being human, because he, Ohsawa, sincerely had his doubts.

Being angry often can be viewed as a sign of being unhealthy. In Oriental medicine, anger is related to a weak liver. Excessive fat, alcohol, and sweets, among other specific foods that tax the liver, then make one more easily prone to anger while healing the liver by avoiding such foods can make one more tolerant and patient.

However, when we do feel or have anger within us, then it can definitely be helpful to express it fully in responsible ways that do not cause anything or anyone harm or damage, physically, emotionally, and psychologically. If you need to yell and scream then, by all means, do so by going out into the woods alone and yelling your head off to your liver's content. Just as crying can be healing, then releasing one's anger can help move stagnated energies within the body, but just do so responsibly.

Unfortunately, I have been angry more times than I care for, and later regretted every time it happened. In my younger years the anger and frustrations I experienced were often uncontrollable. Expressing and releasing pent-up emotions was healing and invaluable to me, and I sought ways to do so constructively. Over the years, I became much more patient, tolerant, and compassionate. Older now and, hopefully, wiser I find no reason to be angry at all. It took me a long time to finally achieve the tolerant, patient, and calm state that my father maintained and displayed throughout his life.

So, if you have anger and if expressing it will make you feel better then don't try to suppress it all. Let it all come out naturally but also try to find out the causes and triggers to your anger and learn to deal with them in other ways and if you keep at it and though it may take a long time, you may find greater calm and peace in your life and be more like Michio. His example continues to be a source of inspiration for me today.

5. Be Grateful For Your Difficulties — (They make life worth living)

First, to clarify, "be grateful for your difficulties" isn't a suggestion to be masochistic. Second, I am also aware that "difficulties make us stronger" is an over-used cliché and telling someone to be grateful in times of crisis is probably the worst thing to say to them and is definitely the last thing they want to hear. Anyone facing an unexpected and unwanted urgent crisis should be focused on nothing else than practically resolving the crisis itself. In that moment gratitude is not a useful sentiment to turn to at all.

Furthermore, even when we aren't faced with any major challenges or difficulties, it is natural to avoid them whenever we can and as best as possible. However, and as we all know, difficulties and challenges come upon us whether we like it or not and our view and attitude towards them can make a huge difference in our lives.

"Be grateful for your difficulties" is a simple and straightforward reminder to appreciate the unavoidable challenges that we all face in our lives. Through our hardships, difficulties, and failures we learn to value and appreciate the simplest things in life. In life-threatening situations we become grateful for life itself.

Our difficulties also serve as reminders to examine ourselves and our lives and to question our long-held beliefs, values, and direction. They serve as opportunities to reflect on our past limitations and explore greater possibilities and new directions that we would have never considered or imagined otherwise.

When I came down with a cold or fever my father would often congratulate me for my good fortune. He was not being mean to me. He never looked at sickness as a misfortune, but instead as a friendly and fortunate reminder that something needed to be addressed and changed in one's life. I found out later that this attitude toward sickness was very much in line with the work of Christoph Wilhem Hufeland, the eighteenth century physician who wrote the first book on macrobiotics titled, *Macrobiotics: The Art of Longevity*. In the preface of his book Hufeland writes:

> The medical art must consider every disease as an evil which can not be too soon expelled; the macrobiotic, on the other hand, shows that many diseases may be the means of prolonging life.

By congratulating me for my illness, my father was simply expressing the macrobiotic understanding of viewing illness as a means to help me live longer. It was good fortune and I only needed to see it as an opportunity for change for the better. Without my illness I would never have known that change was needed. It was a difficulty to be grateful for.

My father did not limit the scope of difficulties to be grateful for to only health issues. Every type of difficulty was to be appreciated from accidents, tragedies, and economic hardships to relationship troubles, social problems, and even war. All challenges and difficulties we encountered were an opportunity for growth physically, mentally, and spiritually.

Challenges and difficulties are not just beneficial for humans but for all living things as well. There is a story about my father that illustrates this point with regard to the difficulties and hardships of plants. Many years ago I accompanied my father to a meeting of advisors for John Denver's Windstar Foundation. In looking to build a utopian community in the Rocky Mountains there was a proposal on the table to create an experimental thriving Garden of Eden inside a protected Geodesic Dome. The prestigious group of advisers that John had assembled all thought it was a wonderful idea except my father. When it came time for Michio to give his input then, with unassuming grace, he gently pointed out that occasionally exposing the vegetation in the dome to rain and other elements naturally occurring in the Rockies might be beneficial for the plants. He suggested that the dome should at least have a window that could open and close to let these external influences in from time to time. Soon it became glaringly apparent to all in the room that exposing plants to the harsh Rocky Mountain climate all the time, from thunderstorms and even snowfall, was the best and most natural thing for the plants in order to thrive in that environment. The Geodesic Dome was not only unnecessary but was in the way of the difficulties and challenges that naturally helped the plants to grow and become strong and healthy. By suggesting a simple window in the dome, my father, in the gentlest way possible, exposed the folly of the whole idea.

In the pursuit of our happiness it doesn't serve us to make enemies of our difficulties and challenges. Like rain storms and bad weather they come and go often, and we must deal with them whether we like it or not. Indeed, they are an essential part of life just as much as are the sunny days and joyous times. By embracing our difficulties we can find happiness in both the worst and the best times of our lives. Be grateful for your difficulties because in overcoming them they not only bring us joy but make life worth living.

6. When An Angel Turns Its Back It Becomes A Devil — (Everything has or becomes its own complementary opposite)
I have heard my father say this in many lectures. He has also said this in other ways such as "Every front has a back and the bigger the front, the bigger the back; everything turns into its opposite and back again," and "there are two sides to every coin." Although not as profound, we can also understand this concept as the process of weighing pros versus cons when making a decision. However, this statement about angels and devils adds a profound moral dimension that many do not consider and have a hard time grasping.

We live in a world defined by the simplistic morality of "good" versus "evil." It's in our movies, stories, and myths. It's in our religion and politics. It underlies all our laws and our society. Many cannot imagine a world without enemies, be it a group of people to fight against, a disease, or any type of unwanted behavior or phenomenon. If we aren't fighting tyrants and terrorists then it's drugs, poverty, or cancer. We make enemies out of anything and look to heroes to vanquish our enemies. We become fearful and build arsenals of defenses so large that, if or when unleashed, destroy ourselves in the process of eliminating our enemies. We can't imagine a world without this duality and therefore the statement "When an angel turns its back it becomes a devil" confounds us.

Yet, there are many examples of how angels become devils. For example, today many individuals rely on medicines, pills, supplements, and diets to cure themselves and stay healthy. But these things also make us dependent and enslave us just as much as they provide us relief. A pill or medicine is both angel and devil at the same time. It may bring us relief but it does not cure us. An automobile is another example that is both a convenience and burden at the same time. We can go anywhere, but then we are also burdened with gas and parking fees, maintenance and repair costs, insurance and depreciation. In the beginning of a relationship we think the best of our new partner and want to be with them all the time, but when the relationship goes sour we want nothing to do with them. The loving beautiful angel they once were becomes a devil, yet it is the same person. Similarly, a mother's love for her child, on the one hand, is nurturing and selfless while, on the other hand, can spoil, be overbearing, and hamper the child's development. A physician whose oath is to do no harm and who can save many lives can also become a most dangerous person, intentionally or not. A policeman whose job is to protect the community and enforce the law can overstep the very laws he has sworn to uphold. A company whose goal is to produce vast quantities of food is also the greatest purveyor of harmful food products. A country, whose foreign policy is to promote freedom around the world has, through its same policies, caused the greatest amount of war, exploitation, and suffering. Angels are devils and devils are angels.

We often cite Hitler as the epitome of evil and Jesus as epitome of good. While it is undeniable that Hitler's Nazi Germany committed various atrocities the ensuing response to his actions and to World

War II has been to create a legacy of heroes and a united and global stand for peace and vigilance against tyranny. With regard to Jesus, whose life was devoted to compassion for all of humanity, then in his aftermath, how many have been killed in the name Christianity? How many cultures and peoples have been destroyed by the spread of Christianity? How much hatred, bigotry, and violence continues to be created toward women, gays and minorities in the name of Christ and other prophets of peace? The work of devils turns into the work of angels and the work of angels become the work of devils.

Many years ago someone once asked Michio what would he be doing if the world were "macrobiotic" already — if we had achieved One Peaceful World. His surprising answer was that he would probably be selling junk food and promoting chemical agriculture. His response exposed the relative nature of our morality. The world today was heading toward global degeneration and destruction, and the biggest game on the entire planet is to work toward creating a world based on natural order, health, and peace. But if the opposite were true — that we lived in a harmonious world of health and peace — then the biggest game on earth would be to move it back toward degeneration and destruction.

There is a larger dynamic at work here that transcends our simplistic morality. We can no longer say who is good and who is evil. We all are complicit in creating our opposite. If we understand that angels turn into devils and devils into angels then, at any given point in time, we may know what to expect in the future and, perhaps, even influence this process toward a direction that we prefer.

When we begin to see that our world is much more dynamic and fluid than we imagined, then we can learn how to manage our own actions and achieve our goals. If I push in one direction then I may create an opposite reaction and result, and the harder I push the greater will be the reaction to me. Similarly, if I drop a pebble in a pond then it makes gentle ripples, but if I drop a big boulder then larges waves are created.

Aggressive and violent actions always produce a violent and opposite reaction, and if stability is our goal, then we will never achieve it through violence. Subtle and gentle movements allow us to better manage the unintentional reactions that we create and can therefore help us to achieve our goals much faster and easier. Understanding the dynamics of angels turning into devils is a neverending study and discipline and makes life a fascinating journey and adventure.

This journey continues to unfold for me, and as it does I reflect on the influence and effects of my own past actions. Failures in business projects and relationships can all be attributed to the aggressive and bold actions I initiated in the past that ended up producing the opposite result of what I wanted. It took me awhile to figure out that remaining passive and simply accepting what comes my way produced results I wanted much faster and easier. My life has become much more satisfying and continues to be a fascinating journey, and it's all thanks to my father's lesson that angels turn into devils.

7. Think Big, Dream Big

At our father's memorial service my younger brother, Hisao, recalled our father telling him to, "Make sure your life's dream is something that you can't achieve during your lifetime." Our father's dream was nothing less than creating "One Peaceful World."

My father's dreams and optimism had a tremendous positive influence on the lives of so many. He counseled thousands with terminal and life-threatening illnesses and always found a way to inspire and uplift them. Many recovered and lived well beyond their original prognosis. Beyond this, his grand vision of world peace through a peaceful biological food revolution inspired many to pursue new careers in alternative healing, organic foods, and macrobiotic education.

His large vision affected my life. When I was young thinking about what to do with my life in the future I asked my father for advice. I told him I was thinking about becoming a writer and he said, "Great! You can be better than Shakespeare! If you want to be a writer then be the best!" I thought he was nuts. I could never be better than Shakespeare. Another time I thought about being an inventor and he said, "Great! You can be the first one to invent a UFO or a machine that provides free unlimited energy," and he would go on and on suggesting many seemingly impossible inventions that would completely change life on Earth as we know it. I asked him once if I could be president of the United States and he replied that I would be a great president, far better than the current one. "Why and how is that possible?" I asked. He said it was because I was much healthier and had much better intuition than the president. The irony was that Nixon was president at the time, and later I came to find out that my father had actually personally met Nixon in the '50s when Nixon was in Congress. Whatever thought or idea I had about my future he always took it far beyond my imagination. He did so to expand my narrow limited mind and have me think and dream bigger. Though patronizing, he was sincere and, more importantly, I believed him. By his own example, he showed me that I could dream and achieve anything I wanted to.

Halfway through high school I became discontent with the direction my life was heading. I was no longer interested in pursuing a normal education and career path. I felt that following the conventional dictates of society was not going to change anything. I was interested in pursuing something much bigger and larger but I was not clear about what it was. So I joined an experimental educational program that was being offered in my high school where students could participate in how their classes were being taught. It was new and different and the vision was bigger than the normal school offerings. I also enrolled in an experimental college. Every major life decision I made involved looking at the larger picture of life. I had big ideas and big dreams, and they gave me the creative inspiration and courage to overcome whatever challenges and difficulties came my way.

I still have big visions and dreams. However they are tiny compared to my father's dream. I asked my father once about his dream of One Peaceful World. I asked him how long he thought it would take for it to be realized. He sat there and thought about it for a long while. It seemed that he was making complex calculations in his head. Finally, he said, "I estimate about 2,000 years." 2,000 years??!! Whoa! His answer took me by surprise. It wasn't so much the number of years that surprised me, but it was the fact that he devoted his whole life to working on something that he expected wouldn't be realized for another 2,000 years. I was amazed at his optimism, dedication, and commitment to pursing a dream that would remain unfinished long after he was gone. His immense vision and dream was and continues to be inspiration to me and I remain joyful and optimistic that we will create One Peaceful World one day and no matter how long it will take. Thank you, Michio!

8. We Are Insignificant — (The first lesson in understanding the universe)

The first chapter of my father's book, *The Book Of Macrobiotics* begins with the heading, "Life Is Vanity." It is an introduction to the ephemerality of life; that life is but a fleeting moment and everything we do will eventually pass away. All of our ambitions, our achievements, our struggles and concerns come and go in the larger view of things. Whatever we do will eventually perish and disappear. Everything we do is in vain. That is the first section of the first chapter in *The Book of Macrobiotics*. That is the first lesson in beginning to understand our universe and its order.

Michio also always talked about the universe as "One Infinity," and how we are living in it, how we came from it, and how we are returning back to it. An infinite universe is immense and our place in it and relative to it is pretty small. In terms of scale, Neil Tyson DeGrasse (rephrasing Carl Sagan) in the TV show, *Cosmos*, pointed out that if the entire history of the universe were mapped out onto one calendar year starting with the Big Bang at midnight on January 1 then all of human history would occur in the last few minutes of December 31.

Such immense ideas are very abstract and difficult to relate to and therefore are easily dismissed. I prefer to be much more to the point by simply saying this: We are insignificant. We are nothing in comparison to the size and scope of the universe. We are nothing and we should be humbled by this fact. We should be in awe of the immensity of everything else.

To bring this to a more understandable scale let's compare the number of insects there are to humans. It is estimated that the ratio of insects to humans is 200 million to one. For every one person there are 200 million insects on earth. That's a lot of insects.

But let's not stop there because insects aren't the most abundant life form on earth. The latest estimate on how many bacteria there are on earth, (according to estimates,) is five million trillion trillion. Bacteria and viruses far outnumber all life forms on earth. At only 7 billion we humans are truly insignificant and compared to bacteria it could be said that we live for them. They are the dominant life form, not us and when taking this into consideration then the idea of antibiotics seems like a foolish quixotic attempt to try and control something that we could never ever possibly do at all.

Once we accept that we are insignificant, and that everything we do is in vain, then what are to do about this? We could become depressed and apathetic and no longer care about anything including our own existence. This option leads nowhere but to our own arrogant self-pity.

There is another option and that is to stop being arrogant and stop taking our human life so seriously. We are arrogant about our beliefs, our morals, politics, our religion, and our identities. We take them so seriously that we will even kill and die for them. Yet they are as insignificant as we are, and once we fully accept and appreciate our own insignificance; that we are nothing but an insignificant end product of an immense and dynamic ever-changing universe, then it becomes impossible for us to be so arrogant. The universe is there for us to discover, explore, and understand and the first lesson to learn is the humility of our insignificance.

Remembering the insignificance of my life has helped me in times of difficulty. It helps me remember that there is nothing worth getting upset or depressed about, let alone killing or dying for. It helps me to remember that there are always others in the world facing much bigger problems than me and even their problems are insignificant. It helps me to remember that I know nothing and that there is so much to discover. It helps me to remember to appreciate this immense universe that created my insignificant life. It helps me to remember to enjoy life and be forever grateful for all that this universe provides.

"We are insignificant" is the first lesson in understanding our universe and our relationship to it. It is the first lesson in understanding the size, scope, and proportion of things. Beyond this there are many other lessons toward understanding the "Order of the Universe" and how it moves and changes (including how angels become devils.) We can study, for example, how we are the product of our environment in its entirety including the foods we eat. We can explore how we are affected by different foods and changes in our environment. We can look at how the earth moves and how it affects us. We can ask ourselves why we have two eyes, one mouth, and five fingers. We can ask why Jupiter is so large compared to the other planets and why did ancient people build pyramids. There are so many amazing things to explore and accepting our insignificance and letting go of our arrogance is the very first step and rabbit hole to pass through in order to reach this magic wonderland.

9. Discover for yourself — (Non credo)

In his lectures my father answered many questions from students. He would give elaborate and detailed answers that might take the class on a fascinating and inspiring journey to the far reaches of the galaxy or back to ancient times and conclude with practical and simple actions like chewing your food 100 times. However, there were also times when, in his typical broken English and a thick Japanese accent, he would respond to a question by simply saying, "Please discover for yourself." Whenever he did this the room would fall into silent reverence of him, with everyone thinking of him as being a very wise sage who withheld answers and challenged his students to actively use their brains and think on their own. Little did they know that his response really just masked his own ignorance on the subject matter asked of him by the student. It was a clever little ploy that he used to encourage others to think instead simply admitting his own ignorance and saying, "I don't know." Fortunately, his ploy worked. The students were inspired to discover for themselves. I was inspired to do so as well. Michio was wise after all.

More than just encouraging me to find answers to my own questions, "Please discover for yourself" had a much deeper meaning for me. It was also a suggestion to never blindly believe anything that anyone said or taught including my father. It meant for me to have a healthy skepticism about everything. It meant to never blindly believe anything 100 percent and to retain at least 1 percent of disbelief. Conversely it also meant to never reject anything 100 percent and retain at least a 1percent possibility that something could be true. It meant to have an open mind about everything and always maintain that nothing is certain. It meant that if I wanted to discover the certainty in anything then it was up to me find it and no one else. It meant that I would have to learn how to learn. It meant for me learn how to use my brain and all other resources available to me. It meant learning how to ask the right questions. It also meant exposing and confronting my own ignorance and to never be arrogant about knowing anything. It meant becoming a self-reliant and free thinker. It meant learning to trust my own instincts and intuition. It meant to "discover myself" and, last but not least, it meant to always retain a humble sense of wonder and awe for everything.

Everything is moving and changing constantly in the universe and what we know is also always changing. Never believe 100 percent in anything. Always allow for a minimum of at least a 1percent possibility that you or anyone could be wrong. Let that percent of disbelief, of "non credo," no matter how small, be your inspiration to "discover yourself." That percent of disbelief, doubt, and self-discovery is your freedom, so never let it go. May you always "discover yourself."

10. Life Is Play
One of Michio's favorite talks was to ask students what they thought was the purpose of life. They would stumble along with a variety of answers and usually settle on "making a difference" but then would finally be corrected by him. He would simply say, "Life is play," and explain that everyone came to earth to play. (Unfortunately, with his broken English accent some people were confused and thought he said "Life is pray." But they would be quickly corrected by their neighbors who understood him) "Life is play"—and that was it and there was nothing more.

In other words, there is no purpose in life other than to enjoy life itself. We can be so serious about life. We fight wars and kill each other. According to my father, why we do this is simply because we forgot that we came here to play. We became so absorbed and lost in playing our roles that we forgot who we are, where we came from, and why we are here. We forgot that we are only actors on a world stage. We forgot that there is no purpose in life other than to play and enjoy it, and when we do remember this then we no longer take things so seriously. We can rewrite the script and choose to play roles that make us happy instead of ones that cause suffering.

There is nothing to be gained or lost but our own enjoyment. Life is play and that is all.

Remembering Michio
Sean, Lianna, and Angelica Kushi

Michio wasn't your average grandfather as I am sure many can imagine. He wasn't the most present, since he traveled the world to teach, nor was he the most cuddly of grandfathers. But, all of us grandkids loved him for his oddities. Michio has fourteen grandchildren: Yogen, Angelica, Tenji, Lianna, Takeo, Alexander, Sean, Alexander, Ryan, Teruko, Kate, Paul, Gina, Ty. We are bonded by the fact that Michio and Aveline raised our fathers, and as a result us, in a very out-of-the-norm way.

Here are a few memories from Michio's grandchildren:

Memory from Sean Kushi, Norio Kushi's third child.
This is the story of how I was given my most prevalent nickname by my *Ojiichan*, Michio. During my years at Brookline High School, I lived with Michio, on the third floor of his home. It was during these years that I was able to experience the most of him with his unique character and personality. One idiosyncratic feature of Michio was in his accent and his pronunciations, and with that, he could never correctly say my name Sean. He persistently pronounced my name as "Shang" or sometimes "Shane" depending on the rough interpretation of his unique accent. Friends and family were so entertained by Michio's inability to pronounce my name that they began to partake in calling me "Shang" regularly. People

used it as their contact for me in their phone, spoke it when greeting me, and addressing me in notes. A few friends even altered their nicknames for fun, like my friend Drew to Drang, or Hunter to Huntang. It was a humorous and endearing nickname that continues to follow me to this day. Shang, my given name by Michio.

Memories from Lianna Kushi, Norio Kushi's first child.
As a little kid, to be honest, Michio was always kind of intimidating. He always wore a suit and was always working. I have tons of childhood memories with my grandmother, but not that many with Michio. But there is one memory that stands out. When I was probably ten or eleven, we were visiting the Kushi house. My dad and I walked to the entrance and Michio was on his way out. Usually, he just gave a quick wave and would say "hello" or "welcome," but in this moment he stopped, looked at me, and gave me a hug. He then continued on his way. Part of the reason this stood out so much, is that my dad was shocked and said, "Wow, he's never hugged me." I realized right away, that was a very special moment.

When I lived with Michio, he would often call my cell phone and leave messages such as, "This is a message for Lianna Kushi, this is Michio Kushi, your grandfather. Please call me back on 617-566-6785."

When I was twenty-one, after living in Japan for almost a year, I had a chance to spend a week with Michio and Midori in Japan. Traveling with Michio to the Kushi Institute of Japan was a wonderful experience on a number of levels. One, we were in Japan together and two, we actually spoke in Japanese together. Michio is infamous for his unique accent, and it was the first time in my life I sat in on his lectures or had dinner with him and listened to him speak without an accent. It is a time I will always be grateful to have had.

After Michio married Midori, I think he had more time and honestly permission to relax. That was the time when I first saw him wear jeans instead of his three-piece suit. One particularly special memory was when my younger siblings were visiting Bucky, the

Kushi house, we all convinced him to play Nintendo Wii. It was so fun to watch him play golf and see him take a break from work. At this point I was already in my twenties, but I think it's a memory my younger siblings cherish.

Angelica Kushi, Larry aka Haruo Kushi's daughter.
Many of my cousins had the opportunity of living with Michio at the Buckminster Road house, aka Bucky. I lived there until I was three, so my memories of that place and many of my interactions with Michio were when I was visiting, romping around as a kid at the K.I. Summer Conferences or later studying and teaching at the K.I. As a child and young adult, I remember coming to visit Boston, driving to Brookline, and turning into the circle driveway of the ominous brick mansion. Every time I visited it was exciting…until, I would walk down the long hallway to Michio's office and bedroom suite and remembered he has X-ray vision. He didn't always diagnose me on the spot, but it was definitely something that happened…a lot. One time, he said, in his very thick accent, "Oh, Angelica, your aura is purple, you've been eating too much chocolate." Oh great, not only can he diagnose my face, he can diagnose my aura. Another time, I remember walking down the long corridor with Lianna and Alexander. We formally lined up in a row to say hi to Michio. He said, "Oh, Angelica, you eat too much cheese, you may develop fibroid cysts, Lianna, you eat too much salt and oil, oh, Alex, you look so good, you are perfect." Meanwhile, Alex ate everything under the sun! Lianna and I were furious. Was that a Japanese male chauvinistic comment, what the heck, we wondered. The truth is I had been eating cheese sandwiches all summer long before I saw him because I was teaching hang gliding on the sand dunes in North Carolina and that was the vegetarian fast food option easily available. It was a good wake up call, Michio's diagnosis; I realized I needed to find better sources of food to sustain my active lifestyle.

Michio wasn't always there for typical grandfather duties. I had been performing in an off-Broadway show in NYC for a few years, and finally after some serious convincing by my father, he agreed to come. About half an hour before the show he tried to cancel, giving the excuse that he and Midori wouldn't understand the play because they had trouble understanding English. That excuse didn't work since the show has no words. They showed up reluctantly. This show, *Fuerza Bruta*, isn't a normal show. You stand the whole hour and 5 minutes, the show happens all around you. It's an immersive theatrical experience with people flying in the air, swimming in a pool above you, dancing on a moving stage, a man running on a massive treadmill getting shot at with a loud rifle, while house music beats are blasting in the audiences' ears.

Michio, with his spiked up grey hair and orange ear plugs sticking out of his ears, watched and took it all in. At first his face was inquisitive, slightly curious, and partly confused…but in the end when the cast invites the audience to dance and join in the fun, his face was beaming with joy. I went up to him, grabbed his hands, and we jumped up and down together to the beat of the music. His smile was so wide, and he kept repeating "AMAZING, AMAZING, AMAZING."

This memory alone will be imprinted into my mind as one of the most precious moments I was fortunate to share with my grandfather. I don't have a traditional job, and for a traditional Japanese man, it may be hard to understand the world of performance, but that night he got it, he understood that I was living my dreams. For the first time, I could sense he was really proud to be my grandfather. As my cousins and I got older, he would express to us about how he wanted us to teach macrobiotics, yet none of us have really taken that path as a profession. But after he came to my show, he sent a really thoughtful card with a beautiful message inside. One that I believe he wishes for all of my cousins and all of humanity: "Walk, run and jump in every domain of every day of your life on you own shining way!"

Remembering Michio
Janet Lacey

Any attempts to describe how much Michio Kushi's life and work have meant to me will fall short of conveying the true impact. He spoke the truth, he gave us the ultimate understanding of universal principles, and he went beyond the greatest religious leaders to share the dietary keys to spiritual development. And with his unmatched sense of humor and play, he lived fully in each present moment: a gift, a prophet, and a shining light for humanity that can never be extinguished.

Knowing Michio has been the greatest joy and privilege of my life.

Remembering Michio
Carol Louro

I first met Michio and Aveline because of my parents. My father had a diseased kidney and went to see Michio thinking that by being on the macrobiotic diet it would give him strength to recover from his operation. Well, he never had his kidney removed and lived until ninety-one years old. He was a musician and owned a music store. My curiosity started when my father was bringing guitars and a flute to Michio. And I asked my father, why are you bringing instruments to this man Michio Kushi?" And my father said to me, "I am not giving Michio enough for what he is doing for me and he has many children." Then my father said to me, "I want you to meet Michio and Aveline." So my husband, my children, and I went with my parents to meet them. Meeting them in my mind and heart was a blessing for myself, my family, and years later my community because Michio came to our area and gave lectures.

When I think of my adventures with macrobiotics, I feel so blessed because I feel that God brought me to Michio and Aveline. My journey began in the late '70s. When I met Michio one of the first things he said to me was that I was going to be a teacher, and that I'd eaten enough butter for this lifetime and the next! My adventure began when I started studying at the Kushi Institute on Station Street in Brookline. Later I became certified, and under Michio's advice I started setting up macrobiotic lectures in my community and teaching, like he first told me I would. The counselors from the Kushi Institute were invited to speak on my local radio station many times. Michio sent Antonio (Toze) Areal to live with us so he could help New Bedford's Portuguese community.

Michio not only helped my father, but also my mother who lived a healthy life to 90 years old. He helped me, my husband, and all four of my children with different health problems: Chris with his kidneys, Tracy with her spine, John with a high fever when he had not eaten well, and Aimee with a fibroid adenoma. They all straightened out with his help. In my family macrobiotics has continued, and some of my grandchildren are practicing the diet.

Michio came to our community to lecture, and many people went to see him for consultations. There were many people who were very sick who became well under Michio's care, and are still friends of mine today. Two couples moved to Hilton Head, South Carolina, a young woman moved to Oregon, and another to Albuquerque, and I am still in touch and friends with them.

There was a young man who was very sick, and his father said to me, "Carol, all I want is for Michio to look at my son; then I know that I've done everything God wants me to do to take care of him." That was over twenty five years ago and that man is still well. Another time Michio came to lecture in Dartmouth. At the end of the lecture he was relaxing in the church and said, "It's so nice to see so many friends here tonight." He looked up and said to a woman sitting in the balcony, "You need to clean out the southeast corner of your upstairs." To this day nobody knew how he saw that. Everyone was saying, "Michio look at me! What do you see?" He was there very late giving advice to everyone. It's been over twenty years and people still remember that lecture.

At one of Michio's birthday parties everyone was standing up telling stories about him and thanking him for all he's done. The stories were beautiful and I wished I had had the courage to stand up and say something about him. Then it was time to serve dessert and tea, and we all started to relax. Michio slapped his hands on the table, looked straight ahead, not looking at me and said "Wait a minute! Isn't there somebody here from New Bedford?" I was totally surprised, sat up straight, and they came up to me with the microphone. While I spoke and thanked Michio he never looked at me. When I finished he looked right at me, smiled, and said, "Thank you very much."

One day at Michio's house I was sitting on the floor next to him leaning on the coffee table. He told me to give Thomas, his secretary, my email address so he could get a hold of me to do a lecture. He said, "Please give Thomas your email address so he can get in touch with you." I told him, "I don't have a computer." Then he said, "Do you have a fax number?" I was embarrassed and said, "I don't have a fax number either." "Really?" he said, "Do you have cell phone?" And very embarrassed I told him I didn't have a cell phone either. "Wonderful!" he said, "You're a simple human like Michio!" And then I felt much better.

I once brought a young couple to his house for a consultation. I was sitting across from Michio on the floor at the coffee table. He told the young man, "You can have one tablespoon of barley malt a week." "Whoa!" said the young man, "I thought you could drink that stuff!" Michio threw his pen down and said, "Ah, Carol…so famous for her barley malt." His humorous demeanor made him so real and fun to be with. Being with Michio was always uplifting, and his insightfulness was truly amazing.

When Michio would come down to lecture he would never go straight home. He would always come to visit with my husband, many friends, and me. Remembering Michio and how warm and supporting he was to our community will always stay in our hearts.

The last time Michio visited New Bedford was June 25, 2004. The local newspaper wrote an article titled "Food for Thought on Fourth of July Weekend." We have a picture of him lecturing that night, and over his head hangs a sign that says "heaven."

Michio is remembered for his passion and dedication to world peace and health. Many people in the New Bedford area feel very blessed to have known Michio, including not only my family and friends, but the whole community. None of us in the New Bedford area will ever forget Michio.

Remembering Michio
Judy MacKenney

Meeting Michio Kushi was a turning point in my life! I had been diagnosed with a Stage IV cancer, non-Hodgkin's lymphoma, and told that it was incurable! It had metastasized from my lymph system to the spine, spleen, pancreas, and mesentery bowel. Doctors were ordering me a protocol of chemotherapy, which clearly stated that it would not cure my condition. The medical professionals indicated that it might give me a temporary remission that would allow me to have a little more time with my family. I was a 49-year old woman — wife, mother, new grandmother, and business owner. Numb and devastated with this prognosis, I started the cancer protocol. The side effects were challenging and debilitating. Then I met Michio Kushi, a profound human being, macrobiotic leader, visionary, brilliant teacher, scholar, and mentor of wisdom. He gave me hope, inspiration, and direction with a plan for healing and wellness at a time that I was being informed (at a prestigious Boston hospital) that my life was almost over and that I should be getting my affairs in order. My family and I will be forever grateful for Michio's teachings! They saved my life!

For nine months (one day per week) I drove three hours from our home in in the Boston area to Dr. Bernie Siegel's Exceptional Cancer Patient (ECAP) Support Group/Class in New Haven, Connecticut to find peace, positive spirit, a way to live and die gracefully. It was there that I met with numerous, seriously health-challenged women and shared in their concerns and witnessed their courage. We were allowed to sign out books and tapes from Dr. Siegel's lending library. There I discovered *The Cancer Prevention Diet* written by Michio Kushi with Alex Jack. I had read a number of books at medical libraries looking for hope. Up to this point, every book I had read regarding my medical condition had been discouraging. I opened *The Cancer Prevention Diet* to the chapter on lymphoma and read, for the first time, that there was hope! All I had to do was be open to change in my ways of eating and choices of lifestyle and my disease could go into remission! The emotions that flowed through me were euphoric! Hope! For the first time I had found the plan I had been diligently seeking!

I called Michio's house in Brookline to make an appointment for a consultation but was told he was traveling abroad. Dr. Marc Van Cauwenberghe was the very knowledgeable macrobiotic counselor recommended to me in Michio's absence. He was very thorough in counseling me and provided me with an excellent healing plan. Three months later, I called Marc back to make a revisit consultation appointment with him but was told that he had returned to his native Belgium. Michio was on another trip so this time, Evelyne Harboun Miyaji, a gracious, lovely, knowledgeable, macrobiotic counselor was recommended to me. She counseled and supported me for many months. With gratitude I thank both these wonderful counselors. To see Michio in person was very important to me. I attended a Winter Conference at the Eden Roc Hotel in Miami Beach, Florida in 1993. My body was responding quite nicely to the macrobiotic diet and lifestyle. Numerous macrobiotic classes were offered at this conference, and I tried to absorb all the information I could from each macrobiotic teacher I encountered.

My husband Larry and several dear friends sat in an auditorium with twenty five or thirty other people to do a group consultation with Michio. Upon his arrival, he observed each person and gave each of us instructions on how to improve our health. He answered my questions and touched me profoundly when he stated, "You have the power to heal and recover from this cancer." I believed him. My prayers were answered. I met with Michio privately the next day. He spoke with me on a spiritual level. He helped to refocus my eyes and aligned my body using energy healing. He was a gifted healer. At the end of the conference, it was announced that Aveline Kushi was looking for volunteers to assist her with a fundraising dinner in a spacious, lovely home on the water. My friend and I volunteered. Aveline was so calm and gracious and taught us how to create the appetizers and elegant dishes for this wonderful dinner. Michio's first lady taught my first official macrobiotic cooking lesson!

Remembering Michio
Larry MacKenney

We first met Michio and Aveline at a Winter Conference at Miami Beach's Eden Roc Hotel in 1993. My wife, Judy attended after undergoing seven months of chemotherapy treatments in Boston's Dana Farber Cancer Institute for a Stage IV diagnosis of non-Hodgkin's lymphoma. We couldn't afford to stay at a hotel in the Miami area so friends of ours invited us to stay at their townhouse in Boynton Beach, a little more than an hour north of the Eden Roc. I commuted between Boynton Beach and Miami Beach twice a day for the entire conference, one round trip to take Judy down every morning and one round trip to pick her up every evening.

Our first encounter with Michio was at his group consultation of about twenty five to thirty people that Judy had signed us both up for. We were amazed at the way he diagnosed everyone without any prior knowledge of anyone's condition. He then proceeded to tell everyone, individually, what he or she needed to do to improve his or her conditions. Then he opened it up to questions and some of his answers astounded us. He was 100 percent confident in everything he said and his suave demeanor earned our respect and admiration immediately. The next day, Judy was thrilled to volunteer to be one of Aveline's assistants for a dinner she was cooking at a private residence for donors and supporters of macrobiotics at the Winter Conference.

In the first couple of years of the twenty-first century, Kushi Institute held three off-campus seminars organized by Phiya Kushi, Liz Klein, and David Kirchner, which featured Michio and Christina Pirello. The first was in Philadelphia, the second was in Tampa, and the third was in Philadelphia again. They were treated like mini-conferences and were quite well attended. At the conclusion of all three of these seminars, Michio held Advanced Training Classes for all teachers and students in attendance. We learned more from these Advanced Training Classes than any other classes we had attended because Michio let us in on many of his trade secrets of diagnosis which, of course, he was a master at.

Judy and I had worked hard at studying and we completed our 6th Level 4 session in December 2001. The night of our Level 4 graduation dinner had arrived. I was looking forward to the special evening meal and the award ceremony that followed. I was proud to have completed all the levels and was carefree and in good humor, as I usually am. I observed my classmates and applauded them all as they were called to the podium with Michio, Phiya, and Liz Klein officiating. When my name was finally called, I rose to the applause and gallantly strode to the officiating body with a big smile on my face. Once I got there, faced the audience, and Michio presented me with my diploma, it suddenly occurred to me that I was being handed this diploma by the man whose teachings had saved my wife Judy's life a few years earlier. At that precise moment, I became humbly overwhelmed with profound gratitude for Michio. The smile vanished from my face and I openly wept before that applauding crowd. It was one of the happiest days of my life, and I knew I would honor this man for the rest of my days!

When I headed up the Counseling Department at Kushi Institute, I had the distinct honor, privilege, and pleasure of scribing for many of Michio's consultations when he'd visit the Institute. To me, scribing for Michio was like being in a one-on-one classroom with the master! The knowledge I gained from those sessions was awe-inspiring, and I'll be forever grateful for those opportunities! Each occasion was nothing short of amazing!

When I was taking the levels at Kushi Institute, I occasionally had the opportunity to attend a class taught by Michio, himself—the master! My classmates always looked forward to it with bubbly enthusiasm. I have to admit, I was always a bit apprehensive as a student with Michio as my teacher in the classroom setting. The reason? I had to read his lips to understand his Japanese accent. He often stated that the older he got, the worse his English got, and I, for one, had to agree with him. I had a terrible time understanding what he was saying on many occasions and, whenever he'd turn his back to the class to write on the blackboard, especially for prolonged periods of time, I'd literally fall asleep. It was embarrassing but, evidently, what MY universe dictated!

Judy and I helped put on a mini-conference seminar in Tampa in 2002 featuring Michio and Christina Pirello. Our eldest daughter, Lauren was going through some uncomfortable medical issues. She was living at our home about an hour south of Tampa at the time. Judy was scribing for a lot of Michio's consultations at this seminar, and Michio took a moment after one of these consultations to ask Judy how she was feeling. Judy remarked that she was feeling great, but that our oldest daughter was having some medical issues and described her symptoms to him. Michio asked Judy to bring Lauren to him after his class the next morning and he would diagnose her. Lauren arrived the next morning and Michio gave Lauren his diagnosis of breast cancer involving both breasts, lymph, and lung (later medically confirmed) and told her what she had to do to start to heal herself, including attending the Kushi Institute Way to Health program. The entire mini-consultation took 15 minutes in the doorway of the classroom. Judy and Lauren absorbed the profound information that he imparted. They were grateful for his advice, and Lauren followed it over the next few months and healed herself of breast cancer with the help of Kushi Institute macrobiotic counselor Luchi Baranda without any further assistance from Western medicine.

Lauren's gynecologists had told her repeatedly that she could never become pregnant and bear children. She remained macrobiotic after her breast cancer recovery and, a few short years later, at the age of forty one, became ill for a number of months, thinking her cancer had returned. It was suggested that she take a pregnancy test, as many of her symptoms resembled that condition. Without realizing it, she had changed the chemistry in her body eating macrobiotically and three separate pregnancy tests revealed she was, indeed with child at the 4-1/2 month mark. She gave birth to a healthy, bouncing baby boy, Steele — yet another macrobiotic miracle!

Judy and I have had the pleasure of being part of the working staff on the annual Holistic Holiday at Sea cruise with Sandy Pukel, and John and Jan Belleme since 2006. It's always been on a huge Italian ocean liner serving macrobiotic-vegan-vegetarian cuisine in the Caribbean and is an absolute blast — combining vacation and holistic schooling in an unbelievable setting. Michio went on the very first cruise in 2004 as the featured speaker. Judy and I were not aboard because that particular week we were facilitating a Way to Health program at the Kushi Institute. Michio declined Sandy's invitations to sail with him again from the second through the ninth cruises.

Finally, in 2013, Michio, at eighty-six years of age, accepted Sandy's request to celebrate the tenth year anniversary cruise. I was selected by Sandy to be Michio's bodyguard/escort/guide (subject to Michio's approval) for the first two days of the cruise. My responsibilities included going to Michio's cabin a few minutes before he was scheduled to make an appearance somewhere on the ship, knock on his door (I told Michio of a secret knock that I'd do on his door so he'd know it was me), then escort him and Midori to his destination. Once finished with his responsibilities there, I'd lead them back to their cabin until his next scheduled assignment. I was also assigned to sit with Michio, Midori, and Judy at each mealtime at a designated table in an obscure part of the dining area to allow Michio some privacy while he was dining, prevent people from taking pictures of him anywhere we went, and generally keep people at arm's length from him in a crowd for his health and safety.

I was asked on a couple of occasions to read a statement that Michio had printed requesting his privacy be honored for the duration of the cruise. Most people honored his request. I only had to speak to a few people who refused to honor this request but I did so with grace, charm, and diplomacy. Man, I was good — so good, in fact, that Sandy told me I'd have this responsibility for the remainder of the cruise! We had some wonderful chats at mealtimes. At one point, feeling rather bold, I asked Michio who he had in mind to replace him as the new macrobiotic leader once he passed on. That question got me a swift kick in the shin under the table from Judy! He discussed the possibilities but never disclosed an answer to that question.

Just before the cruise ended, Michio asked Judy and me if we'd join Midori and him sightseeing the Miami area for a couple of days once we disembarked the ship, to which we excitedly responded in the affirmative! The first thing we did after disembarkation was to take Michio and Midori to the hotel that Sandy had selected for him. Upon entering the hotel lobby, we encountered construction workmen, complete with hard hats, hammering and power sawing, and construction dust everywhere. They were remodeling and the lobby area was in total chaos!

We followed the temporary signs and strode to the makeshift lobby desk where Michio graciously cancelled his hotel reservation. We returned to our vehicle and drove to a couple of quieter hotels. They selected a simple yet elegant room in the second hotel, which was situated in a peaceful neighborhood where they could stroll near the water. No chaos here! We helped them unload their luggage, allowed them some time to unpack and settle in, then returned to pick them up and begin our sightseeing expedition.

We were to spend the next two days playing with Michio! The first place we went to was the Coral Castle Museum in Homestead, a few miles south of Miami. Michio was fascinated with the sculpture garden in stone, the nine-ton gate that moves with just a touch of the finger, a Polaris telescope and functioning rocking chairs—all made entirely of stone built by one man using nothing but homemade tools. We completed the castle tour, had a light lunch at the tiny restaurant at the castle, and then drove back to Michio's hotel where they rested until dinnertime. We joined them for a delicious dinner at a simple Japanese restaurant within walking distance of their hotel, strolled the peaceful neighborhood, stopped for a tasty dessert, then walked them back to their hotel—the end of a wonderful day playing with Michio.

Late the following morning, we picked Michio and Midori up for lunch. We had a lovely lunch at a cute little al fresco Japanese restaurant then proceeded to an elegant hotel on Miami Beach. We followed Michio, strolling straight through the lobby of this exquisite hotel to a lush garden at the rear of the property which then emptied right out to the beach, filled with bikini-clad young ladies (some of them topless) and muscular young men. Almost everyone on the beach seemed to be sipping on a cocktail at his or her beach blanket/towel. I got the distinct feeling that Michio had been here before and wanted to relive an earlier visit. It seemed important for Michio, in his three-piece suit, to spend time at this beach, and he plopped himself down on a beach chair in the middle of this crowd who, by now, were amused by his unlikely beach attire.

Walking through the sand had tired him out somewhat so he rested in the chair for about 30 minutes as Midori, Judy, and I stood close by him amid the smiling gawkers. After resting, Michio asked me to help him to his feet and we followed him back, off the beach, through the garden and hallway to the lobby, out the front door to the sidewalk where we resumed strolling in front of the sprawling Miami Beach hotels. We eventually came upon another Japanese restaurant, ate another sumptuous dinner, and then returned to our vehicle for the drive back to their hotel. During the entire day, the four of us treated the occasion like a double date, enjoying light chatter, relaxed humor, and carefree fun. It was joyful watching their playfulness, how devoted they were to each other, and we realized that they were as relaxed around us as we were around them. They were catching a flight back to Boston early the next afternoon so when we reached their hotel, they thanked us for our companionship over the previous days, bid us adieu, and we headed for our home on Florida's west coast, basking in the euphoria of having spent quality time with "the master" on an enchanted weekend!

Remembering Michio
Bob Mattson

Back in the mid-Seventies when I joined the "nonviolent biological revolution" by working at the pioneering Erewhon Natural Foods Company, it was announced that the leader of the company would be addressing the warehouse employees. This meeting was my very first exposure to Michio Kushi who spoke to those of us who had convened on the third floor of the Farnsworth Street warehouse among the fifty-pound sacks of brown rice and wheat berries and other wholesome, organic food products awaiting distribution.

While I can't recall the content of his presentation, I do clearly recall that during the question and answer period at the end of his talk, one of the staff members who seemed to want to engage Michio in a political discussion asked: "Michio, which do you think is better: a capitalist system or a communist system?" Immediately Michio responded: "Any system is OK as long as the leaders are healthy." For me, that statement described what I think of as the "macrobiotic mission," that is, to begin the movement toward establishing a new world leadership that will help to return humanity back to its normally healthful and peaceful condition. How fortunate I was to be present at this historic era when the turning point, the revolution, was just beginning.

My very last encounter with Michio took place a few months before his passing on. It was during the 2014 Kushi Institute Summer

Conference at Becket at which Michio made an important presentation during which he reminded his audience about how we originated from our parents' blood, which came from food, which came from the soil, which came from minerals, which came from preatomic particles, which came from the world of vibration, which came from the infinite universe. Here's some of what he had to say, according to my recorded notes:

"Some people think that to fly is a miracle, or to walk on the water, and so forth. Those miracles are nothing compared to your miracle. From the infinite universe, you are here, and you are eating here. This is a miracle of miracles. And *you* did it. *You* have done that miracle. Beyond that you don't need to seek any miracles. You just enjoy your life and you appreciate your life that came from Infinity. That is your origin. And you are living within that Infinity. You came from Infinity and we are living in Infinity.

"Where do we go from here? To where do we go? Just like a candle, we are burning. Everyone has body temperature, burning; everyone has temperature. In order to burn, we must take oxygen and we burn. That's why everyone has a body temperature and burning bodies. Whatever we eat, the body is burning, resembling the candle, the fire goes. In the same way, you have an aura, burning. When you feel other people's hands, you feel the warmth. That is burning. Then this burning furthermore goes; all vibration goes. That burning is mind—mind. There is body and there is mind. That mind becomes more and more; vibrations become higher, more refined vibrations. We call that "spirit," or you may say "soul."

"That means what we create becomes body, mind and spirit by burning. And then what we do from here when burning goes, all this is returned to the soil as ashes.

"Your body returns to the soil. But your mind continues and your spirit continues. All go to that world of vibration. Your image, your understanding, your memories are all there. *And you never die.* Yes, your human life may end, *but your life never dies.* Your life continues as mind, as spirit, as vibration. But where do we go? We return to Infinity. And then from there, where do we go? And then coming back from the world of vibration, the world of preatomic energy, the world of elements, the vegetable world, the world of food, the world of parents' blood; everyone is universally reincarnated. *And we never die. We never die.*

"Everyone has eternal life. You must really understand. . . . And you never get scared. You never think, 'Oh, my life will end.' You never think that. Your life is eternal. You have no experience of death. You only experience change, the changing process. Our stages are changing, *but we never die.*"

Remembering Michio
Mitsuko Mikami

I recall my life at the Kushi House in Boston for almost four years was the entrance to the new world that has been guiding my personal evolution.

The Kushi House was a very busy, exciting, and perfect place for me not only to learn about macrobiotic theory and method but also to learn the significance of macrobiotics through the daily routine.

My days at the Kushi House as a housemother started at 5:00 a.m. by making soft rice and miso soup for the house people before going to school. I had to go to college to keep my student visa status, along with daily work as a main cook for the people at Kushi House, usually more than ten people. At that time, I also made special food for Aveline and gave her regular foot massage. Usually I started to do homework, prepare for a quiz or test for the next day late in the evening, and I was often nervous when I didn't have enough time. However, I always had help when needed and learned cooking from the people who helped me, and I rather enjoyed being busy.

I also remember the enjoyable trips to Japan and Amsterdam with Kushi family and Chris Akbar, an assistant to Michio. To cook special food for Aveline during the trip, we had to pack all the ingredients and cooking utensils, including pressure cooker, suribachi, cutting board, knife, chopsticks, and many other things. And as soon as we arrived at the hotel, Chris and I started cooking mostly for Aveline. Since Michio loved soba noodles, it was easy to cook for him.

I remember Michio used to write something in the living room next to the kitchen. Once, I cut my finger very deep while cooking and got much bleeding. Luckily Michio was there at that time, so I immediately ran to him and asked if I needed to go to the hospital. It seemed to be a deep cut. Taking a glance at my bleeding finger, Michio just told me to put much salt and a Band Aid. I followed his advice and found it was so painful when I put salt, but then the bleeding stopped soon and I could continue to cook. Amazingly, the wound disappeared in a few days. If I didn't have to keep on cooking, I thought I could put a small piece of nori instead of Band Aid. This is one of the macrobiotic solutions I experienced from daily life at the Kushi House.

One day, when I was cooking as usual, Michio called me from the living room. I was curious and went there. Then, suddenly Michio told me that I was going to teach the Five Transformations and Nine Star Ki in the future. It was like a prediction. And he started to write the ancient Japanese Kannagikuruma calendar and a circle to explain about Nine Star Ki on a piece of paper. At that time I couldn't understand any of it and just listened to him with surprise. Honestly speaking, it was too complicated for me and thought teaching it would never happen to me. But strangely enough, I kept studying Nine Star Ki for nearly nine years with a ninety-five-year old Japanese lady to whom I was introduced by Edward Esko, and now it is my most favorite topic when I give classes.

Michio's teaching of the Five Transformations and Nine Ki cosmology to explain the fundamental macrobiotic theory — "everything is energy" and "everything changes" — is one of his big achievements. I hope macrobiotic companions can take over Michio's original idea, "One Peaceful World," and cooperate with each other to make it possible.

Remembering Michio
Tom Monte

We were sitting in his living room at a low Japanese table in the late afternoon. It was autumn, 1987, and the sun was starting to wane. He was dressed in his customary dark blue slacks, white shirt, and dark blue vest. He hadn't been traveling for a few weeks and he looked good—strong, energetic, and healthy.

"You seem happy," I said to him.

"I'm not happy, or unhappy," he said with a smile.

I got the point—he was asserting that he didn't indulge in such dualities—but I couldn't help but press the observation. "Well, you *seem* happy," I said, with a laugh.

I was writing a book about AIDS, HIV, and gay men in New York who had adopted a macrobiotic diet to treat the illness. Both Michio and his wife, Aveline, had a great interest in helping people with the disease, and he had asked me to write something about their work.

Talks like this one occurred regularly through the 1980s, ostensibly because I was often writing something about him, his work, and about people who had adopted a macrobiotic diet to treat some kind of serious illness, and I often needed to interview him to get his perspective on the subject, or the person's recovery.

Inevitably, our conversations would drift off into philosophical matters, especially about the state of the world and his concerns for the human race.

"Human health is declining," he said. "Human judgment is getting weaker. More delusional way of thinking is happening. Meanwhile, technology is becoming more powerful, especially biotechnology. Biotechnology changes DNA for profit. If we don't change our way of eating and thinking soon, it will be the end of human beings."

He was known as the leading teacher of macrobiotics, and was often seen as focused primarily on food, which in fact was the centerpiece of the vast majority of his teachings. But the food was his way of teaching about the underlying energetics of life, the quantum physics of all existence. Food is, in fact, packets of energy. And each food, as a bundle of energy, resonates with specific organs of the body. He taught people how to understand the energetics of food and their resonant effects on the human body in order to restore health.

He stressed that human beings had emerged in nature as a consequence of eating plant foods, especially whole cereal grains, whose unique characteristic, the very essence of their nature, was their nutritional and energetic wholeness. The natural energies that created whole grains—the forces of heaven and earth—were captured in grain, which meant that those who ate whole grains would consume that unique energetic matrix, and thus inevitably experience greater wholeness, health, and a more holistic view of life. One consequence of a greater wholeness would be an enhanced ability to understand many different sides of a challenging issue.

Processed foods, more the product of the food factories than of nature, often contained chemicals that were poisonous to the body. But they were also nutritionally and energetically deficient, robbing the body of what it needs for health and wholeness. Processed foods were, in essence, partial foods, and thus would create a partial, one-sided point of view.

When you can only see one side, the other side looks like the enemy. With such a mentality, conflict is inevitable. "This is more and more the way people think — one-sided, dualistic mind," he said. "We cannot understand each other. Without understanding, you can't have peace."

To this teaching, he gave himself tirelessly in the hope of improving health and creating greater understanding among peoples — the work he referred to as "the dream of One Peaceful World."

"What motivates you?" I asked him on that sunny afternoon in 1987.

He let out a good-natured laugh, as if the question touched a small note inside of him that he usually kept to himself.

"I never wanted to do any of this," he told me. "I did it because I saw the need. And because Aveline kept creating more and more projects." That brought another round of laughter.

"I am a poet by nature," he said. "After so many years in the America, my English is still not so good, but I spoke beautiful Japanese." As he said this, his posture rose and he gave a big smile, as if the thought of writing beautiful words elevated his life condition. "I loved language and poetry. That's much more my nature — to reflect and be inspired and write poetry."

Destiny intervened when he met George Ohsawa, the Japanese philosopher who recovered the macrobiotic philosophy from both modern and ancient writings. Ohsawa introduced him to the connection between food and health, and to many of the underlying principles of macrobiotics. But he could not remain a student of Ohsawa for very long.

"I could only stay with him for a couple of weeks," he told me. "Ohsawa was so dominant. He treated every man like a woman. You had to be a woman to get along with him."

He left Japan for New York City in 1949, still largely unconvinced of Ohsawa's teachings and philosophy. But once in New York, he began studying people's lives, their dietary patterns, and their health, and soon understood the importance of macrobiotics to health and world peace.

It was at this point, in the early stages of his development and understanding, that some kind of enormous personal and spiritual transformation took place. He was no longer a teacher of diet and health exclusively, but a philosopher and spiritual teacher of the first order.

In post-World War II America, the leading nutritional teacher was, of course, Adelle Davis, who focused primarily on individual nutrients and supplementation. Michio, by contrast, was teaching the unity among diet, the origins of humanity, human health, the evolution of human consciousness, the forces that cause spirit to become matter, the destiny of mankind, and the nature of the universe itself.

He based his teaching on the ancient philosophy of yin and yang, or what Ohsawa had called the Order of the Universe, and on the spiral of materialization and spiritualization. These two understandings — the philosophy of yin and yang and the spiral — were the two most important tools for understanding life available to us, he maintained.

He was, to be sure, a man of extraordinary abilities, many of which I witnessed first hand.

In January of 1980, when our first son was just three months old, Toby, my wife, and I met Michio privately in his hotel in Baltimore, Maryland. He had just given a talk before a large audience and, before arriving in Baltimore, had been traveling and teaching for some time. When we entered the meeting room, I noticed that he seemed a bit tired, but he wanted to talk to me about moving to Boston and coming to work for the *East West Journal,* the magazine he started to spread the teachings of macrobiotics.

For our part, Toby and I were eager to know what guidance he might give us concerning our son. Jacob was bundled up in hat and heavy clothing, which obscured virtually all of his features. All that was visible was a little bit of his cheeks.

"Should I take off his hat and coat so you can see him?" Toby asked Michio.

"No, it's not necessary," he said. He pointed to Toby and said, "Your father is with him. He's trying to help your son."

Toby's father had passed away when Toby was ten years old, and now, when we met Michio, Toby was only twenty six years old, an age when one easily could have assumed that Toby's father was still alive. But Michio had not only seen that Toby's father had passed from this world, but that his spirit was watching over our son.

On another occasion, when Michio and I were having lunch at his house in Brookline, Massachusetts, he asked me, "How is your family?"

Though the question came out of the blue, it was in fact my central concern.

Toby was pregnant with our second child, but our midwife could not determine when Toby had conceived. Based on the midwife's calculations, the baby was not developing normally. She informed us that very likely our child was deformed in some way and the odds were that Toby would eventually miscarry.

After I told Michio all of this, he paused and entered some kind of strange reverie in which he seemed to study the area over my left shoulder. At length, he said, "Your wife became pregnant three months and seventeen days ago. The midwife will soon realize all is OK. Everything will be fine."

A few weeks later, the midwife was able establish the true date of conception and found that our child was developing normally. She consulted her little conception date calculator and gave us the date when Toby had become pregnant. I did the math, determining the length of time between Toby's conception and my lunch with Michio: Three months and seventeen days, on the button.

And indeed, our daughter, Christina, was born at home, and was both healthy and beautiful.

On another occasion, Michio and I were sitting at his low table eating a meal together. We had been talking about life in general, and at one moment the conversation reached a pause and both of us were silent. Suddenly, he looked at me and said, "You can have anything you want in life." And with that, he picked up a cigarette lighter from the table, held it at shoulder height, and let it fall on the table. The smack of the lighter against the table caused a noise that seemed to explode in my nervous system. The sound fairly shocked me. And with deadly seriousness, he said, "But you have to give your life for it."

Talks like these were the real reason I kept showing up at his house. Indeed, what I learned during the meals we shared was a big part of why I kept writing books and articles about macrobiotics, individual recoveries, and Michio's exploits. Over time, he told me many things about myself that were of a personal nature that I treasure to this day. And much of what he said continues to inspire and fuel my life, as his teachings have done for tens of thousands of people around the world.

More students, of course, meant more teaching, more travel, more projects, and more demands — all of which brought a considerable cost. Michio's son Norio estimated that more than two thousand students stayed with Michio and Aveline at their home in Brookline, Mass. over the years the two were teaching. People from all over the world called them on a daily basis with desperate pleas for help, often at 2 or 3 in the morning.

Virginia Harper, who cured herself of Crohn's disease using macrobiotics, remembers making such a call to Michio at 3 a.m., terrified that she could not stop her intestinal bleeding. Aveline answered the phone, listened to Virginia's plight, and then consulted Michio. Soon Aveline was back on the phone with instructions. "Very strong miso soup, with extra wakame seaweed," she said. Drink the miso soup every hour. Bleeding will stop, she told her. Sure enough, the "very strong miso soup with extra wakame" stopped the bleeding, and it wasn't long before Virginia would cure herself of an illness that medical doctors had told her was incurable.

Time and demands take their toll. Fortunes change. In the mid-1990s, the shadow fell, and a long period of suffering followed for Michio and the Kushi family, beginning with the loss of daughter, Lily, who in 1995 died of cervical cancer. Lily's death broke his heart and changed him in fundamental ways. In 2001, Aveline, his wife of more than forty years, passed away of the very same disease. Three years later, Michio himself was diagnosed with colon cancer. And on December 28, 2014, he passed from this world.

But at our meeting in the autumn of 1987, his spirit was still strong, and he was very much engaged in all of his many activities. By then, he had already achieved more than most men dream of. He started numerous businesses, including Erewhon, the first major whole foods distributor; *East West Journal*, a magazine for holistic health; the Kushi Institute, a center for Macrobiotic learning in the Berkshire hills of western Massachusetts; and he had written dozens of books, many of them with writer Alex Jack. He had received many awards, and would go on to receive even more. In the late-1990s, his papers would be installed for permanent exhibit in the Smithsonian Institution. But most important, he had affected the lives of millions of people, and helped to heal untold thousands of them.

As our conversation wound down on that autumn afternoon, I asked him, "What is your greatest success?"

Without missing a beat, he said, "I have no successes. But I moved everything forward."

In his simple, poetic way, his words captured the essence of what he gave us all.

He wasn't perfect and indeed he was a man of many contradictions, some of which were baffling, others truly vexing, and most of them beyond explanation. But in the end, little of that matters. Because he was true to his word: He gave his life for what he wanted, which indeed was a worthy cause.

And that is the measure of a great man.

When I left him that day, he saw me to his front door and bid me goodbye. And as I watched him close the door behind me, I saw that he had already turned inward, preoccupied perhaps by yet another challenge that needed to be moved forward.

Remembering Michio
Rich Myers

Other than my parents, no person has shaped or contributed more to the quality of my life than Michio Kushi.

As I was approaching age forty I was experiencing the gradual onset of health issues which commonly afflict middle age Americans—elevated blood pressure and cholesterol levels, arthritic joint pain, weight gain, frequent headaches, susceptibility to colds, and reduced stamina and energy.

Intuitively I felt these ailments might be caused by the calorie-rich diet I had been eating for years as a career Navy man on ships and shore stations—high in fat and animal protein, highly processed and chemicalized foods, refined flour products, and excess sugar. It was back in the early 1980s when I remember asking my doctor if these ailments would go away and my health and energy improve with a diet change. He chuckled dismissively and assured me the military's four basic food group menu was balanced, nutritious, and healthy and there was no basis for me to criticize or change my diet.

Aware of the health benefits people experienced on the macrobiotic diet I decided to give Michio's dietary teachings a try. With the help of macrobiotic friends and support groups I succeeded in transitioning to the macrobiotic way of eating. Stunned by dramatic improvements in my health and energy level I kept a diary in which

I recorded the disappearance of these ailments and over twenty other positive changes in my physical condition. Rather than embracing the dominant scientific nutrition and medical orientation of that time I listened to my body instead. Today at age seventy I continue to be blessed with excellent health and energy and am in better physical condition than my three siblings and most other friends my age who remain on the standard American diet. I believe following Michio's dietary teachings have added a decade or more to my life span.

From Michio's arrival in the United States in 1949 until his death in 2014 he devoted six decades in selfless service to others. Investigated and harassed in early years by the FDA and FBI for teaching and promoting the diet-health link and dismissed by the dominant medical and scientific communities, he remained a voice in the wilderness for more than half a century.

Besides being a prolific writer and author of many books, Michio gave countless lectures and seminars and established and sustained macrobiotic conferences and the Kushi Institute with no government funds. These educational activities have educated thousands for over thirty years, molded a following of gifted and certified educators, provided testimony to government agencies, and inspired physicians, government officials and a worldwide network of macrobiotic learning centers. His pioneer work importing macrobiotic food staples into America helped trigger a natural foods industry, a network of wholesalers, and thousands of natural food stores and even supermarkets. Tofu, miso, brown rice, tempeh, soy sauce, and soy products are well-known items and are available everywhere. Most dramatic of Michio's achievements perhaps was his nutrition counseling in which he helped thousands upon thousands of seriously or terminally ill people regain their health through dietary change.

Over the decades his teachings ceased to be a counter-culture movement. The accumulation of scientific evidence, the 1977 Senate Select Committee's bombshell report *Dietary Goals for the United States*, the introduction of the epochal Food Pyramid guidelines starting in 1992 have validated the health benefits of a macrobiotic diet centered on organically grown, pesticide-free whole grains, vegetables, fruits, beans and minimally processed, low-fat and low-sugar foods. Clearly Michio's teachings and lifelong works have been imprinted on the country. While thousands of accomplished and dedicated people have contributed significantly to this movement, I challenge anyone to identify a single individual who labored longer, more passionately, and in so many different ways to change the country's perspective on what constitutes healthy eating and to improve people's health. Michio Kushi was truly a great man and deserves to be honored as such.

Thank you, Michio, from the bottom of my heart.

Remembering Michio
Gideon Nelissen

Good afternoon everybody. I am Gideon Nelissen. I am the oldest son of Adelbert and Wieke Nelissen from Amsterdam and I am going to play some piece of Bach. I played many times when Michio was in Holland or in other places where we met each other. I chose Bach because that comes the closest to the grain, the whole grain. Thank you.

Gideon performed Sonata No. 1 for Solo Violin, 1st Movement, Adagio by Johannes Sebastian Bach.

Remembering Michio
Wieke Nelissen with Horriah Nelissen

Hello everybody! Dear friends, my name is Horriah Nelissen. I am the oldest daughter of Adelbert and Wieke Nelissen from the Kushi Institute of Europe in Amsterdam. I will read a message from my mother, Wieke Nelissen, and in the spirit of my father who recently passed in the beginning of September.

Both Wieke and Adelbert, my parents, have seen Michio and Aveline as their great teachers and guides on their path of macrobiotics. For their children, I am the oldest of five children; Michio and Aveline were like grandparents to us. For a long period of time Michio and Aveline were both present several times per year in Amsterdam and other Dutch cities where seminars took place. Their first encounter was in 1975 when Michio and Aveline visited Europe for the first time.

At that time Adelbert and Wieke were already practicing macrobiotics eight years. They started in 1968, learning from the book *Zen Macrobiotics* by George Ohsawa. Their understanding of macrobiotics was very limited at the time. They wrote down in a diary: "Horriah" (that's me) "got one raisin! Oh, oh, oh, will that be okay?" I read that diary and, oh, I'm glad that I'm still alive! They started already the first macrobiotic food store in Amsterdam and sourdough bakery called Manna.

The first Michio Kushi Seminar of Europe took place in London, and Michio was speaking there for a group of acupuncturists. My father was there, and he attended those lectures, and he was so overwhelmed by Michio's teaching that he immediately phoned home to all the workers of Manna company, which was growing at the time. They had to drop their work immediately and come to Paris where Michio and Aveline would teach next, as soon as possible.

Paris was for Michio and Aveline like entering the lion's den since in France several of the old students of Ohsawa were teaching there, and Michio was a little bit seen as an intruder with too many modern ideas about macrobiotics. The seminar was very successful, and Michio and Aveline took the most challenging step into the world of European macrobiotics successfully.

That same year in the fall, Michio came for the first time to Holland and taught for over three hundred very grateful students. For Adelbert and Wieke, Michio and Aveline made order in their macrobiotic life — their daily experience. Suddenly everything made more sense to them so that one raisin became a normal box, I think.

And it was the beginning of a long relationship between my parents and Michio and Aveline. Adelbert organized more than forty seminars with Michio and Aveline with students from all over Europe in many different languages. Perhaps you cannot imagine, but all the teachings had to be translated in up to eight different languages.

The Kushi Institute of Europe was established in 1978 as an educational center for leadership programs. Here are some of the highlights of the seminars and conferences Adelbert and Wieke organized for Michio and Aveline. In the '80s a conference for medical professionals was organized for the World Health Organization in Brazzaville, in the Republic of the Congo, and led to a conference in France, in Bergerac, for very interested doctors.

In Brazzaville Adelbert visited markets in preparation for Michio's visit, and in small villages he would gather different kinds of products as samples to present the macrobiotic standard diet to the World Health Organization doctors. He even found brown rice and tofu. So it became clear that in a poor capital like Brazzaville, a macrobiotic standard diet was possible to eat.

In the 1980s the Kushi Institute in Amsterdam organized a number of conferences on AIDS and cancer. Although Michio and Adelbert had various meetings with the chairman of the governmental cancer organization, interest in the healing power of macrobiotic food was very low at the time. Healthcare in Holland was so well organized, why would people take care of their own health if the government paid everything? On the contrary, and at the same time, there were numbers of people very interested in the health of family and children, which became, in the end, one of the trademarks of the Kushi Institute of Europe.

Between 1980 and 2000 Michio and Aveline conducted several times, four levels of spiritual development training in the south of Holland in a monastery. And other very popular seminars were "New Medicine for Humanity," "The Destiny of Mankind," "The Cause of War and the Art of Peace," and "The Essence of Macrobiotics."

When Michio and Aveline came for the first time to Holland, Wieke and Adelbert made them taste sourdough bread from their bakery. Aveline especially immediately grew very fond of this traditional Dutch bread. And also they introduced them to tempeh. You might be familiar with tempeh now, but tempeh was originally a fermented soybean product from Indonesia, a former colony of Holland. And Aveline and Michio didn't know this food, since it was not originally Japanese. So they immediately decided to put this delicious, healthful food, together with sourdough bread, into the macrobiotic standard diet, and now tempeh has spread all over the world.

Michio loved Amsterdam but not the weather. Some of you may not either. He would always make a joke saying, "Welcome to the Winter Conference!" even in the middle of the summer. And once he tried to adapt to the Dutch habits by trying to ride a bicycle. But he didn't get very far. After a hundred meters he actually gave up. In Holland you have also bikes with side wheels. Maybe we should have given one like that.

The last time Michio visited Amsterdam was to celebrate his eightieth birthday. Many of his old students gathered for a big party with delicious food and artistic performances of professional macrobiotic musicians and dancers. It was a wonderful evening during which everybody could express his or her gratitude for Michio's teachings. In Holland his many students, and especially our family, will remember and cherish Michio and Aveline for their wonderful teachings and guidance for so many years. Adelbert always spoke so highly of them and always felt extremely connected with both of them.

May their spirits guide us all to One Peaceful World. Thank you.

Remembering Michio
Mayumi Niimi Nishimura

I came to the U.S. to study macrobiotics with Michio in January 1982. I had previously read about macrobiotics in Japan from George Ohsawa's books and from Michio's *The Book of Macrobiotics*. I knew very little about living in the U.S. and of the English language. Yet, despite this, with some savings I was determined to study and fully learn macrobiotics.

My first meeting with Michio was at his house in Brookline. My friend Joji Araki was living there. His father was a good friend of Michio's. I don't remember if he was really into macrobiotics, but he had a beautiful girlfriend who came to study macrobiotics from Canada. Joji introduced my then husband Jinn and me to Michio and Aveline. We were so excited to meet them and study macrobiotics. We were low on money and were hoping to live at the Kushi Institute somehow. We thought that maybe we would get lucky and be able to live with them, but that didn't happen right away. At that time, Michio and Aveline were busy with Erewhon, their natural food company. When we met them they asked if we wanted to purchase a rice cake machine from Erewhon. At that time we needed help with room and board and had no funds to purchase a rice cake machine. So our meeting was short and sweet. I made sure that Aveline remembered me as someone who knew how to fillet fish as I was born into country inn by the sea in a small island in Japan. We were hoping to move into the Kushi House so we could continue to attend classes but we had no idea how to do this.

One rainy day in May I received a phone call from Aveline. She asked if we could move into the Kushi House, and if I would be able to cook for everyone in the house. I explained how little I knew about macrobiotics, but she insisted that since I was Japanese I should be able to cook macrobiotic food with no problem. Well if Aveline said so, then I thought maybe I can. I did not forget to ask her if we could stay at the Kushi House in exchange for work and tuition for classes. So, my husband became Michio and Aveline's chauffer, and I became the house chef.

We moved into the Kushi House at the end of June. Michio and Aveline were away teaching in Europe. Nobody at the house knew we were moving in that day and that I was the new cook. Unable to speak English, I had a hard time communicating with a house full of Americans. Flo Nakamura was Michio's secretary. I thought I would be able to communicate with her, as she was Japanese. No such luck. Flo was from Hawaii and spoke very little Japanese. However, she did understand that I needed to find kombu and shiitake mushrooms. She pointed me to the pantry. I was able to find everything I needed to cook my first meal at the Kushi House. I don't recall what I made that night, but what I remember is that when Michio and Aveline returned after several weeks, I made an azuki bean dish of some sort. I was a bit nervous because the beans were not well cooked. I thought I knew how to cook azuki beans and I made them the way I thought my mom made them back home in Japan, but they did not come out right. Michio called me from the dining room and asked,"Did you soak the beans before you cooked them?" " No, I didn't," I replied. He said, "Well you should soak beans always." I thought my mom never soaked them and they always turned out fine. However I never actually watched her cook, and so really didn't know how she actually cooked them. I never really had an interest in what she was cooking. Now I know that if you are lucky some of the azuki beans will cook fine without soaking, but if you want to make sure always turn out perfectly, soak them for 6 to 8 hours. That was my first lesson from Michio, "Soak your beans almost always."

We moved to the Berkshires of western Massachusetts after Michio and Aveline purchased their property in Becket. We were there to help start the Kushi Institute. It was envisioned to be a residential center where students could fully experience macrobiotics in theory and practice. We began our days there by dusting every room one by one. The property was huge. The land was bigger than the island where I grew up. The Main House used to be a hunting lodge for a railroad tycoon. It was later sold to the Franciscans.

There was a dormitory for priests in training. It needed a good cleaning and a new floor for the main classroom. We were busy with all that for the first year. We had one fun dinner with local macrobiotic friends who were helping us to place the new floor in the dormitory. They knew quite a bit about wild foods in the Berkshires. One evening they made dinner with wild mushrooms that happened to be the kind that makes one laugh for no reason. The dish tasted good, and we enjoyed laughing over dinner. But then we had to visit Michio and Aveline in Brookline that same weekend. We made a report to Michio and Aveline about how things were going in Becket. Afterward he said to us, "Do not eat too much mushrooms, OK?" How did he know we had eaten wild mushrooms that made us laugh? So my second lesson from him was, "He is a wizard. We can't hide anything from him!"

I got used to living in the countryside. I had my first child in the Berkshires, a daughter, Lisa. She came with extra thick hair and was a very healthy baby. I had no problem raising her on a macrobiotic diet but was asked by a co-worker if I taught my child English. It was more important for me that she understood Japanese because she would have no problem learning English while living in the U.S. There were no Japanese speakers around except the occasional visitor from Japan. The same person questioned me about my position at the Kushi Institute. I was a caretaker, chef, and cooking class assistant. I felt unwelcome at the Institute because I had a baby. I asked Michio what he thought about me raising my child while working at the Institute. He said, "Well, since you can do both why don't you do so. There will be a time when you have to choose between one or the other." That was his third teaching: "Do two or more things while you can." I've kept this very close to my heart after thirty years.

I started cooking for Madonna in 2001. I had to let go of full time mothering, as the new job was also full time. I did so because I had to earn money for my kids' college tuition and living expenses. I was divorced then. It was not easy to leave my two kids (I had a son, Norihiko, born in 1988) to do that job. Almost every year I wanted to quit. I couldn't stand not seeing my kids regularly during the first three years. After that I wanted to quit because of the job itself or because of co-workers. One day I had a bad argument with Madonna's assistant. I don't remember what it was, but her assistant was really upset with me and I was not happy with that. I called Michio at his home and told him that I wanted to quit and asked him what I should do. He asked, "Did you submit the resignation letter to her?" I said, "Not yet." He replied, "Why don't you wait for three days before making a decision?" The very next day my mood brightened. I decided not to quit my job. I stayed on as Madonna's chef. That was my fourth lesson from Michio: "Nothing lasts for more than three days, even rainy days — everything changes."

I'd like to share what Madonna thought about Michio after having lunch with him in Los Angeles. "He is very charming," she said. I think we all agree about that, don't we?

I keep these lessons in my heart and think about him often. I will keep walking the path you showed me, Michio. I hope that I am not making mistakes. Love you and miss you.

Remembering Michio
Patricio Garcia de Parades

My mother, Luisa Baranda, was a weakly child from birth, and eventually her condition deteriorated to the point that her doctors thought that she would never recover. But because my brother and I were little at the time, she decided to try doing something on her own to improve her condition. For a few years she experimented changing her way of eating and became vegetarian, but to no avail. In 1975, while shopping at Macrobiotic Zen, a natural food store and restaurant featuring macrobiotic food in Barcelona, she saw advertised a seminar by Michio and his wife Aveline Kushi and decided to attend. In those days there was a growing interest about macrobiotics in Europe, and Michio would come several times a year to teach at various locations. After the seminar, my mother began to make changes in her way of eating and implement various lifestyle practices that Michio had recommended. About a year later her condition had greatly improved and she was full of hope. The next time Michio came to give a seminar, my mother decided to bring me and my brother along so that he could check on us and make sure that we were doing fine. And that's how I got to meet Michio for the first time when I was six years old.

I remember going into a room where Michio was sitting, and as we were approaching him, I realized that he was looking intently into my face. As soon as we got close, he pointed at my face and said "too much shoyu." In Spain, it is common to keep salt and other seasonings at the table and people would adjust the flavor according to their preferences. Since beginning to eat in a macrobiotic way, my mother had also added shoyu. And since I found the new food to be a little bland to my taste, every meal I would pour shoyu everywhere. So when we went back home after the seminar, my mother took the seasonings out from the table and food became bland again. This is what triggered interest in cooking for me, because when I cooked, I could season foods strongly and the way I liked it without my mother noticing. Although I was not yet aware at the time, this was my first encounter with the art of making balance, an important and profound approach not only useful for cooking or eating, but also how we live and manage every aspect of our lives.

Michio's lectures were the driving force behind the macrobiotic movement in those days. Not only were they stimulating and entertaining due to his charismatic personality and often humorous way in which he delivered his talks, but because they were highly motivating and inspiring. His talks would cover a wide range of topics and the views he presented were very new and unique. He seemed to always be looking at life from a large, all-encompassing perspective yet his message was clear and his teachings would be expressed in a straightforward way. It is hard to know or quantify the impact Michio has had on individuals, families, society and the world as a whole. But there is no doubt that for many of those who attended his talks, their lives were changed forever.

Central to his teachings was a way of life in harmony with nature and a well-balanced way of eating based on natural quality foods and traditional eating patterns. Michio was among the earliest proponents for the use of food and lifestyle as the most fundamental way to promote personal and planetary health. And he also introduced, many times taught, and encouraged the use of various traditional techniques for physical, mental, and spiritual development and less invasive methods of healing to help people strengthen their health, including Shiatsu massage, palm healing, Do-In and other forms of bodywork, Aikido, Judo, meditation, imagery, chanting, breathing techniques, certain traditional herbs, moxibustion, acupuncture, and many others. My mother, like many others in those days, after experiencing the healthful benefits of a macrobiotic way of life opened a natural food store, began to teach and give cooking classes, organized seminars, and dedicated themselves to help other people. They promoted organic farming, helped make natural-quality foods available, taught about the benefits of consuming unrefined grains and other whole foods, and guided people to improve their dietary habits by reducing animal food, sugar and other highly processed foods in favor of more wholesome natural-quality foods and an eating pattern mostly based on a wide variety of plant foods.

The macrobiotic approach to eating and enhancing health through more natural means was very new in those days, and it was sometimes met with certain opposition and seen with some reluctance or disbelief, particularly by nutritionists and healthcare professionals. However, since then things have greatly changed, and now dietary and lifestyle changes are being recommended as the single, most important way to tackle the epidemic of chronic disease by many nutritionists and medical professionals, as well as governments and health organizations. And although differences about details abound, the consensus has been reached that, in order to prevent chronic disease and help relieve many common health conditions, we need to reduce animal food, sugars and highly processed, chemicalized foods and move towards a traditionally oriented, whole food, plant-based diet, as has been suggested by macrobiotics from the very beginning. Meanwhile, diet and lifestyle along with many of the natural healing modalities introduced by Michio and other macrobiotic teachers are currently being actively used by countless people around the world and form part of what is now being referred as alternative, complementary, and integrative methods of healing.

Through his teachings and his books, Michio strived to present a unified view of life by integrating traditional and modern views and by complementing the seemingly differing views and ways developed by Eastern and Western societies. His teachings of traditional Oriental culture and way of thinking have been very valuable for developing a better understanding of life and closing the gap between East and West. However, Michio's modern interpretation of Oriental culture and traditional way of thinking was practical, dynamic and alive, which is very different from other more academic interpretations. The emphasis was placed on reviving old ideas, grasping the essence and applying the principles in our everyday life so that it could be implemented in simple ways by anyone. The goal was to use this understanding as an effective tool for enhancing personal health, improving quality of life, and achieving greater happiness as the foundation for a better world. His teachings included studies of key Oriental concepts such as Ki or the invisible energy flowing throughout the universe, the environment and our bodies, and the yin and yang view of life and its countless applications for maintaining balance and creating harmony within and around us. Throughout the years, many people became interested to learn more about these, and they are becoming increasingly known in contemporary society. Actually, now that I have been living in Japan for more than fifteen years, I am surprised to see that the number of people who are familiar with these concepts or interested in their practice is very few compared to in the West. A clear indication of the far-reaching influence Michio's work has had.

Michio was repeatedly ahead of his time, and many of the things and ideas that he introduced have, in a relatively short period of time, become well known and appreciated by many people. Together with his wife, Aveline Kushi, he popularized many traditional Japanese foods, including grains and grain products such as brown rice and seitan; vegetables such as daikon and shiitake mushrooms; tofu, soymilk and other soybean products; sea vegetables, pickles such as umeboshi; seasonings such as miso, shoyu, and rice vinegar; and natural sweeteners such as rice syrup and amasake among many others. And they also shared other aspects of the Japanese food culture including many new ways of cooking, food processing, and ideas for creating balanced meals through maintaining a variety of colors, flavors, and textures, as well as ways of harmonizing our way of eating with the changes in the seasons. Other examples include simple, practical aspects of everyday life such as eating with chopsticks, sleeping in futons or removing shoes before entering a house. I remember that when my friends or other family members would come to my house and see us eating with chopsticks, eating sea vegetables or sleeping in futons, I frequently felt kind of awkward. Interestingly, a recent documentary in

Japanese public television covering on the three trendiest aspects of Japanese culture in Barcelona showed that Japanese food and the proliferation of Japanese restaurants, futons, and manga were the most popular.

The macrobiotic way of eating that Michio spent large part of his life creating, teaching, and promoting has many times been misinterpreted as a strict dietary pattern mostly limited to the recovery of health. But nothing could be further from the truth. In fact, the macrobiotic approach doesn't really prohibit any food. But it does suggest to maintain a certain basic food proportion and to choose the highest quality foods available as a practical way to maintain balance. If we observe current eating patterns, most problems are related to excess or deficiencies. A clear indication of this unbalanced eating pattern characteristic in modern society is that about one-third of the world population suffers from problems related with overweight and obesity while another one-third suffers from problems related to hunger and malnutrition. Macrobiotics is about becoming aware of the profound influence that food has on our lives and little by little making conscious, more responsible choices when it comes to selecting our food and practicing a style of eating. It is not about following rules and regulations. In addition, the macrobiotic way of eating should not be practiced in a rigid manner but with flexibility, taking into consideration individual preferences and respect for diversity. The key element to keep in mind is moderation.

Restrictions commonly associated with the macrobiotic way of eating mainly originate from modifications aimed at increasing the possibility of recovering health by those who have lost it. Unfortunately, many people learn about the relation between diet and health late in their lives or decide to implement dietary and lifestyle changes once they have run out of options. How many times we hear from people who come to study macrobiotics that, "I wish I knew about this before." As a result, a large number of people who decide to give macrobiotics a try are frequently due to serious health concerns that often require limiting our way of eating to help correct unbalances and have a greater chance of regaining health. Needless to say that Michio has made a very valuable contribution to develop the idea that "food is medicine" and through his dietary advice countless people, including my mother, were able to recover their health and start a new life. And those who were able to regain their health and their families and friends will always be grateful for it.

But we should also know that the purpose of the macrobiotic way of eating is not reduced to the recovery of particular health conditions. And few people acknowledge the enormous contribution the macrobiotic way of eating that Michio and Aveline Kushi taught and disseminated through their books, seminars, and cooking classes have had helping improve dietary habits around the world. These include supporting organic agriculture and natural methods of farming without the use of chemical fertilizers and pesticides; promoting natural and traditional ways of processing that maintain the integrity of the food; teaching about the benefits of whole foods; reintroducing and popularizing staple foods such as whole grains and whole grain products including sourdough bread; increasing variety and availability of vegetables and showing new ideas for cooking with them; recommending beans and introducing soybean products such as soymilk and tofu that are now increasingly found in many healthy kitchens around the world and are helping replace meat, dairy, and other animal products; introducing sea vegetables that were new for most people but are now being harvested in the United States and in various parts of Europe; teaching how to make natural sweets using milder, unrefined sweeteners that are contributing to replace sugar and other artificial sweeteners; introducing new seasonings such as miso and shoyu with many cooking possibilities and health advantages; encouraging consumption of locally grown, seasonal foods; and many others. And besides strengthening the health of millions around the world and helping prevent chronic disease, since many families, mothers, and young children are now benefiting from these foods; we are also talking about improving the health and wellbeing of future generations. These efforts are important aspects to create a new world food culture that over time, and, as it continues to spread around the world, will eventually help regain our innate, natural human health, and sickness will simply cease to manifest.

Michio had no doubt that food is a powerful tool not only to enhance personal health, but also develop society, help solve the environmental crisis, and eventually realize world peace. Another important aspect of the macrobiotic approach promoted by Michio for over fifty years that is often overlooked is the contribution to a more sustainable and efficient food culture, a more humane way of producing our food, and a more socially responsible and equitable way to feed humanity. And now that in recent years the environmental and social implications of our food are becoming clearer, this should also be better recognized. Livestock production caused by the unprecedented increased consumption of animal food around the world along with intensive, chemicalized farming and the modern globalized food system that relies heavily on highly processed foods and drinks is now being linked to a wide range of environmental issues and extensive damage to the planet.

Livestock production alone is one of the biggest contributors to global warming and climate change; water, soil and air pollution; environmental degradation, water scarcity, deforestation, decline of biodiversity, soil erosion, and many other problems. According to the United Nations, livestock is responsible for 18 percent of global greenhouse gas emissions, which is more than the 14 percent allocated to transportation. However, according to a 2009 report called *Livestock and Climate Change* by two World Bank environmental assessment specialists found that the environmental impact of the livestock sector has been underestimated and that it accounts for at least 51 percent of global greenhouse gas emissions. In the report, the quickest and most efficient way to mitigate the impact of global warming and climate change suggested is by replacing livestock products by plant-quality substitutes such as soybean products and seitan (sometimes also referred as wheat-meat). And these foods have become known and popularized around the world thanks, to a large extent, to the efforts of macrobiotics. My mother, for example, learnt how to make seitan, soymilk, tofu, and tempeh from Aveline Kushi at a time when soybeans were unknown in Spain and she had to drive to France in order to get them. Later on she made them at home, sold them in her natural food store, taught how to cook with them and introduced them to many people.

Meanwhile, the socio-economic impact of our food today is also great and can't remain hidden anymore. These include rising health care costs caused mainly by poor dietary habits that weaken our health, poverty, hunger, malnutrition, food loss and waste; water scarcity, and depletion of natural resources among many others. For example, it is estimated that about one-third to half of the global food being produced for human consumption every year is lost or wasted before reaching a human mouth while one-third of the world population experience lack of food or food insecurity. And this alone is responsible for about 14 percent of global greenhouse gas emissions or about the same as transportation, as well as a tremendous amount of pollution. The combination of these issues put a lot of pressure on families, communities, and societies, and is a major underlying cause for conflict and war in modern society. So when evaluating the macrobiotic way of eating, we should not just fix our attention exclusively on small aspects, but seriously consider these larger issues because they endanger life on this planet and threaten our very survival. Michio, his students, and associates deserve credit for tirelessly teaching and advocating a sensible way of eating way before scientific reports were available and the association between our food and various environmental and social issues became noticeable.

As many have noticed and mentioned before, Michio was an outstanding teacher of life. During the last years of his life he periodically came to teach in Japan. On those occasions, he encouraged everyone to continuously develop their human potential and to try to think and judge things by themselves. He also emphasized not to follow him or his teachings, but to use macrobiotics as a tool to discover life by ourselves and to surpass him whenever possible. He would point out that our life is always changing and our consciousness constantly growing. Therefore there are always new mountains to climb and higher heights to reach ahead of us. He also frequently talked about the meaning of the last supper of Jesus with his disciples. And mentioned that the day humanity partakes of a similar quality of food and drink, it will result in a similar quality blood, a harmonious type of mind and a kindred spirit among all people, and that all humanity will become like brothers and sisters sharing this planet and playing from morning till night as part of our endless journey of life.

Michio was a very compassionate person. Constantly devoted to his dream, clearly aware of the tremendous challenges we are currently facing and fully committed for the well-being and destiny of man kind. Being quite close to him for many years, I can attest that he was not afraid or concerned at all about losing his life for his dream. Not caring for himself and generously giving away his time and understanding of life to others was his way of sharing his love and his life for all of us. I feel tremendously privileged to have met Michio and to have had the chance to play and share precious moments with him in this life. I am also eternally grateful to him for helping my mother regain her health and for patiently teaching me and helping me grow. And because of that, I will always be indebted to him. I would also like to express my deepest appreciation to all his students, my teachers, who have also supported and contributed to my development. I hope that macrobiotics will continue to unfold and flourish as we all participate in the creation of One Peaceful World. We are all part of this legacy now.

Remembering Michio
Zlatko Pejic

Apart from the words in his books, and thoughts he shared with us at many lectures we had a chance to attend, my memories of Michio are those of the moments we spent together—moments determined by a variety of circumstances.

On imperfection, with eyes wide open

Soon after my days spent at the Kushi Institute in Switzerland, I went to the Kushi Institute in Becket. On my first day there, I was walking the distance between the dormitories and the Main House feeling a bit pensive, or maybe it would be more appropriate to say a bit anxious. I had two reasons for the anxiety I felt: I had a severe cold and sinusitis, and such a severe headache that it felt as though my head was about to explode. The second reason is that prior to my arrival, a rumour spread that I was 'a cool guy,' who could do this and that, and who knew this and that. But, due to the cold and the headache, I did not feel good at all. On the contrary, I felt a bit useless, defeated, and ashamed.

At the moment when this lousy feeling reached its climax, Michio 'materialized' in front of me: "Would you like to accompany me to the General Store? A friend of mine will take us there." His invitation surprised me, but I accepted it: "Why not"—concluding that this might be an opportunity for me to feel more useful.

After a quick ride, there we were in front of the General Store. Before I had a chance to ask what we were doing there (or supposed to buy), Michio went to the bar. Reaching the bar, Michio, loudly and to a certain extent dramatically, ordered a cup of coffee. My jaw dropped. Looking at my wide-open eyes, Michio said: And what would you like?" Pretending not to notice my astonishment, he did not wait for my reply. "A juice and a muffin? Have you ever had a muffin? You must try it!"

And so there I was, standing at the bar with a muffin containing all the wrong ingredients—sugar, eggs and everything else that I had been avoiding for years! Presumably in order to ease the state I was in, Michio continued: "Imperfection does not necessarily have to be a bad thing. Sometimes we can find a little bit of pleasure in it. It is in that pleasure that we find a motive to improve ourselves and to lessen our imperfection. Also, when aware of own imperfection, one finds it easier to set priorities, and to see whether it is more important to try to do some greater good or to devote time contemplating whether or not to binge and drink coffee. Am I right?" Not leaving me much time to reply, he continued: "It is OK to be imperfect. Aspiring to perfection can be deceitful, and it can also be illusive and arrogant. Awareness of our weaknesses keeps us humble."

I looked at the muffin and had a bite. It was tasty, maybe too tasty, and we continued discussing the evil of imperfection—the fate of Narcissus, the idea of the *Ubermensch*, as well as the grief and misery such aspirations can inflict on us.

On higher causes, futility, and a bit of charm

In 2003, the lunch with the President of the Republic of Croatia, Stjepan Mesić, along with his councillors, and generals, was a great experience. While happily munching on a macrobiotic meal, both Michio and our president broke the silence with a series of jokes. These moments and the murmur took me back in time to 1988 when, after the public lecture and the workshop held for medical doctors in Zagreb, we all went to Belgrade where we were to deliver the same public lectures for thousands of people at congress and concert halls.

There, the mayor of Belgrade, as well as the representatives of the Federal Government of Yugoslavia welcomed us. The event was a major success. I think I could say that the whole visit was spectacular, but, being exhausted as I was, I could not help feeling a sense of hopelessness and guilt. The familiar feeling of "sublime futility" overwhelmed me! So I asked Michio whether it was worth sharing our philosophy with people that, most likely, had no interest in macrobiotics. I also questioned whether the whole idea was a mistake. Since my defeatism could not, in any way, undermine the intensity of Michio's enthusiasm, he replied: "Imagine a field. It cannot move anywhere: it cannot move towards you, and it cannot run away from you. That field does not demand anything from you. You are the one possessing seeds, hence you should go into the field, plant seeds and wait… two to three months and something will grow. This is exactly what we are doing today — planting seeds. We might not get to see the Golden Harvest, but somebody will. Nothing is futile!"

Some fifteen years later, another seemingly futile event took place - our reception at the office of the president of the Zagreb City Council. Michio was very enthusiastic. The reception was nice. We were served roasted seeds, dried fruit, and everything else that the president and her colleagues considered appropriate for the macrobiotic guests. At the end of the reception, according to the strict protocol, the president apologised for not having time to show us around the city council due to other obligations, and informed us that her deputy will accompany us instead of her. Michio thanked her for sparing some of her precious time for us, and asked if he could say a few words. He looked her in the eyes and said: "How come the women in Croatia are so beautiful?"

She smiled, blushed a bit… and, of course, she decided that she was going to show us around, and stay with us much longer than it was planned by her strict protocol. She also saw us to the main entrance of the building and greeted us warmheartedly.

On peace and war

Michio was dreamily drawing domes of the "shrine of peace," as well as planet orbits with his fingers in the air, while Aveline was quietly apologizing to me. She kept repeating that if not today, then certainly tomorrow Michio would listen to what I had to say about the situation in Croatia.

It was 1992, soon after the war in Croatia broke out. I was in the States on a short lecture tour. Several peacekeeping NGOs and American media invited me. Since they were all really interested in what I had to say, I expected that Michio would be interested even more than anybody else.

That evening in Boston, during a dinner in a Japanese restaurant, while Michio was talking about the "shrine of peace," about the importance of macrobiotics etc., I was wondering whether it made any sense to talk about the war and killings in Croatia. I have to admit that, at that moment, I felt a bit confused, even offended, since the dinner was organized on the occasion of my visit to the States. At least Michio stated that in his toast! And, of course, knowing that, I expected that Michio would show more interest, understanding, empathy, or, perhaps, compassion.

Finally, I gave up, determined to let go of all expectations, and to start enjoying the delicious food as well as listen attentively to Michio's contemplations about the universe, history of civilization, his magnificent stories about the power of food, and the meaning of health and happiness. As Michio was talking, radiant gestures of his hands either preceded his words, or rounded up his thoughts, and emphasized the meaning of what he said.

Mesmerized by the chef's delicious food, and impressed by Michio's words, we were about to leave. Only then Michio quietly told me: "You know so many people are so intensely focused on evil, on wars… So, if we will talk only about the evil, and if we will dedicate too much of our precious time to tragedies caused by people's delusions and stupidity, and if we will base our history textbooks on fear, catastrophe, and the figures concerning the killed, humiliated, and victimized… in our eyes the evil will gain importance, and it will become a part of our value system! Imagine people of the future reading about our civilisation — they will think that we were ignorant and idiots."

Slightly confused, I experienced an epiphany, and came to a realisation that only a few words denoting peace exist in our language! Also, it seemed to me like we have managed to perfect the culture of evil. Paradoxically, international law makes a distinction between more 'humane' regular bullets and 'inhumane' expanding bullets, beside the fact that both can kill! The war in Croatia was just another episode of the tragic soap opera about the human stupidity and the merciless production of evil sponsored by the military industry...I spent most of the night thinking about that.

The following morning, as I went for breakfast eager to share my new "revelations" with Michio, everybody was already sitting at the table. As I was about to say that I realized what Michio was talking about the previous night, he simply said: "So, how is it there? Do you have enough food, clothes… are the children dying?"

Aveline looked at me and quietly said: "You see?"

On postponement and enthusiasm

In the summer of 2013, my wife Jadranka and me, among other people, received the Aveline Kushi Award. As we were leaving the hall, Midori approached me saying that Michio is looking for me. I stopped and waited while he was walking towards me with an envelope in his hand. He gave it to me saying that I can read it immediately, or later, but that we should meet and discuss it. I stepped aside, opened the envelope and read the hand-written letter while Michio was answering a question about pancreas or some other organ asked by a woman that interrupted us abruptly. I turned to Michio, interrupting the lady, and said: "Of course, Michio, we would really like for the Makronova Institute to formally join the Kushi Institute, and to continue promoting the program of the Kushi Institute."

I also told him that I was sorry that we did not join the Kushi Institute earlier, and that maybe we did not show enough enthusiasm in that matter. I also told him how much we were fascinated and inspired by his enthusiasm. Michio smiled, raised his arm and said: "It is important to dream. But it is even more important to make ourselves better people than we were yesterday. And it is not good to rush into something, especially if you do not have to. It is not necessary to do today all the things that one can leave for tomorrow. If we do them all today, what are we going to do tomorrow?"

I thought to myself — "Hm, I'm not sure if things really are that way... But, who cares, it sounds good!"

After all, maybe it's a pity that we did not manage to do everything we dreamt of, but I am sincerely grateful that Michio helped us find something that we liked doing; something we have now been doing for more than thirty years with the same passion and devotion as when we first started. And I hope that, inspired by Michio's enthusiasm, we will have enough strength and wisdom to carry on working for a better tomorrow!

Remembering Michio
Christina Pirello

I was diagnosed with Stage IV leukemia in 1983. No one held out much hope; not my doctors, my family, my friends or even me. Through a friend, I met Robert Pirello who turned me on to macrobiotics as a way for me to regain my health and vitality. I had no idea what I was doing but with Robert's guidance, I began to find my way.

I remember it like yesterday. I was nine months into my macrobiotic practice (and seeing improving blood test results), and Robert, (my cooking teacher turned love of my life) asked me to go with him to hear Michio Kushi speak at the Friends Meeting House in Philadelphia.

It was a night that would change everything.

I had no idea what he was talking about most of the time, but Michio held me rapt while he spoke. From the most basic food advice to the most esoteric theory about the natural Order of the Universe, this guy lit my fire.

At the end of the lecture, Michio shook every single person's hand. He smiled graciously and spoke warmly to each individual who had attended the lecture. He took my hand, looked into my face, and smiled…and asked us to wait for him on the side of the room until he was through greeting people.

I have to say that I was nervous. I had cancer and I was sure he was seeing something I was missing. I was sure he had bad news for me. Robert held my hand and tried to reassure me. I couldn't hear him. Why else would this great man want to see me, I thought.

Instead, Michio sat down, took both my hands in his, smiled, and asked…for the first of many times in my life, "How are you?" Anyone who has met him has heard those words and has seen that little tilt of his head and the mischief in his eyes as he asked. He went on to speak about my illness and how well he thought I was doing (I was doing well and had the blood tests to prove it, but how did he know that?) He told me where I was still weak: kidneys, liver, etc. Then he said, "If you take responsibility for your illness and recover fully, you will become my most well-known teacher of macrobiotics. OK? OK." He smiled, patted my hand, and left me there, jaw agape.

It was the first, but certainly not the last time Michio would leave me wonder-struck at what he knew about me. Forget what he knew about the world, the universe. Impressive as that is, I am always struck at how he sees to the core of people.

After that fateful meeting, I went on to study with him for years, any chance I could. I would sit by his side and simply listen as he spoke, take note of what he said, and saw as he counseled people on their health and made recommendations they could use to regain their vitality. I studied with him in seminars as he shared generously from his deep well of wisdom. I asked him so many questions; it became a joke between us. He would make a point and look over at me and say, "Yes?" He patiently answered anything I requested of him.

Each time we met, he would come up to me, kiss me on both cheeks, and say, "How are you?" My answer was always the same: "You tell me. How am I?" He would laugh, look deeply, and then nod his head and say "Very good. Please rest more." And then proceed to blow my mind with some prediction about my future

...that was always true.

I remember sitting around a large round table at the end of a weekend seminar during which we had hosted Michio and several other teachers from the Kushi Institute. As we decompressed from three long, but inspiring days of classes, lectures, counseling, cooking, and working together, we sat at an Italian restaurant listening as Michio drew the Order of the Universe on a cocktail napkin, all spirals and arrows. Suddenly, he looked up and studied my face for the longest time. I grew uncomfortable and said, "What do you see?" I wasn't sure I wanted to hear.

Michio smiled and said, "In five years...yes, five years, you'll be teaching macrobiotic cooking on television." Huh? At that moment, a TV show was not even a glimmer in my thoughts. I still struggled with stage fright for a cooking class and he saw me on television?

Oh, well, I thought, even Michio can be wrong, I guess.

Almost five years to the day of that dinner, *Christina Cooks* launched on national public television. I was on television, cooking macrobiotic food. And as he predicted, we were a hit. I think what I was cooking was odd for America, but it was what I said that resonated with them.

To this day, what I hear most often is that no other chef on television speaks about food like I do. And that's true. One of the many gifts Michio gave me was an understanding of how food works in the body; not the science of the nutrients and minerals (which is great to know and I am thrilled that I do), but how food works; how the energy of food creates who we are.

As I studied for my Master's Degree in nutrition science, I was often struck by how accurate our macrobiotic esoteric "energy-speak" (as I call it...) aligns so accurately with conventional nutrition wisdom. To this day, studies will reveal the latest breakthrough in understanding of food and its impact on health and I will always think: "Man, Michio has been saying that for years."

There really are no words to describe the impact Michio has had on my life. With the wisdom he so generously shared with me; I rebuilt my health and wellness and built my career. Prior to being diagnosed, I felt lost in my life, not sure of why I was here or what I should be doing.

Cancer was the gift of my life, much as Michio said it would be. Through my illness and recovery, my eyes were opened to the truth. I finally knew my purpose. I knew that my calling was to share what I had learned about food and living natural lives as real humans.

But how?

I had studied and studied and decided to seek Michio's counsel on how best to share what I knew and had experienced in my own healing.

We met in the sitting room of his Brookline, Mass. home, the sun streaming through the large windows at the backside of the house. I told Michio my grand plan. He smiled and said, "You will make a wonderful cooking teacher."

Cooking teacher? Seriously?

I bristled and said I had no intention of teaching cooking but wanted to lecture. Why did I have to teach cooking? Because I am a woman?

Michio smiled again and advised me to reflect and let him know what I decided to do. As I had many times before, I left him feeling like Grasshopper in that old *Kung Fu* show, sent off to reflect.

I decided to lecture. After my first adventure in teaching, I lay in bed that night thinking of all the questions people had asked…and how many of them had to do with food. I realized that I could serve people and their health more effectively if I taught cooking…and lectured while I did so. I came to the conclusion that I could lecture all day about carrots and what they do for us. But if people left that lecture not knowing what to do with a carrot, did I do them any good? Did I help them in an effective way? But if I taught them how to chop a carrot; how to cook a carrot and how the nutrients and energy of that carrot could alter their health, I was giving them something. I was providing tools they could use.

I went back to Michio to explain why I would become a cooking teacher.

He smiled and said, "Very good."

And so, in 1989, I started teaching cooking classes in my home. We began with four students, which became eight and then sixteen. The classes grew with each one that I taught until finally, in 1995, my husband decided to take what I was doing to television with a cooking show on national public television…just three years after Michio's prediction. And two years later, we launched *Christina Cooks*, the first and only macrobiotic cooking show on national television. We remain that to this day.

This should be the happily ever after part, right? Not so fast. In 1998, in our first year as a national television show, I had a brain aneurysm burst at the base of my brain. It's a long story, but in short, the aneurysm was genetic and due to low Vitamin B-12 levels, homocysteine levels rose too high and one of my aneurysms burst. Twelve days in the neuro intensive care unit can really make a girl think…and think hard, even with worst headache you can imagine. How did this happen? What had I done (or not done) to cause this latest crisis?

I got lots of unsolicited commentary from the community. I heard that my ambition had gotten the best of me and that I ate too much flour. All amusing ideas but not really all that useful as I tried to heal.

We went to Michio for advice on the best path. He asked me why I chose to live my life like someone without a history of illness. He asked me why I didn't rest more. He advised me to sing a happy song and be sure to rest as much as I worked. He said to continue to follow the dream that Robert and I were building. I ate well, rested, worked and healed.

I often hear Michio in my head.

When I was new to macrobiotics and studying cooking, things seemed…well, grim, not to put too fine a point on it. Everyone took everything so seriously. And yet, I was reading Georges Ohsawa who spoke of love, passion, joy, lust, and freedom in his books. I adored him!

The classes I took were serious to the point of clinical. I did not see passion or joy or lust. I went to Michio and asked him where I might find Ohsawa. He told me he had passed away (Too much passion I wondered?) I regrouped and asked Michio why macrobiotics as I was studying it was so serious and why no one was having any fun. If it was meant to create a great life, I had yet to experience it.

Sensing my obvious frustration, Michio cocked his head, smiled, and said, "Please study well and then teach happiness."

And so…as I always have…I took his advice. With Robert I created the great life promised us by understanding macrobiotics. I studied everything I could get my hands on about natural health and healing. I continue to study to this day.

And I teach happy…and I rest as much as I work.

Michio remains a guiding force in the work Robert and I happily do together. He remains one of the most influential people in my life and the person I credit with opening my eyes to the truth about life. He gave me the tools to lift the veil from my eyes and see clearly.

He will always have my love and gratitude.

Remembering Michio
Jessica Porter

The first time I met Michio Kushi was through his tome, *The Book of Macrobiotics*. My sister had purchased it when I was fifteen, and after a cursory scan, she packed it away on a bookshelf. Every time I went into her bedroom, I saw its spine, with the word "macrobiotic" jumping off it, followed by its author's foreign name. It was both odd and memorable, although not particularly enticing to a teenager.

Roughly seven years later, I took my first macrobiotic cooking class, having been hypnotized by that book, its dignified spine, and its mysterious title. I went out and bought my own copy, although after glancing through it, I felt repelled. The ideas were too dense, and its topics a little scary, for my mind to comprehend. I chose to put it down, thinking, "I like this food, but I guess I won't be getting into the theory!"

But I cooked, and I cooked. And I ate, and I ate. And sometimes I even chewed. The cells of my body enrolled in my education long before my ego did.

After almost two years of eating macrobiotically, I picked up *The Book* again. This time, it melted me like brown rice syrup. My brain was ready to receive the Order of the Universe. Rather than dense and scary, its words were like music, singing the song of nature. It resonated with my whole body and spirit. It was then that Michio and I were properly introduced; I saw into his mind, and he expanded mine. It was a life-changing moment, for which I am extremely grateful.

About a year later, I moved to the Kushi Institute. Within a month, Michio made his first visit. Let's just say the place was abuzz; it was like Elvis arriving at Graceland, but without the fried chicken. Back in New York City, reading his books, I had only dared to imagine meeting him, let alone sitting in one of his classes. It was perhaps my first macrobiotic dream coming true.

Later that night, sitting *seiza* in the dorm of the Kushi Institute, I experienced another Michio mind-blow; the concepts he dealt in—with such charm and ease—were gigantic, even galactic. Again, I felt my consciousness expand by a thousand-fold, and yet the insights remained orderly, even comforting. No other teacher has ever had that effect on me. It was transcendent.

Michio was a human, and I had the privilege to know him as such. He was funny, self-effacing, inspiring, infinitely wise, and obviously a genius. But I didn't know him as well as many others did; as a grand-student of Michio's, he remained at a slight distance, and yet his teachings burrowed into me deeply—perhaps as deeply as they had into anyone who'd known him better. Michio, even from a distance, created intimacy. That was part of his magic.

So we remember both the ideas, and the man. The yin and yang of Michio Kushi. Separate, and yet one. We have lost the body of the man, but we will have his ideas forever.

Thank you, Michio *sensei*.

Remembering Michio
Michael Potter

Greetings, I'm Michael Potter from Michigan, Eden Foods. I say, "Hello" to the Kushi family and to all of you. We have lost—humanity has lost—a friend, a teacher, a great man. Our condolences go out to the family and especially to Midori, his wife. I like to believe—I like to think that Michio is in a more peaceful place now than he was here on earth. Wendy Esko and I were commiserating the other day after learning of Michio's passing, and we concluded that Michio's passing is the end of an epoch, about a sixty-year epoch—1954 to 2014—sixty years.

I really do believe he is in a more peaceful place. And speaking about "peaceful:"

When I was a young man, a teenager—eighteen years old, nineteen years old—I was of the opinion and of the school of thought that revolution was a violent thing. Political power grew out of a barrel of a gun—Chairman Mao—things like that, and I was involved with radical elements in my community. And, thank God! My sister handed me a book, *You Are All Sanpaku*! And I made a decision, as a teenager, OK—I'm not going try to change things by being violent. I am going to change things more fundamentally, more completely, more thoroughly, more effectively by focusing on diet; by focusing on the wisdom that my teachers, my macrobiotic teachers shared with me. The *Order of the Universe* publications that I was reading at that time, they changed millions of people's lives. They changed the direction of medicine, education, diet, and agriculture. But, you know, I continue to experience opposition to the change that wants to happen; that has been encouraged; that has been seeded by Michio. I was also reading publications put out by the George Ohsawa Macrobiotic Foundation in California that encouraged a similar way of thinking.

The impact on humanity of macrobiotic teachings would be hard to overestimate, in my opinion. Macrobiotic teachings stimulate—have stimulated, the evolution of humanity, and there is resistance to it.

Immediately preceding the beginning of the natural foods movement were the teachings of macrobiotics that were released to us and carried to us. After that, after the macrobiotic teachings happened, the natural foods phenomena began to happen all over the planet—Europe, Australia, Japan, and the United States. Macrobiotics was the origin of the natural foods movement. It's largely been co-opted by big money interests, but that's another story.

Macrobiotic teachers changed universal consciousness. Mine, yours, humanity's consciousness has been changed and, you know, I watched as the planet changed. I watched as this universal consciousness was impacted by macrobiotic teachings. It's more than spoken word or written word in books and lectures. It's a consciousness amongst humanity that was impacted by macrobiotic teachings and macrobiotic principles—thank God I learned of them. You know I like to think that—I tell people Eden Foods is a principled company—it's a principled natural food company. I don't often get to tell people though that those principles are the macrobiotic principles as defined, shared, and taught to me by Michio Kushi.

A reporter from the *New York Times* was in my office a little while ago, and she was trying to get some understanding from me, "How did things start?" I didn't know how to answer her question accurately. I couldn't even begin to think of a suitable answer. I went in to my closet and pulled out a stack of old *Order of the Universe* magazines. I put them on the table and I said, "That's what started Eden Foods." She got it.

In this environment and with you all, I just want to share what I was thinking about coming here. As I was driving in my car, I thought "What am I going to say?" and I heard a song, "How do you sleep while your beds are burning?" Ladies and gentlemen, our food and our medicine are being poisoned! Our beds are burning! How can we sleep? We have to address these matters agriculturally, food-wise, and medicine-wise. Thank you.

Remembering Michio
Sandy Pukel

Throughout the forty-five years I knew Michio Kushi, dozens of people would come up to me and ask me, "How do you talk to him, what do you have to say to him, I am too intimidated to start a conversation with the man." That perception was far from the truth. In knowing this remarkable human being, I discovered he was a friend to all, always, and I mean always willing to engage in conversation with anyone, anywhere, anytime, sometimes to the fault of being late for his very next lecture or appointment.

A small unassuming man in physical appearance, he was truly a giant of a man when it came to knowledge and ideas about world affairs and the health of the planet and all of its souls.

I first met Michio in the summer of 1970 at a camp retreat in upstate New York. He was wearing Bermuda shorts, high knee socks, and a short white sleeve shirt with, of course, a tie. Even then, out in the woods, his wisdom was beyond anything I had ever experienced in any of my classroom studies throughout college and law school. His audiences always appreciated his gift of explaining things in a simple fashion. Of course when he started to talk about aliens, spacemen, and pinpointing where they landed on earth, everyone's eyes bulged out to uncharted territories. I remember one afternoon when he gave a lecture in my backyard, blackboard in place, he had fifty of us buzzing with excitement as he calmly talked about his intimate knowledge of aliens visiting earth.

During our forty-five-year friendship, I had the privilege of hosting Michio and his wife Aveline in my home at least one week a year. With his presence, of course, came hundreds of guests seeking his counsel on a variety subjects, in business, but mostly health issues. It was not uncommon for him to see clients all throughout the day, ending in the wee hours of the morning. Always smiling, he greeted his next appointment with the friendship accorded to your long time best friend. Unlike many leaders in various fields in our society, Michio was "just a guy" to the general population, always accessible.

Every year the Macrobiotic Foundation of Florida, which I started with his encouragement, would host a weeklong seminar and for thirty-plus years, Michio was our headliner. One of the best lessons he taught me during one of our winter retreats, and a lifelong lesson I will never forget, was going over and saying to him after his lecture how brilliant I thought the talk was, and how new and exciting the information he shared. He turned to me in his straightforward manner and said, "Sandy, this information is basically the same message I have been sharing for years. It is you who have finally really heard it for the first time." A lesson and a reminder that both he and George Ohsawa have repeated over and over…the potential greatest disease of all humanity is called "ARROGANCE." Thank you, Michio, for a lesson well learned.

This scholar, this statesman, this world leader, had a heart bigger than the Grand Canyon. He would go anywhere to the ends of the earth in promoting his mission of One Peaceful World.

Michio would not hesitate to sing at our annual seminars, even in costume on stage during one of our talent shows, and he even donned his now famous look of his Superman outfit during one of our interviews for our *Joy of Life* magazine. He was one of the most positive individuals I have ever met, and I am sure this is a contributing factor of my proclamation in considering myself the world's utmost eternal optimist.

Do I have stories to share about the man who I traveled with and hosted for almost four decades...of course, and I am happy to share some of them with you.

When in Florida one year, we were barnstorming throughout the state visiting seven cities within a one-week time frame. Just as we were ready to leave Gainesville, one of the organizers said to Michio that he had a friend with a small plane that could take him to his next destination and save a few hours driving. Michio turned to me after looking at this tiny plane and said, "Sandy, I drink too much coffee, you make the decision." Or the time he and Aveline were flying from Miami to Venezuela to give a lecture and when we get to the airport we find out he needed a visa with the plane leaving in ninety minutes. Being the good sport he was, we went to my car, cut up the poster from his just completed lecture in Miami, pasted his picture from the flyer onto the application and in his gentle way said to me, "A true life example of turning yin into yang," and off he flew on his way. How about making soba noodles with Michio at 2 a.m. after returning home from one of his lectures.

Thirteen years ago when I started the Holistic Holiday at Sea cruises, Michio, of course, was the only choice to be the headliner for the initial cruise. It was quite an interesting conversation explaining to him that he would be on the ship for an entire week, with no escaping, as we would be in the middle of the ocean, and he would be lecturing and giving consultations almost everyday. Just a few years back I once again asked him to be one of our headliners for our tenth anniversary sailing for which he most graciously accepted. Michio was always giving, always smiling, always the man to try and cure all the world's problems. Michio you were and always will be the man for all generations, and I thank the universe for the honor of having you as a friend.

Remembering Michio
Arthur H. Robbins

"Le temps est une rivière sans rives." – Marc Chagall

In 1986 I left behind my cozy domestic life in Montréal to become one of Michio Kushi's counseling assistants.

Michio was the recognized leader of the worldwide macrobiotic movement, and assisting his private consultations was a part-time, unpaid learning position. It was a coveted role, usually reserved for budding macrobiotic teachers and advanced students who intended to pursue careers in the healing arts. I was also given a paid job managing the bookstore and helping to organize conferences.

I had spent the previous year or two traveling back and forth from Canada to study at the Kushi Institutes in Massachusetts. There was a "K.I." in Becket, a small town in the Berkshires, and another one in Brookline, near Boston. I was excited about this adventure upon which I was embarking, and just as excited that I was going to stay at the Kushi House.

The Kushi House on Buckminster Road in Brookline was the principle residence of Aveline and Michio. I believe the road had been named for a relative of Bucky Fuller, who grew up in a town nearby. The house was an enormous old granite building that had once been a convent school. It was an imposing structure that rather looked like a small medieval castle sitting on a couple acres of land in a quiet suburban neighborhood.

Approaching the house, by vehicle or by foot, you passed under a massive arched portico that sheltered the oval driveway by the front door steps and porch. Memorably, the interior of the home was separated from the world outside by an enclosed, tastefully carpeted entrance room. From within this quiet space, French doors with lace-curtained windows provided a slightly veiled view of where you were headed. Before proceeding into the house, guests and residents deposited their shoes on a multi-tier wooden rack, so as to enter the Kushi's home in real Japanese style.

Once inside, you were greeted by high ceilings, glistening hardwood floors, an upright piano maybe twenty feet ahead, a plush antique couch with a landscape painting above it to your left, and a big spiral staircase with walnut banisters off to the right. Further along, beyond the piano and a formal dining table that served as a handsome pedestal for flower arrangements, was the rear of the house and an expansive flagstone porch overlooking the grounds. The kitchen was in the west wing, somewhere between the main office and the *seiza*-style common dining area.

There was an understated grandeur about it all, a light-filled breezy spaciousness. Call me a hopeless nostalgist, but it seems to me now that gusts of fresh air infused with a whiff of the ocean, and glistening shafts of sunlight, or shimmering beams of ethereal moonlight were always streaming in from the rear windows and doors that opened-up to the south.

Going to the Kushi House, being invited to the Kushi House, taking your shoes off to enter into Aveline and Michio's private home environment, well there was an unmistakable sense that you were crossing over into something. Maybe not a place of worship per se, certainly not a shrine, but a functional day-to-day living and working domicile quite like none other. You just knew somehow that you were gaining admittance to a spiritual sanctuary of sorts, and that it behooved you to leave behind some of your more worldly thoughts and baser concerns.

The Kushis lived there with their five children, and their children's children, who were not always there at the same time, and a house full of residential guests. There was a continual flow of visitors, too. Friends, teachers, doctors, writers, publishers, business associates, clients and students came from every far-flung corner of the world. That Michio and Aveline shared the intimacy of their family living space with this constantly transmogrifying tide of humanity never ceased to impress itself upon me.

Most of the residential guests at 62 Buckminster Road were assigned chores in exchange for their free board. Michio's personal assistants and secretaries often occupied rooms, as did some of the Institute's students and staff. Having been trained as a restaurant chef in Montréal, and being something of an all-around handyman, it was given that I would help mend the occasional piece of furniture, share in the grounds work, and when asked, I would do some of the cooking.

Food choice and preparation is a fundamental theme in the teachings of macrobiotics, and the kitchen is considered to be central. Health and happiness or sickness and chaos, it is all said to begin in the kitchen. So being invited to cook for the Kushis in their very own home was a great honor and a privilege indeed.

Before coming to Brookline I had apprenticed with chefs at "Le Vent d'Est" restaurant and "La Boulange" natural bakery in Montréal. Culinary artists such as Denise Lussier, Lobie Daughton, Gilles Arbour, Raymond and Gérald Forget, Daniel LeGris, Michel Lauzon, René Lefebvre, Georges Nicholson, Norbert Argiles, Francine Payment, and not to forget my own mother long before them, had all contributed to my epicurean sense of discrimination and culinary skill set, such as it was. After twelve years of macrobiotic cooking and baking, of study and practice, I was thrilled and intoxicated to have ascended the ladder of karma straight into the very epicenter of macrobioticity.

My professional cooking experience had mostly taken place in spacious, white-tiled commercial kitchens, befitted with large marble counters, voluminous double sink basins, brick-lined ovens and shiny stainless... everything. I was shocked therefore, the first time I entered the Kushi House kitchen. It was small. And narrow. And old. How was I gonna cook for the Kushis and their entourage with such a dearth of equipment and lack of counter space? I had brought along my roll of high carbon steel Japanese knives, but... *oof*.

What they did have in the Kushi Kitchen was a beautiful old six-burner cast iron gas range, thank goodness, and some pressure cookers and well-seasoned iron pans and *donabé* earthenware pots and bamboo steamers and serving bowls, and bottled well water, and essentially the basics, ya know. But to cook in such a confined space, I would have to stay focused, and keep myself very well organized.

And I would have to do this all the while being jostled by perpetually ravenous "Macrobiotic friends," who invaded my creative space to get a snack, a cup of tea, or to invite themselves to prematurely sample one of my edible masterworks in progress. *Humph!* To achieve a successful eating experience for two or twelve or twenty, from within the Kushi House kitchen on Buckminster Road, well you just had to be *yang* about it, and maybe that was the whole idea.

So, when I was not actually working at the bookstore, or doing client intake or follow-up, or scribing for Michio's private counseling sessions — when I was not driving Michio around in my little yellow Renault *Le Car*, nor raking by hand the massive leaf fall on the grounds, nor rewiring lamps nor fixing a mailbox or the bathroom showers or some plumbing — when I was not doing any of this, I was sometimes asked to cook a full course macro meal, soup to nuts and pickles to pudding, for the entire household.

More frequently, I was summoned to the lesser task of making Japanese-style udon noodles in shitake, ginger, scallion, bonito, and tamari broth. This was a preferred snack for Michio, later in the evenings usually, when his long distance telephone counseling sessions were finished. I especially delighted though, in concocting wild-fermented whole-grain sourdough bread, which after rising, I then "baked" in a lidded ceramic "Oshawa Pot," which I placed directly inside of a large pressure cooker. No hot drying oven air for me. Powerful energizing steam heat was the better way. When it came to my bread, you got — *steam heat!*

All of this work and cooking was a source of enormous satisfaction, especially when Michio complemented me on my minor carpentry, or when Aveline Kushi, one of the most famous and influential cooking teachers in the entire world, had praise for my edible creations. In my mind, that was as high as a naturally leavened chef or baker could hope to rise.

Once, in my roll as carpenter, I removed the oversized wooden mailbox from the outside front wall of the house, and carried it down to the workshop table that stood hidden in a musky corner of the cavernous basement. There I stripped the maple box of its old yellowed finish and eroded surface wood, and sanded it all the way down, inside and out, to nice clean xylem. I then revarnished the box with enough layers of semi-matte pine resin to impermeablize a rowboat, and befitted it with shiny brass hinges and thick felt dampers. The lid of the good-as-new mailbox would now make a pleasingly resonant, quiet little thud upon closing—*blubpt*. When my restoration work was done I reattached the mailbox to the wall from whence it came and went about my business.

Ya see, I had for some years been an honest-to-goodness, all-weather, toting and traipsing mailman in Québec, and I was very conscious, in the days before electronic communication, of the importance of the written missive. Michio and Aveline's many cards and letters, which came from near and far, would now be received at 62 Buckminister Road in proper style.

What I wasn't expecting was that Michio would not only take notice of my handiwork, but that he would interrupt his day to invite me outside and thank me personally for what I had done.

Standing together in the driveway, Michio looked at me with a glint in his eye and a big open smile. "Oh, Asa-san," I recall him saying in his most rich and mellifluous Japanese accent, "this mailbox, that you have made so very beautiful, this will be here hundred years after you and I are gone from this world. *Né.*" Michio was always reminding us of our body's mortality, and our spirit's eternity, and he did it in the most charming, delightful, and playful manner. I get chills up my spine just thinking about him now.

Although Aveline departed this world in 2001, and Michio passed away in December of 2014 at the age of eighty-eight, they remain very much alive in my heart. I will always remember Aveline, so beautiful and graceful, with her deep, quiet lilting voice and her long thick braid of lustrous black hair. She had an elegant sense of fashion and style as well, and very good taste in art. And I will continue to think of Michio as I knew him best when he was in his forties and fifties: tall, strong, brilliant and charismatic. He was flexible and funny too, and always thought-provoking. Michio was a proverbial font of wisdom and universal love.

Today, Michio is perhaps most widely remembered for his vision of One Peaceful World, for his teachings about our interconnectedness with nature, and for the profound influence he had on the way we think about diet, agriculture and health. But I will never forget what I saw him do in the privacy of the counseling setting.

Many of the people who came to see Michio were in grave distress. More often than not, Western medicine had deemed them incurable and given them up for lost. They would sit with an assistant at first, someone like me, who asked the standard questions and helped fill out the forms. Their pain and anxiety was obvious and palpable. They bore the repressive weight of the miseries they had endured, and they were frightened by their prognoses. I would try my best to encourage them with the possibility of healing and of change, but I was just some little organic-fed whippersnapper. The real transformation would only began to take form after they had sat beside Michio for a while and told him of their suffering and pain and woe.

Michio listened intently. In small words and nonverbal cues he conveyed great empathy and understanding. He might have nodded his head, or said something like, "Yah, yah, um hm." Sometimes he would stand up and go to them, so as to examine their hands or arms. He might briefly massage their shoulders or look more closely into their eyes. No matter how dire the situation, Michio never appeared to be consumed by their dread, nor convinced of the inevitability of their premature demise. In the face of terminal diseases and impending death, Michio would look at you unflinchingly. He would gaze at you as if he was admiring the remarkable beauty of your soul. And he would smile, reassuringly.

In the subtlest of ways, again and again, I saw Michio gradually begin to weave before us a healing tapestry, a vision of wellness. He would describe, in great detail, the dietary and lifestyle changes that would lead towards recovery and health. He would talk about *Shiatsu* massage and *Do-In* exercises, and meditation and a spirit of gratefulness and playfulness, and singing and prayer. He might look at an unwell husband and say, "So, first, no more ice creams. OK?" and then with a great big friendly smile he'd point an open hand towards the wife and add, "Beautiful wife is sweet enough for you, right?"

But beyond the diet, beyond the healing techniques and strategies, beyond the whole grains and miso soup, the fermented foods and small red beans and sea vegetables—beyond a prescription for pinches of *gomashio*, or teaspoons of grated daikon radish, or cups of warmed carrot juice, or hot ginger compresses or burdock root or *umé* tea—beyond all of that, when Michio sensed that his visitors were ready, he would explain the deeper meaning and origin of their problems. He might glance at his assistant ever so briefly, before gently inviting his clients into a perception and prescience that he observed as plainly as the noses and earlobes and philtrums on their faces.

Sometimes Michio would astonish his clients by telling them things about themselves, or their parents or grandparents, things that the rest of us could never have known. In a relaxed and confident manner he would describe the positive qualities and strengths that had been passed on by their ancestors, and he would recount the challenges and misfortunes that had befallen them. Michio would explain the generational karma and consequences that had ensued. At this, their eyes would widen and their faces go pale, and they would straighten themselves in their chairs and stare back intently, and respond in measured staccato as if in a trance. "Yes, yes," they would say. "Yes, it is true. That is how it was. That is who they were. That is what they did. That is what I did. That is how it happened. That is who I am."

I experienced this remarkable Michio effect first-hand, during my own initial consultation. Towards the end of our session, I asked Michio if he didn't have any particular spiritual advice to offer me. Sure enough, he smiled and surprised us with impossible knowledge about my own ancestors, family secrets known only to me and mine. This so astonished and frightened my partner Danielle, that she grabbed ahold of my shoulder and exclaimed aloud, "Arty, Arty, Arty, how can he know that, how can he see those things?!"

In these transcendent moments we felt as if through Michio, we could ourselves begin to sense, to almost feel and touch the spiritual realm within which we all exist. Instantaneous metamorphosis sometimes occurred. Suddenly you knew the cause of your challenges or misfortune, the reason for your illness or unhappiness. You understood how you got to where you were. In a flash you could see before you a new path beginning to materialize, an alternative trajectory emerging that lead away from suffering and disease, that lifted you on invisible wings towards the promise of health and harmony and a better, more sunlit tomorrow.

Such was the transformative power of Michio's macrobiotic counseling sessions, that he helped to heal and to save many thousands of persons during his lifetime. Yet Michio was so much more than an extraordinary healer. His altruistic influence and diverse accomplishments would be difficult to catalog or overestimate.

I guess I always knew somehow that I was not destined to become a macrobiotic teacher or counselor. I think Michio knew that too. Nevertheless, observing the interpersonal dynamic in these sessions was so powerful an experience, that it reshaped my view of life and death, and shifted my direction in this world.

Watching Michio transmute suffering into hope and healing was the reason I enrolled in a counseling degree program. Though I did not ultimately become a health counselor or a psychotherapist, I did go on to a sort of mentoring and lecturing position for a while. In my own humble way I attempted to assist, and to empower people. During my entrepreneurial phase, it was Michio who had most inspired within me the confidence to speak before large audiences, and the audacity to dare to try to be of help, or of succor, or of guidance or leadership or inspiration.

I lived in the Kushi House for just about sixteen months, divided into several stays over the course of a few years time. A brief enough interval, and yet those days and weeks were among the happiest moments of my life. I not only made the acquaintance of many who were to become my closest friends and business allies, but I had a wide variety of formative experiences that have stayed with me ever after. Above all though, was the generosity of the Kushis themselves, and the many gifts they imparted.

For in this fleeting life of rare beauty and impermanent happiness, of ephemeral splendors pre-joined to the inevitability of change and transition, and sometimes to the challenges of chronic pain or the heartbreak of permanent loss — the gift I received in 1986 and 1987 was a special one. I had been allowed to spend five seasons of my life in the home and hearth and kitchen and presence of Aveline and Michio Kushi and their family and their eternal dream.

Remembering Michio
Evan Root

Michio means "man of the way." Michio = Man of the way.

First off, I'd like to just acknowledge that we're here for Michio; Michio that lives inside us. Michio that is in each other who's here as we greet each other; Michio's work in the world beyond us in all the people who couldn't come here and now, of course, Michio in the heavens. All here for Michio and I want to thank the family so much for this occasion to do this, not just now but also for sharing Michio with us for all these years. Can you imagine sharing your parents with thousands of people around the world? Sharing the time and then the family giving the community this opportunity? I am so grateful, thank you.

I first met Michio in 1965 in New York City. I was hanging out with Michel Abehsera, and Michio was coming to town for a weekend seminar so a friend of mine and I, of course, went there. And what an evening it was! It was the beginning of the rest of my life. It was a small group as things were in those days, maybe six or eight people around a coffee table in a living room and Michio just picked something—I'd forgotten exactly what it was. It was something like a bean on a plate and then he began to talk about it. And then he began to draw spirals on the blackboard and the interrelationship of yin influences and yang influences and the next thing you know across the day, step by step, stage by stage, we were at the parameters, if there is such a thing as a parameter of the infinite universe, and there he left us for the day. We went home. Came back the next day. He took us step-by-step back down through, right back home to the bean on our plate, and "poof," you know, that was it!

I'm sure all of you have some kind of a similar experience to that. So my friend and I, when we left the building, spontaneously started jumping and dancing in the street, twirling, whooping! And that's how we made our way home to our apartment that night, literally jumping, dancing, and whooping. The joy exploding in our hearts from the vision that Michio, the beacon, broadcast into the world that reached those who were ready to hear it.

A few months later, Michel took me aside and said, "Got a call from Michio. They're getting moved on from Wellesley. They were, you know, kicked out of Cambridge and went to Wellesley and set up a wonderful East West Institute, Aikido Dojo, etc. Next thing you know the town fathers, Board of Selectmen, said to them, "You gotta leave town!" So, at this point there was no 24/7 guy around. It was just family, some others had left because the Institute wasn't able to operate anymore.

So he put out a call, "You know a helper down there by any chance?" We went out to a café and he said, "You know, Michio needs some help up there. Would you like to go?" I packed my bag and left the next day and showed up here, and that was the beginning.

I met the wonderful group of people here today, kids at that time, and the love that exuded from each one of you was just such welcome that it still warms my heart after all these years. So together we moved, and they started the study house at Gardner Road. We started up the Erewhon store. The lectures before they were here at the Arlington Street Church were just on bags — the people coming, again half a dozen or so — sat at on the bags of grain that were in the side storage room at Erewhon. And that worked up until a point, until the FDA (Food and Drug Administration) raided the place, and we had to be very careful and segregate education from food.

Never the twain shall meet. So, they located that little room on the side entrance of the church, and it began to build, little by little, you know — eight, ten, twelve, fourteen people around that. And you know, I saw a fair amount of dancing and twirling after those things on the street right here. It was an explosion really for those who were ready for it.

But it wasn't without its difficulties even though they'd been moved from town to town. Gardner Road was always on edge. Anybody who was visiting from Japan was a relative. That way the single house family thing didn't come into question, and then all these other people were just visiting.

But that wasn't the only thing. They had tabs on us, and there was often a plainclothes car parked across the street watching. Some of the community members were even stopped by authorities. The amazing thing was they knew everybody who was involved, including names. And sure enough, Michio, there was a full press to send him out of the country. And it was thanks to Wally Gorell's father who was very close with senators. Was he a senator himself? I can't remember. But anyway, he explained to a very good friend that this guy had saved his son from a life of drugs. At that time there was a lot psychedelic action and young people getting into drugs, and macrobiotics wasn't that. It was a way out of that for a lot of people. So that sort of righted the ship.

The first year at Erewhon was kind of slow. It took a year before people started coming. But one by one more people came and everybody who came wanted to help. People came because they wanted to learn and they wanted to help. They wanted to share — this was a dream that was shared.

So, as more people came Sanae restaurant opened up, and then people could eat — sort of developed a motor — to buy food there, get introduced to it here, eat there, go there, and then Tao Books came in where Erewhon used to be, and then it was like a three-way motor. And it was, then Boston became like a school really. We're here to learn and we were here to help.

Michio was very strategic. He had a plan. It was always kind of a moving target, but it was to establish the way of health, the way of peace, and the way life in the age of humanity here on the planet earth. And so, when we would meet around the table at night at Gardner Road, there was always a talk 'til 2 a.m. around the table. And it was, "You go to Italy! You go to Spain! You go to…" It was a grand scheme of people who were going to train here. And he always thought that it was up to the Boston group. There were other people teaching macrobiotics here and there in the world — including students of Ohsawa — but he said to me, "They are very good and very confident, but this is up to Boston friends. This world change is up to Boston friends." So, that strategic planning was for health, freedom, and happiness worldwide.

I want to say and I think that it probably goes for a lot of people in this room — at least to some large degree — he was the most influential person in my life, outside of my parents, without question, except maybe the person who introduced me to him.

So, thank you Michio for the love, guidance, help, and encouragement and, in reviewing my life with Michio for this talk, I had gotten many letters from him. I was amazed how much he put into us. Detailed letters, who's doing what, I got in Japan. And in every single letter he always said something about loving one another, guiding each other, helping each other, and encouraging each other. And as the new ones came along to help them, guide them, and so forth. He wanted to know that there was peace and cooperation in the family and that the energy was flowing. He always wanted that for us and we have that in our macrobiotic DNA now. So thank you for this opportunity, dear family, to speak about the man who changed my life and our lives. Thank you.

Remembering Michio
Michael Rossoff

Michio Kushi passed away in Boston early Sunday morning of December 28, 2014, surrounded by his four sons and his wife Midori. His oldest son, Norio, wrote that they all shared a magical and beautiful experience. Michio was peaceful and happy, free of pain, able to say his farewells to each and ask for harmony among all. Michio was eighty-eight years old.

He left behind many thousands of people whose lives were changed for the better because of his influence. Some found healing and new life, while others were inspired to start businesses in the natural foods industry, and still others took on the responsibility of teaching and sharing this wonderful way of life. I count myself among the latter.

Combining the philosophy of Oriental yin/yang with a strong Japanese emphasis, his vision spanned from the practical, such as organic, seasonal and local foods to a spiritual consciousness. His teachings, which extended over fifty years, directly and indirectly, changed many thousands of people's orientation to greater health, myself included.

His expression of macrobiotics always came from a larger view of life, inspiring people to seek their greater potentials as human beings. He taught that our foods are our connection to nature and the best means to bring health and harmony to our personal life and our world. Though we may fall short of these goals, we can remember that they are vital to seek. I am forever grateful to his inspiration and early guidance.

Michio Kushi Memorial
Saturday, January 31, 2015, Boston, Massachusetts
On a very cold winter's day in Boston, with snow piled high along the sides of the street, about 500 people gathered to show their gratitude and respect for Michio Kushi. Inside Arlington Street Church where Michio taught weekly during the late 1960s and early 1970s, there was a warmth and friendship that pulsated throughout the church. Many people had not seen each other for ten, twenty, thirty, or more years. They all shared one thing in common — having studied with or been deeply inspired by Michio and Aveline Kushi's teachings.

Though I have been in Boston a few times over the past years — seeing friends, colleagues and students — it was another thing to be among people from the distant past, whose lives had taken them in different directions. I lived in Boston from 1969 to 1972, in several "study houses" and in an apartment of my own. I also worked at Sanae restaurant for two years and knew many people from that time. For me, it was a total immersion experience, plus a time of great experimentation. There was a common link despite our many differences. That link — an enthusiasm for macrobiotics and the shared deep appreciation for Michio and his teaching of the macrobiotic way of life — brought us all back together. People came from across America, Europe, and Japan for a celebration of Michio's life and dream, plus a reunion and sharing.

In his role as master of ceremonies Michio's son, Haruo (Larry) Kushi, set the tone and focus for the memorial. Speaking for Michio's four sons and wife Midori, Haruo said that we, Michio's students, are as much a part of their extended family as they feel a part of ours. Each speaker brought some unique remembrance of Michio's life, his impact on his or her life and on the much larger scope of society and the world. The speakers were:

- Midori Kushi, Michio's second wife
- Masao Kushi, Michio's younger brother from Japan
- Evan Root, friend
- Eric Utne, friend
- Alex Jack, Kushi Institute director
- Aldebert Nelissen's (created the Kushi Institute in Amsterdam) two children:
- Gideon Nelissen, played a Bach violin sonata
- Horriah Nelissen, shared a message from her mother, Wieke Nelissen
- Chico Varatojo, director of the macrobiotic center in Portugal
- Toyofumi Yoshida, president Mitoku Company
- Michael Potter, president Eden Foods
- Dennis Kucinich, former Congressman from Ohio
- Hisao Kushi, youngest son

This was a wonderful commemoration of Michio's life, accomplishments, visions and dreams. Following the memorial service, there was a gala reception at a nearby hotel with music, food, and a unique opportunity to meet, greet, and catch up with many people from around the country and the world.

Gratitude to Michio Kushi and Recalling the Early Days in Boston
I first met Michio in 1969 when I was twenty-four years old. After hearing him lecture on a Sunday afternoon in a house in Brookline, Jim Ledbetter (Michio's early assistant) introduced me to him. Michio told me to do macrobiotics for one full year, then decide if this was right for me. His advice was profound because during that year I went through important personal changes, and by the end of the year my life had a new direction and purpose. I never looked back.

In July 1969, I moved to Boston and spent my first year in one of the "study houses" in Brookline, Mass., where around twenty strangers lived together because of our common interest in macrobiotics. I made several lasting friendships from this yearlong adventure.
In those days, macrobiotics was practiced in an extreme way. Pressure cooked brown rice was served daily (rarely other grains), along with miso soup, beans (very occasionally tofu, but tempeh was not available then), plus overcooked vegetables for the main fare. Once

a week we had fish and a dessert—usually cooked fruit. Everything was very salty, with tamari, gomasio, umeboshi, and miso all used liberally. Eating raw salad was considered a sign of weakness. Fried vegetables, or tempura, were welcome treats, with oil meant to fill our "yin cravings." So, going out for a beer on the weekends was popular.

At that time, Michio gave weekly lectures on Tuesday nights at the Arlington Street Church in downtown Boston and often taught another class on Sunday afternoons in a private home. Further, the couple who ran the study house also gave talks two evenings a week. These talks delved into the cosmology or the Order of the Universe, levels of judgment, philosophical topics and spiritual realms. An intensity and enthusiasm inspired and motivated everyone.

Michio was a powerful early teacher for the direct connection of foods to health. His ability to express Oriental philosophy of yin/yang in practical terms of everyday life was unique. He could speak easily, moving from the mundane to the profound, and showing the interconnectedness of all. His focus was on the application of this philosophy to foods, nature, and healing. The idea that we could take charge of our health by simple eating and practical lifestyle changes was revolutionary. It was challenging and freeing at the same time.

Occasionally Michio would invite other guests to speak at his Tuesday evening lectures. One of those guests was J.R. Worlsey, a teacher of acupuncture who was just starting a school in England. While now there are well over fifty acupuncture schools spread across this country, in the mid-1970s there were none. So I traveled to England to study with Worsley, a teacher whose influence in acupuncture education in America has been extensive. I credit Michio for introducing me to this great Oriental medicine healing tradition. Ever since then, for over forty years, I have combined acupuncture with my macrobiotic counseling and teaching. This remains my passion, my life's work.

In Boston, my first job was as a gardener for six months before I started as a dishwasher at Sanae restaurant. This was the first macrobiotic restaurant in Boston, seating about forty people. An early menu shows several choices of fish with a side of cole slaw and vegetables for only $3.50. The restaurant was like a school, in an apprenticeship style, with each position training the next person coming up. I "graduated" to short-order cook and finally to head chef. The pay was low, but the spirits and camaraderie were high. It was a special time.

Michio was a student and follower of George Ohsawa who is well known as the "father of macrobiotics." In the U.S. Herman Aihara and his wife Cornelia joined Michio and Aveline Kushi as dedicated teachers of the macrobiotic way of life. During the 1970s in America the macrobiotic movement seemed radical and strange. Now the U.S. government and many advocates of healthy living and eating are on board with the macrobiotic emphasis on grains, especially whole grains, and vegetables along with primarily vegetable protein.

Michio had a big heart and a strong spirit that inspired me and thousands of others. His contributions to personal healing, social change, and world peace will be part of his lasting legacy. I am grateful for having known him for over forty-four years. I remain inspired by his teaching of the unique principle, Order of the Universe, and *non-credo*.

Remembering Michio
Naoki Sakaguchi

When I met Michio for the first time, it was 1984 at his lecture for the Japanese people who lived in the Greater Boston area. It was held in his house in Brookline and about thirty Japanese people came. There was a Shiatsu class by a Japanese teacher, Michel Matsuda, and also Michio's wife, Aveline Kushi, made us soba noodles in broth.

At the time I was working at a Japanese restaurant called *Genji* located on Newbury Street, and two chefs at the restaurant were practicing macrobiotics. They often talked to me about macrobiotics, and I understood the concept but I was very attached to sugar, alcohol and meat, and I was not ready to accept their kind offers to engage in macrobiotics then. I had an aunt who lived in Boston and who participated in Michio's first lecture, and she was the one who recommended I attend. I do not remember all the details of Michio's lecture, but I do remember that what he taught made total sense. But what surprised me the most was the price of the lecture. It was only $5, including the Shiatsu class and also the bowl of soba. I could not even buy a bowl of soba with $5 at any restaurant. After the course I realized that the most important thing I had learned was about Michio and Aveline's "humility," and I sensed that within this humble spirit resided the real strength of their knowledge. After the course, I decided to stop meat and sugar.

Seeking the truth, striving to understand the truth, and having the courage to live the truth shows our strength. And the truth is the order of universe itself. Later on I tried not to ask Michio too many questions because I wanted to come up with the answer by myself, but I remember once I asked him a question while visiting his house. "Macrobiotics is the science, the true science of this universe, isn't it?" He answered me right away, "Yeah, that's right," with a big smile on his face. At the time, I noticed that this smile showed his strength and expressed a deep understanding of life lying behind. In Buddhism, it is said that there are three offerings that we can share with people: offering of the law of the universe, offering of money or material things, and offering of no-fear. Even if you do not know the law nor have money, still anyone can offer no-fear. And I heard that the offering of no-fear to the people around you is to smile. I wanted to know more about the strength behind his smile so that I started to dig into macrobiotics deeply.

Michio taught about life not only in lectures, but also in a myriad of interesting ways. Ways that often required your own attention and careful observation. Michio did not have a driver's license so usually somebody gave him a ride when he needed to go out. On one occasion, while Michio was visiting the Kushi Institute in Becket, I gave him a ride. We went to the General Store in Becket, and as we sat on the stools at the counter, there was a tray full of famous doughnuts in front of us. I tried not to take unknown quality oil and fat and too much sugar, so I ordered a bagel. Michio right away knocked on my bagel with his index finger and made a sound without saying anything. He was telling me about the hardness of bagel. I knew that the hardness of food also affects our health but I digested the idea at the counter while eating my bagel with him.

In Michio's Spiritual Seminars many curious things happened, but the session with Chris Akbar was something special. She was Michio's private secretary and had recently healed from breast cancer through macrobiotics. We all made pairs and tried to send energy from forehead to forehead, an area of intense energy known as the "third eye." I had been feeling a tingling sensation on this area all the time when I received energy from someone else. I practiced many times because I attended the Spiritual Seminars for three years, but was still skeptical about the sensations on my forehead. It was her turn to send energy so I was waiting for the familiar feeling to arise. I waited for ten or twenty seconds, but no such feelings arose on my forehead. I started to think that since she had cured cancer, she must have been eating well for some time, and she was probably able to send a lot of energy to me. So, why was the sensation not coming? As I was asking this question to myself, suddenly a shower of light came upon her. It was really a horizontal shower of golden light and it was so bright. When I asked her what had happened right after the session, she said, "This time, instead of sending energy as a beam, I put a mirror at 45 degrees in my head."

At the time I could get the answers to all my questions: aren't the sensations on my forehead the product of my imagination? Why does the tingling feeling occur? How much light does a person receive from heaven? And then I realized that Michio already knew all answers to these questions, and then developed this practice to lead us to the answer by ourselves. It became clear to me that if you keep knocking on the door, life will lead you to open the door by yourself. While I was working at the Kushi Institute, Michio once told us at a staff meeting that it would be wonderful that by the time the students finished Level I they developed politeness, sympathy after Level II, and compassion after Level III. This idea has stayed with me ever since. He would teach us about these qualities with remarkable patience, in front of our eyes, for those who could see. Now the world is increasingly becoming confused and our egocentric ways often leads us to abuse and kill each other in order to obtain advantages, grab lands, or impose our beliefs. It is our narrow and often egocentric views that separate us from each other. Feelings of anger toward others and attachment to things are signs that we need to work on ourselves. We need to develop a larger view of life. It's time for us to raise our consciousness one step at a time whenever the opportunities present. And in order to do that, we need to pay more attention to our foods, the way we eat, as well as improve our attitude and try to behave better.

Macrobiotics is a way to develop our consciousness. Continuing to change and to develop, to help change, and improve our world, and striving to maintain unity while following a middle way within a seemingly divided world is the core teaching I learned from Michio.

Remembering Michio
David Sergel

"Stay Boston one year. Teach Kushi Institute. Enjoy four seasons. OK?"..."OK!"

I had come to Boston from Tokyo, with my new wife Toko, in the summer of 1982. We planned to stay for a few months and then return to Sydney, Australia, my hometown. Toko had studied macrobiotic cooking with Lima Ohsawa ("She's like the sun," Toko said after her first class), and I had studied Shiatsu with Shizuto Masunaga, whose approach was, to my understanding, in harmony with macrobiotic principles. Michio had heard about me, and a few days after I arrived, requested I give him Shiatsu.

I went to his house late, nearly 11 p.m. We worked in the large library, and in the process, Aveline came down to watch. He didn't say much; when he asked me about Masunaga, I realized he was quite different from what I expected—more serious, purposeful, with a sense of gravitas. We finished around 1 a.m. and he called a taxi. As the taxi passed the gate, I turned to look back, and Michio gave me a wave and remained there until the taxi disappeared. It both surprised me that he was still there, and impressed me. It was very late, he'd had a long day, he was obviously a very busy, important person, and I was a novice. I think this incident is a good place to begin relating what Michio means to me. Toko and I came to Boston to learn from him. To me that not only meant knowledge but also who he was as a person, how he lived his life.

Waiting until I was out of sight before leaving, that sense of respect and consideration, was a quality I saw in different ways when he allowed me, along with other teachers, to observe his counseling sessions. I remember him saying to a "client," as I recall Michio calling those who came for consultations, to call him if there were any problems. When asked what was a good time to call, his response was, "after midnight!" His counseling was most insightful, educational, thorough, methodical, orderly, clear, and simple. Equally important I think was the rapport he established with the person seeing him. He was patient, totally committed; he didn't keep to a schedule, (which caused other problems for his staff and students as he was often late); instead, he answered all questions, carefully, in a charming and often humorous way. Above all, he "elevated;" he always lifted up and encouraged, he was always positive and totally supportive. He gave people confidence that they could heal and the inspiration to follow his suggestions. Smiling, "That's great!" was a common expression.

These same qualities came through in his teaching as well. There were some added insights since he faced the class, while in counseling we were off to the side and behind him. Again, he put his whole heart into it. He nearly always went overtime; he had incredible endurance. It also became more noticeable however, how tired he could be. He often looked exhausted and depleted. Giving his all appeared to take a heavy toll on his own health; he stooped as though he was carrying the weight of the world on his shoulders, which in a way he was, but he just kept going. Amazingly, one could see him a day later and he looked great; he had amazing recuperative powers. Again, his teaching was clear and orderly, and again he could be funny and charming, and always, perhaps underneath it all, cheerful. He answered every question, and he made himself accessible to anyone who showed genuine interest in macrobiotics.

Michio impressed me not only in terms of the breadth of his knowledge, but also its depth. What really interested me though, was the way he thought: big mind grounded in this reality.

Again, going back to the early days of our arrival in Boston. I was familiar with what is known as the Five Elements, this ancient theory from China, that all phenomena in this relative world could be classified in terms of one of five natural phenomena: Wood, Fire, Earth, Metal, and Water. Michio presented this not as something static, elemental, but as an energetic process of transformation. To me, by changing one word, this whole theory opened up in a way that his approach could be easily understood, along with the real meaning of it. That one change was *Wood* to *Tree*. Both words, as I understand it, could be translations of the Chinese character, but one, *Wood*, as dead and stiff as the word "element," and the other, *Tree*, full of life, and imagery. Since a tree grows from the earth, rising into the heavens, we could easily see the association he made of *Tree* with rising energy, which flowed into *Fire*, the most active energy, and so on.

This same approach could be seen in the relationship with food and how we could see its effect on our own physical condition and mental outlook. Root causes could be seen easily in this way, and solutions to problems likewise. The basic movement was from a bigger view, in this case the food we eat, to us. It was a process of bringing the emphasis of change back to the individual. If the individual followed the changes that were suggested, and opened up to assistance from those with more experience and knowledge when needed, one could change one's life in a positive way: greater health and happiness. For many of us the changes were profound.

Personally speaking, I felt more comfortable in this body; more flexible, more relaxed but more alert, with a much keener desire to learn and grow; and much more accepting of, indeed at home with, the idea of change, which is so central to the macrobiotic way. However, beyond this was another horizon that perhaps was Michio's most important motivation: world peace. I personally felt more at peace within myself; my thought process moved further and further away from a competitive mindset to one of co-operation. Those committed to macrobiotics have become participants, perhaps to some extent even unwittingly, in Michio and Aveline's dream of One Peaceful World.

It has been more than forty years now since I began macrobiotics. I have no regrets. Since Toko began macrobiotics in 1980, we, along with our two children, have never experienced any but the most minor health issues. In addition though, we all get along, we like each other, and I think, both children play active social roles in life, have an interest in macrobiotics that was never forced on them, and our two grandchildren are likewise healthy, and also, joyous. I have my own macrobiotic project that I work on that has arisen out of my studies with Michio. Without exaggeration I wake each day keen to develop the ideas I have been working on. I have something that is both meaningful in my life that I look forward to sharing with others, and something I believe that will hold my interest, until this earthly experience is over.

Thank you Michio.

Remembering Michio
Rudy Shur

As a relatively young book publisher in 1981, I had just discovered the virtues of the natural health movement. I may have been a little behind the time, but when I realized how manipulated our society was in terms of the foods we ate and the health problems those foods caused, I knew the direction my company had to take. Although my business was located in Garden City Park, New York, I had a number of authors in Boston. One of these authors, Steven Blauer, told me about a group of people involved in the macrobiotic movement. He advised me to learn more about what they were doing, and invited me to Massachusetts to see for myself. When I arrived, Steven filled me in on Michio Kushi and his organization's many accomplishments, from the Kushi Institute to Erewhon Foods to the macrobiotic restaurants that were popping up around the Boston area. Steven was also kind enough to set up a meeting with Len Jacobs, the publisher of the *East West Journal,* a macrobiotics-focused magazine dedicated to improving American diet and lifestyle.

As we walked down the halls of the magazine's headquarters in Brookline, I noticed a room filled with people doing yoga. I sensed that I liked this place. When I was introduced to Len, I asked him about the yoga class, and he said that the *Journal* offered various classes to their employees. I asked why, and Len explained that it made for a better work environment. After inquiring about the magazine's philosophy and mission, I questioned if they would be interested in having my company publish books that could be culled from the magazine. He said it wasn't a bad idea, but that he would have to think about it, learn a little more about my company, and then get back to me. We wound up publishing several books for the *Journal*, from cookbooks to collections of articles.

As I worked with the magazine, I learned more about macrobiotics. I discovered that the founder of the movement was George Oshawa, and his most dedicated students were Michio and Aveline Kushi. Michio had been the moving force behind the Boston-based group, which was growing and spreading throughout North America. I asked Len about the possibility of speaking to Mr. Kushi about publishing his books. At that time, a company based in Japan was producing his English language books. I thought we might be able to reach a larger market in the U.S., since we were becoming a fairly recognizable health publisher. Len arranged for me to meet Michio at his home, which was also in Brookline. I was not quite prepared for the experience.

I later learned that Michio's home had been a private girls' school, and it was a beautiful example of late nineteenth-century architecture. As I walked into the large foyer, there were people moving everywhere. Apparently, the Kushi house was home to many folks, including family, guests, and students. To the left of me was the library, and I was ushered inside. There, too, people milled about. Sitting on the couch was the gentleman I quickly realized was Michio Kushi himself. Edward Esko introduced himself to me and took me over to meet Michio. As he did, Edward asked the others to leave so that we could have a private conversation. The room cleared out, and the stained-glass doors to the library were closed. I was on. I may have appeared a little nervous — which I was — and Michio offered some bancha tea. He told me it was good for the nerves. I, of course, accepted.

Between sips of tea, I explained who I was and what my company did. I told him that while I understood that he already had a number of books available on macrobiotics, we could, perhaps, make a few of them more accessible to the average reader. We could also provide his titles with wider distribution. Michio was very gracious. He asked me a few questions, told me about his long-time relationship with his Japanese publisher, and said he would think about what I had proposed. I inquired if I could ask a few questions about aspects of macrobiotics that I didn't quite understand. He bowed his head and said yes. That gesture of answering the questions of a relative stranger exemplified Michio's kind and generous nature.

Twenty years later, when I sold my company, I had published over a dozen of Michio and Aveline's books and had them translated into no less than eighteen languages. Michio's book *The Macrobiotic Way* had become a bestseller. Over the years, I had enjoyed the privilege of speaking to Michio quite often about his writings, his lectures, and his travels. He continued to be generous with his time. Because of the agreement I had signed with the purchaser of my company, I could not publish books on health or speak to any of my old authors for three years. I hated that, but I kept to the agreement.

Two months after I sold my first company, I established a new company called Square One Publishers. After being in the business for twenty-three years, I had found myself at Square One…again. Three years later, when I could speak to my authors legally, I immediately called Michio, and just like that, he was happy to renew our relationship. I was grateful for his continued trust. Of course, I explained why I hadn't called him in all that time, but he simply said he it was good to hear from me again. Over the last few years, we have published new editions of *The Book of Macrobiotics* and *Macrobiotic Home Remedies* to very positive reviews. We plan to bring out several other of his titles. Just as Michio was committed to us, we continue to be committed to him and his legacy.

Beyond the macrobiotic philosophy I have incorporated into my life, I learned a great deal from my time with Michio Kushi. He was never pretentious or conceited. He always tried to give of himself to friends, students, and colleagues. He had a tremendous entrepreneurial spirit, which not only inspired a wealth of innovative ideas but also launched the careers of so many others. His life was not al ways easy, and yet he found the will to see it through. I am thankful for having the opportunity to know you, Michio.

Remembering Michio
Kezia Snyder

What I do every day has been influenced profoundly by what I learned from Michio. My studies began in 1969, when I attended one of his lectures after reading George Ohsawa's three little books earlier that year. The lecture was at the Japanese-American United Church in New York City, on Seventh Avenue and Twenty-Fourth Street. A more recent addition to that neighborhood is a Whole Foods store, the first one in New York City and one of many across the United States that represent a direct outgrowth of the spread of macrobiotic teachings. As the importance of natural foods has entered the greater food culture at large, thousands, if not millions, of people have come to understand the vital connections between food and health that, owing to the conjunction of various social forces, had eluded many for decades.

This is a revolutionary advance, and the writings and teachings of Michio Kushi have been a vital link in this transformation. I'm one of the fortunate ones to have been present as his galactic perspective unfolded before us. Representative of his scope is his theory of "the spiral of materialization," beginning in distant time and space and moving down to the most practical and basic daily details of life. Included in his revelations were his at times shockingly specific comments to us, revealing his knowledge of our dietary indulgences of the past few days, weeks, months, or even years. These were extremely obvious to Michio, prompting the admiration and the inevitable curiosity: how? Then came more study — and we learned.

Michio discussed our ancestors and our grandparents with amazing accuracy, deepening our admiration and respect, but not without a sense of humor. I recall a consultation with a woman who said to Michio, "I love peanut butter!" He answered with disarming sincerity, "Do you want to marry peanut butter?" From the cosmic to the comic, a truly astonishing range. I remember shaking hands with Michio after a lecture and feeling a powerful electric charge from my hand up to my elbow. Most of all, because of Michio's simple question: "What is food?" and his answer: "Everything we take in, in any way; air, water, physical substances, what we see, hear, read, and so on," brings us invaluable insights into our lives and how we live them. So many have been helped, healed, and enriched by the teachings of Michio Kushi. Our society has been and continues to transform because of his tireless efforts to effect positive change on this small blue-green planet.

Thank you, Michio Kushi, we are very, very grateful. Your dedication to the evolution of humanity lives on.

Remembering Michio
Bill Spear

I was living in Denmark when I first began to practice macrobiotics. I'd seen the book *Zen Macrobiotics* through some college friends in Cincinnati but had not explored the principles beyond a few conversations and some brown rice. Eventually, I spent time with students of Georges and Lima Ohsawa in Copenhagen, and the way I first started was extremely strict and narrow. A few years later, back in the U.S., I was living in Virginia and attended my first lecture with Michio. Although his broken English and thick Japanese accent was hard to understand, I was captivated by his presence and immediately signed up for a consultation.

I still have those scraps of yellow, lined paper on which Michio wrote notes on what to do. Though they reflect almost exactly what became known as the Standard Macrobiotic Diet, it wasn't the dietary advice that was as meaningful to me as the brief exchange we had near the end of the short time I was given to meet with him.

"What do you want to do with your life?" Michio asked after handing me his recommendations. That was easy (or so I thought) as years before I'd started a free clinic, a suicide hotline, worked in various capacities in health care and was now working as a drug and alcohol rehabilitation counselor at a halfway house for teenage runaways.

"I want to be useful. I want to help people" I replied, confidently.

"Ah, useful. Want to help all kinds of people?"

"Yes" I assured him. "Everyone."

Michio grinned and shook his head. "Hmmm…all kinds…like you help murderers?"

"Of course," I assured him. Murderers needed help, too, after all.

"So you help Nazis, too? And friends of Adolph Hitler?" he asked, his head tilted slightly.

I gulped and said nothing — completely taken aback by his preposterous question.

"Please study macrobiotics so you can help people, all people," Michio declared. "All same. Be useful *that* way."

In that single moment which I recall as if it were yesterday, Michio planted in me a seed of equanimity and a sense of oneness with all men and women no matter where they came from, how rich or poor they were, good or bad, right or wrong. While helping one of the world's most notorious mass murderers was the furthest thing from my young mind, his question caused me to consider how alike we all are — not how different and how I might begin to be useful in the world.

Not long afterwards, I began to accompany the Kushis when they visited many European countries and had the opportunity to observe hundreds of private consultations. I certainly felt useful helping him arrange these sessions, seeing to it that he had good food at the breaks and following up with the many clients he saw. Sought out by ministers, superstars, and extremely rich individuals, Michio seemed unfazed by anyone's status, stardom, or wealth. When it came time to offer advice, he sat across from "everyman" and "everywoman" and gave them something of value — something they could use to change their lives.

Soon, the Kushi Institute opened in London and not long after, in Boston. Those of us who had studied together over many years became its first teachers, eating well and busy with families and the larger communities we helped to create. I tried hard to be more useful to others, and I tried to remember the "all same" mantra as my own teaching and counseling practice evolved.

Late one night, after returning from a long trip overseas with Michio, I went back with him to his home in Brookline. We sat on the floor at his dining room table and sipped the last of the rich tamari broth left over from a bowl of soba noodles he prepared for both of us moments after we set our bags down in the hallway. I was deeply content, fulfilled and sated by more than just that midnight meal. My huge smile turned to laughter and soon, both of us were doubled up with laughter for no apparent reason other than the affectionate joy we shared at that moment.

Finally calmed down after we returned to some sense of decorum, it was my turn to ask him a question.

"Michio, you often said that to develop ourselves, all we really needed to do was to eat well and be physically active. I've certainly been doing that now for many years, and I can't say I have ever been as happy. Is this the way other macrobiotic friends feel, too?" I rattled off the name of a few other teachers, incredulous that they, too, might be as blissed as I was.

"One more thing," Michio said, his open palm chopping through the air to make his point. "Give it all away—and please be sure it is useful."

"What do you mean?"

"Anyone can give a box of clothes away to—how you say—Salvation Army?"

Smiling, I commented, "Ah, yes—the Salvation Army—like the thrift store."

"Yes, thrift store. Give your old coat. Easy, right? But not give away yet, not yet good. Must be useful. Then, later you see a man on the street wearing your coat! You go, bow to him, and say 'thank you very much for wearing that coat.' Now the coat is useful, you gave it away and made it benefit someone. Then you must thank him. Right? You understand?"

And yes, I understood. I saw why, at the end of a weekend seminar, or evening lecture, when the audience stood up and said a collective thank you, he bowed and said, "No, no—thank *you* very much." We'd say, "Michio, thank you," and he'd bow deeper still, with, "No, thank *you* very much."

Michio inspired in me a life of purpose, a path of helping others. He taught us all how to be useful in the world, and his own life was precisely that for millions of others he never had the opportunity to thank. I feel certain that especially to those close students of many years—though it was more difficult for him to actually do so—he would bow in gratitude.

Remembering Michio
Jane and Lino Stanchich

When an honorable human being of such magnitude as Michio Kushi has lived and now has passed away, our hearts are filled with the deepest gratitude, respect, and love. Michio's life was dedicated to teaching people the way to achieve peace, health, and freedom by learning and following the principles of humane, compassionate, organic, ecological living, all principles to foster world health and peace.

Brilliant teacher, macrobiotic leader, prolific author, humorous and loving mentor, and dear friend, Michio Kushi passed away peacefully December 28 at age eighty-eight, in Boston, Mass., surrounded by his beloved wife, Midori, and his sons Norio, Haruo, Phiya, and Hisao. He was fully conscious until the last moment and passed with a smile on his face. Michio had developed cancer, the disease he helped untold numbers of people worldwide prevent and reverse. In his last public lecture, Michio taught that each of us is a "miracle" and "there is no death," believing in eternal consciousness. He truly is a man of the ages, of infinity. As Michio said,

> *To all of my friends and associates around the world, as well as people everywhere who are true peace promoters, I am grateful for your heartfelt efforts and for the opportunity to be together with you on this beautiful planet with all of its wonderful difficulties. I pray that we can*

always love and help each other and together realize One Peaceful World.

Michio studied at Tokyo University and with George Ohsawa, a passionate proponent of world peace through health. A true visionary, young Michio, with the aid of famed Norman Cousins, left Japan for America following World War II. Seeking paths to world peace, he consulted with world leaders, famous writers, and philosophers who offered no solid solutions. Michio profoundly realized that until people were truly healthy within, peace among families, communities, and nations was impossible. For over sixty years, Michio taught and counseled people of all faiths and walks of life throughout the world. He met and maintained mutually respectful relationships with all people, as well as leaders in fields of medicine, science, academics, fitness, politics, and the arts.

Michio and his first wife, Aveline, were stalwart believers in and proponents of the powerful connection between one's diet and environment… and one's health. Since 1949, these beloved visionaries spread the philosophy of macrobiotics, the nutritionally sound, balanced, and healthy whole foods diet and natural lifestyle now accepted and respected in the medical and scientific world. The United States Congress has honored their work and their macrobiotic archives are now housed at the Smithsonian Institution's National Museum of American History.

Working and writing tirelessly, Michio and Aveline Kushi published over seventy books traveling throughout the world teaching the macrobiotic philosophy and way of life. Due to the inspiration of the Kushis, macrobiotic centers were created in dozens of countries, teaching multitudes worldwide how to achieve personal health of body, mind, and spirit through a natural way of living and eating. Acknowledged pioneers in the natural food movement, the Kushis strongly advocated organic farming, natural products, local foods, and healing home remedies and cooking.

Michio and Aveline courageously taught what were, in the 1960s, (and still today!) revolutionary philosophies about natural medicine, healing foods, and cooking to balance health conditions. Through their groundbreaking health food store Erewhon, they reintroduced organic traditional whole foods to America. In almost daily classes, they taught the health properties of whole grains, land and sea vegetables, beans and bean products such as tofu and tempeh, as well as nutritious high-probiotic fermented foods such as miso, shoyu, umeboshi plums, and natto. Countless scientific studies have shown, throughout the past decades, these macrobiotic foods to be powerfully nutritious, disease-preventive, and healing.

The Kushis taught the wisdom of a diet centered upon eating these whole, organic, ecological foods, conscientiously prepared and humanely harvested. Now these concepts are familiar in our mainstream culture, gaining increasing credence and acceptance. Eons ahead of his time, Michio with Aveline, totally devoted their lives to helping others, often sacrificing their own personal health and well-being in devoted pursuit of world health and peace.

Michio also dedicated his life to teaching spiritual development and living in harmony with all of nature and humankind. Forever seeking solutions towards world peace, Michio was a leader in matters of philosophy, spiritual practices, the development of intuition, ecology, history, natural medicine, the Unique Principle, and the Order of the Universe. His many books can be read and savored as one gleans priceless wisdom for wellness, world peace and harmony in the universe.

We bow to you Michio, with most profound gratitude, for being so courageous, wise, kind hearted, humorous, and humble. You are the true example of what one man can do in the world. You left a legacy of knowledge at the Kushi Institute, as well as throughout the world, in centers, libraries, museums, and in the hearts of those who knew and were privileged to have met and learned from you.

Friends, let us continue the teachings of macrobiotics, of the ecological whole foods organic diet, sustainable living, pure air and water, personal freedom, and peace among all people, as did Michio.

Remembering Michio
Sanae Suzuki

I started practicing macrobiotics under the guidance of my first macrobiotic teacher, Cecile Tovah Levin, in Los Angeles. I was diagnosed with ovarian cancer in 1993 and was on my path to healing with macrobiotics. When I found out that Michio Kushi and his wife Aveline were Japanese I really wanted to meet them. I was not sure how macrobiotics would work, but it surprised me how quickly I felt so much better and stronger as I created my foundation step by step and I was able to travel the following year.

In the summer of 1994 I visited the Kushi Institute in Becket, Mass. and was surprised to see many people from Japan. I met two charming girls who lived in a Kushi House in Brookline, near Boston. They invited me to go with them to the Kushi Summer Conference at Green Mountain College in Vermont in the bus that Norio Kushi (one of Michio's sons) drove. Because of them I met Michio and Avleline Kushi and was so lucky to be a part of the Japanese macrobiotic supporting community. I really enjoyed talking to the Kushis in Japanese and receiving their teachings directly.

After I enjoyed my first Summer Conference, Cecile told me that Michio and Aveline were looking for a live-in assistant and thought it would be a great opportunity for me to go Boston. They were looking for a U.S. permanent resident or citizen who spoke and wrote Japanese and English and could also drive. I fit the bill, but I couldn't go because I had a dog and cat family, and I could not abandon them. Instead I kept in touch with the Kushis and visited their house almost every summer and worked at the Summer Conference as a second cook.

I have many stories about Michio, but here are a few.

When I was taking Levels 1, 2, and 3 at the Kushi Institute in Becket, I lived in nearby Great Barrington with my dog Kin and cat Mai. Sometimes Kin went to the Kushi Institute with me and waited for me while I was taking classes, having fun running and chasing wild animals. I heard that Kin also went to visit Mark Esko's dog Hash as well as the Becket General Store in Becket Village. One day I was looking for Kin and some people told me they saw Kin at the General Store with Michio, eating donuts. I thought they were making a joke, but one day I asked Michio if it was true that he gave donuts to my dog. He said, "Oh, was that your dog? She was a good dog and really enjoyed the donut with me, but not to worry, she has a strong constitution and she can eat donuts occasionally." I laughed so much!

Another time I saw him at a Smithsonian Institution's fundraising party in Laguna Beach. My husband Eric and I cooked for the guests with other macrobiotic chefs. Michio and Aveline were so proud of the macrobiotic movement in the U.S. We really enjoyed the lecture about how they started macrobiotics in the U.S. Eric cooked his macrobiotic meal for the first time publicly, and I think that was the decisive moment for Eric to become a macrobiotic chef from then on.

I learned so much from first Level 4 that Michio taught in 2001, and some of the teachings helped me embrace all of life, good and bad. Michio instructed us to "never move vegetables when you are water sautéing them." He said that vegetables have their own energy and they blend together perfectly and do not need our help. I was not sure if this was true, but every time I water sautéed vegetables I remember what he taught me and feel the vegetables' own energy that needs no disturbing. I respected his teachings, even when he included the bathroom cleaning duties as part of the curriculum of Level 4. It was a lesson of being humble and letting go of one's ego even as you train to become a macrobiotic teacher. Too bad the curriculum has changed and bathroom cleaning is no longer part of Level 4 study,

I am very happy to have received his unique principles of teaching.

This memory is very special for my husband Eric and me. Eric told me that Michio made a phone call to him while I was in a coma for three days at the Intensive Care Unit in an Arizona hospital. He told Eric I am going to come back with more strength and not to worry so much, and to just pray for me. As some of you know I had a near-fatal car accident on my way home after finishing my first section of Level 4 study in Becket in 2001. It totally changed my life, and the doctor told me that I would not walk again. I was bedridden for one year and spent three years in a wheelchair. I did not give up and continued practicing macrobiotics, resolving to walk, so I went back to the Kushi Institute in 2005 to complete my Level 4 study. Gradually I could become ambulatory, and I am happily teaching, counseling, and living a life of macrobiotics more than ever before, thanks to what Michio said to Eric.

Michio was a very busy and active person, so I hesitated to take his precious time. The last time we really got together was in Tokyo in 2007. He and his second wife Midori invited Eric and me to have lunch at an Italian restaurant. They were very casual and smiling a lot. We felt that they were such a harmonious couple. He told me how happy he was that I continued and kept up my macrobiotic practice after the car accident. He said he knew that I would be able to come back even stronger than when I overcame cancer. The only suggestion he had was not to eat too late at night, and to find time to have fun amidst our busy city life. He was so intuitive and not afraid to speak out. Eric and I really appreciated his advice, and we try to stop what we are doing to enjoy a meal at the right time, and to go to the beach or hiking, and treat ourselves to other diversions that we enjoy together.

Michio was always polite and attentive. His teaching style was thoughtful and deep, but also very funny and playful, making people laugh. I thought he should be on the David Letterman show.

His teaching method was truly in keeping with the principles of yin and yang. When I was working on my cookbook, *Love, Sanae*, I asked Michio to write a foreword, so I called him frequently. He was very friendly and made jokes all the time. But when I made a mistake, he would turn into a serious, but kind teacher and correct me instantly and assertively. Mostly what I cherish are the moments I spent with the wise, benevolent, charming teacher and friend who helped me relax every time I talked to him.

I feel extremely fortunate and grateful that I was able to learn from Michio, who helped my macrobiotic seed grow and multiply as I pass on his teachings to the global community.

With all my love and gratitude to Michio *sensei*!

Remembering Michio
Bill Tara

Michio and my father were the two men who most influenced my life. My father instilled in me an enduring love and appreciation of nature, and Michio taught me how to connect the dots. The gifts of these two difficult men have served me well, and I am grateful for them both.

The day before I heard of Michio's death he showed up in a dream. I would love to say it was a profound dream announcing his departure, but it was not. It was a silly dream. The uniqueness was only in that I had never dreamed of Michio before. Now he only lives in dreams. Some of those dreams are the dreams of remembrance of those of us who knew him. Some are visions he wove in his life and have become reality. Michio was a dreamer and consistently worked to make his vision real.

I have never met a person who was more focused on his vision than Michio. His dedication was unconditional, sometimes myopic, but always moving ahead. His mind was constantly in motion and focused on how he could better express the macrobiotic philosophy and demonstrate its practical application. Like all great men he was a walking contradiction. He was a man who taught natural law but was very ambivalent about nature.

Aveline called me up once in Boston and asked if I would drive Michio on a camping trip. I was amazed to hear the words "Michio" and "Camping Trip" in the same sentence.

It turned out that two girl students were concerned about the fact that Michio was working too hard and wanted to take him for a weekend in the country. Michio begrudgingly agreed if I would come and be the driver (it was one of my jobs in those days.) I agreed.

I arranged sleeping bags and a tent (just in case) and all the camping equipment and went to pick up the campers. Michio presented himself in the three-piece black suit with no tie (the casual look) and wearing a brand new pair of snow-white sneakers! The girls showed up with a month's worth of rice balls.

We drove the better part of the first day going north trying to get out of the rain and ended up in Maine. Michio saw his first moose (WHAT IS?) and slept the night in a sleeping bag with the suit neatly folded on a rock, sneakers on top.

The next day we were driving in a blustery wind out to the coast. The girls tried their best to get Michio out of the car and into the delights of sea spray and wild beauty; he respectfully said he would look from the car. I joined the girls and returned in an hour to check on him. He was fast asleep and I tried unsuccessfully to get in and not wake him.

He opened his eyes and said, "What a strange dream."

"What was it about" I asked.

His expression was very serious, "I dreamed I met a man who was sick and had a strange disease. No one had ever seen such strange symptoms; they kept changing. As much as I tried, I could not think of a cure."

"What do you think it means?"

"It means I must study more," he said and then began to laugh, "It is a dream disease."

"Can we go to the town now and have coffee?"

Michio was big on dreams. He also had a great sense of humor.

We attended a dinner in Paris in the 1970s where Michio was still viewed with suspicion by some of the old Ohsawa students. The place had a low ceiling, everyone was packed in tight, it was hot and there was a cloudbank of cigarette smoke swirling from about five feet off the floor.

Innumerable speeches with slow translation dragged on till finally dinner was served. Seitain steaks with dry brown rice and a slight sliver of vegetables served as the entrée with enough salt to make your teeth ache. This was followed by a tiny thimble of beer, (Oh how the desperate eyes of the faithful gleamed with their naughty treat), and more speeches.

When we finally worked our way to the door and were saying goodbye with much kissing of cheeks, and I noticed Michio nodding his head toward me and then to the side of the hall. There was a table with a fruit display — unbelievable, oranges and bananas. He was giving me the universal big eye signal "go for it." I worked my way over to the table and filched a couple of oranges into the pocket of my overcoat and was joined by Aveline. With her Japanese innocence for cover she managed to get a couple of bananas into the sleeves of her kimono.

We left and walked briskly up the street and around the corner where Michio stopped and said, "What did you get?" I held out the oranges and he nodded. Aveline started laughing and pulled out two bananas. Michio then put on a worried face and looked around as if we might be followed. "We should get back to the hotel fast before they come after us. This could be dangerous!" He loved the slapstick comedy of life, and it was one of his most charming qualities. He could be the inscrutable mystic, the charming raconteur or the stern professor as the mood moved him. So now he is gone and the stories will be told, and mythologies constructed, but none of them will ever provide a true picture of the complex tapestry of his life. He made a valuable contribution to the way we think about the healing power of food and was capable of intuitive and exciting insights into natural law and the human condition. He challenged us all to follow our dreams and then showed us how to dream big. Now he is part of a dream even larger than his own.

Remembering Michio
Eric Utne

My name is Eric Utne. I came to Boston to study macrobiotics with Michio and Aveline Kushi in 1967, when I was 21 years old. My first address was on Commonwealth Ave. in Brookline. The church next to my study house had a small marquee out front with a quote from President James A. Garfield. It read, "The truth shall set you free. But first it will make you miserable." That marquee got it right.

During my ten years in Boston I lived in at least five study houses, managed the Erewhon natural foods store on Newbury Street, lived for a time with Michio and Aveline and their kids on Gardner Road, chopped vegies at Sanae restaurant, met and married my first wife, ran the study house on Warren St., sold ads and wrote articles for *East West Journal*, and stole the *EWJ* mailing list to start *New Age Journal*.

Michio's students
That first summer I attended Michio's lectures here, in the Arlington Street Church. I was the most eager and earnest student imaginable. But so was everyone else.

Michio attracted some of the most interesting people I ever met. Some found their way to macrobiotics because they were drawn to Michio's teachings about Yin and Yang, traditional Japanese culture, and the Order of the Universe. Others were sick with cancer, or diabetes, or some other health concern. Others were spiritual seekers, trying to raise their consciousness. Still others were psychedelic tripsters seeking the ultimate high. Some were all of the above. We all had at least one thing in common: We were deeply doubtful about the conventional wisdom of mainstream American science and religion, especially allopathic medicine, and we were searching for alternatives.

Letter-reading at Michio's lecture

The first time I attended one of Michio's lectures, I took a seat in the front row. It was soon apparent that Michio began each lecture by having people in the front row read letters from some of his students who were traveling and studying abroad. I was too shy to stand before the fifty or so people sitting in the pews, so I moved to the back. But after one or two lectures, I decided that I was being a coward, so I forced myself to sit in the front row.

Sure enough, Michio called on me. He handed me a letter. It was seven pages long, typed single-spaced on onion-skin paper. I began reading and I burst into sweat after just two sentences. The letter was about the Japanese macrobiotic community in Brazil and their recipes for miso. I was making a bollocks of it. Michio watched as the perspiration dripped off my nose and elbows, forming a puddle at my feet. Before I'd finished the first page, Michio patted me on the back and thanked me as he peeled the letter from my hands. I rushed down the center aisle and into the church basement, removed my shirt, and rung it out in the men's room sink. Michio never mentioned it again, and he never asked me to read another letter.

Living in the Kushi household

About a year after arriving in Boston a place opened in Michio's home and I asked if I could take it. I wanted to be as close to my teacher as possible, to learn as much as I could, and to see if he was living what he was teaching. Michio said "OK."

The house was a big old New England colonial on Gardner Road in Brookline, with yellow clapboard siding, wooden shutters on all the windows, and white trim. It was enormous, like all the other houses in the neighborhood, and unobtrusive. The household included Michio and Aveline and their children Norio, Lily, Haruo, Phiya, and Hisao, plus about six other students.

My most vivid memory is of sitting in the second floor kitchen listening to Michio be a father to Norio.

"Norio," he would say, "Please Norio, go to school. Please, Norio, please, go to school." I don't know if it worked.

Another memory is of dinner. Aveline always made delicious dishes for the kids like egg drop soup and tempura shrimp and deep-fried mochi, while we students got miso soup, brown rice, seaweed and veggies. At the time I thought we students were getting the better deal.

Swollen Ankles
During the hot summer of 1970 my ankles swelled to almost double their normal thickness. I must be too yang, I thought.

I was working very hard, drinking very little water, and definitely eating too much salt, all very "yang-izing." Then again, maybe my problem was that I was still too yin. Tall Nordic types were constitutionally yin from generations of eating too much dairy food. "Cow's milk is for cows," Michio used to tell us, "not people."

Eating by yin and yang could be very confusing.

After trying to sort things out on my own for several weeks I finally sought an audience with Michio. He was a very busy man, and I didn't want to bother him with my stupid problems, but I was unable to solve the puzzle of my swollen ankles, and I was desperate.

It was late in the evening. Michio was sitting alone at the kitchen table preparing his next lecture. I reluctantly asked him if I could have a few minutes of his time.

"Hmmm!" he grunted softly, almost inaudibly, with a slight nod of his head. He lit a cigarette, cocked his head to one side, raised his eyebrows, and gave me an inviting smile. "Yes. What is it?"

"Michio-san," I started, "I hate to bother you, but I've got a question."

I stood and lifted one foot unto the seat of the chair next to Michio and raised my pant leg. "I've got swollen ankles and I've tried everything I can think of but they just keep getting bigger and bigger."

"Hmmm," he grunted again, looking at my elephantine ankles.

He squeezed my ankle between his thumb and forefinger. "Very interesting, don't you think?"

He took a long draw on his cigarette, and let the smoke hover around his face as he closed his eyes in contemplation.

"Take five umeboshi plums (Japanese salted plums) every day for five days. See if that helps." Then he turned back to his notes without another word. Audience over.

"That's it!?" I thought. "Five salted plums! Every day! Is he crazy? That'll kill me."

Later, as I thought about it, I decided that what Michio was really saying was, "Trust your own judgment, (you idiot). Figure it out for yourself." Michio was a great teacher.

World Peace
About a year ago I learned that on August 6, 1945, the day the atomic bomb was dropped over Hiroshima, Michio was a nineteen-year-old soldier in the Japanese Imperial Army, stationed near Nagasaki. After Japan surrendered, on August 15, Michio rode by train through Hiroshima on his way home to Tokyo. He saw firsthand the effects of the bomb and its radioactive aftermath. Michio decided then to devote himself to world peace.

After graduating from Tokyo University in law and international relations, Michio came to the U.S. in 1949 for graduate studies in political science at Columbia University. He soon began to question the possibility of achieving peace through political or social means. He then interviewed many prominent scientists, authors and statesmen, including Albert Einstein, Robert M. Hutchins, Thomas Mann, Upton Sinclair, Pitirim Sorokin, and others, asking them their thoughts on how to achieve lasting peace. No one had the answer.

Michio eventually embraced the teachings of George Ohsawa, whose lectures he had attended in Japan. Ohsawa taught that food is the key to world peace because only truly healthy people can be peaceful. Michio changed his diet and began to teach macrobiotics.

Michio's Legacy
Through more than fifty years of writings and lectures, Michio Kushi sowed the seeds for today's natural and organic foods revolution, and thereby sowed the seeds for world peace.

Perhaps more importantly, he built bridges between the East and the West. Arnold Toynbee, the historian, said that the most important phenomenon of the 20th century, even more important than the invention of the automobile, or the telephone, or the television, or the atomic bomb, or the computer, or space exploration, was the coming of Buddhism to the West.

I was a member of the Executive Committee of the Nobel Peace Prize Forum for seven years, and I met many of the winners of the Nobel Peace Prize.

I think Michio did as much as or more than anyone since World War II to build bridges between Japan and the United States, between science and spirit, and between Yin and Yang. I think Michio Kushi would have been a worthy winner of the Nobel Peace Prize.

Michio also deserves Japan's highest honor, the Collar of the Order of the Chrysanthemum. I hope the committee awards it to him.

We are fortunate to have known Michio and Aveline Kushi. Their legacy lives on.

Remembering Michio
Chico Varatojo

Hello, good afternoon, Midori, Norio, Haruo, Phiya, and Hisao. Thank you so much for asking me to pay this last tribute to your husband and father. It's an honor and pleasure. Everyone has spoken a lot about Michio in different ways. I will talk a little bit about my relationship with him and what I knew about Michio as a human being.

I got to know him in 1977, I believe August 16, 1977. I am not sure of the date, I am sure of the month. I was sixteen then. I was a young kid just starting macrobiotics and Michio, Aveline, and some of the children and some other friends — one of them, Bill Spear, is here this afternoon — were there. So I went to the seminar. I sat in the first row and Michio called me on stage. I was extremely nervous, more than I am now, and I am a bit nervous. As some of you know, we had this nail clipper demonstration — this famous counter-clockwise, clockwise experiment — I got the counter-clockwise spiral, and I thought he was reading my mind, knowing everything about my life, my past life, I really thought so! I was scared to death. So, I think he put his hand on my shoulder and it was obvious I was pretty nervous.

You know he had this mantra, which he said to many, many people, particularly young people, which was, "Please come to Boston!" So

I think he spelled that mantra—I mean he used to say this to everyone. I remember him in every consultation saying, "Please come to Boston," and in classes. So, I got it, too. And this was like an enchanted word. It would actually make me fly to Boston a few months later in February. It was very, very cold like now, I remember. I landed in Logan Airport. It was 15 degrees Celsius in Lisbon, and it was minus 20. It was the coldest day of the winter, similar to the time we are in right now, for what was the biggest adventure of my life, which was studying macrobiotics.

And over the years I was actually quite lucky to get to know Michio in many of his facets: Michio the father, Michio the husband, Michio the teacher, Michio the counselor, Michio the philosopher, Michio the politician, Michio the businessman. Michio could embody all of these really well. He was one time discussing politics, and the other time he was closing a contract. And at the same time he was giving advice to someone who was sick. So, Michio had this personality that really embodied lots of personalities, but I think for those of us present here—the teachers, the students, especially the teachers who studied with him—I think Michio was, more than anything else, our teacher. The one who drew spirals on the blackboard and the one who made the relationship with everything, like Evan Root was saying, or taught Oriental diagnosis or gave us consultations.

For me Michio was somehow—and someone else said this already—my second father, not taking anything from you others. Michio and Aveline were like my second parents. He was always the great teacher. One of his capacities was of really drawing people. I remember people in his lectures, people could hardly understand his English, which was actually pretty bad most of the time. And yet they would feel drawn by his energy. They would feel drawn by his quality. I remember one time we were in an airplane in Brazil, and Michio stood up to go to the toilet, and a lady came out of nowhere on the plane and exclaimed, "Oh my God! You are a saint! You are something!" And I thought, "What is going on?" Yet, she did not know him. She just picked up something and went after him and, of course, as usual, I had to rescue him as a bodyguard. That was one of my functions—very often, driving, body-guarding, and running away from places.

If I would say something about him, Michio really had a huge dream. He wanted everyone on the planet to eat well, he wanted a pristine environment, and he wanted to discover transmutation and many of those things that some people are following right now. But he always wanted that with good manners and elegance. Michio had this thing about good manners and elegance. You had to shape up and dress well, speak well, and be gentle. Even in war, he thought things should be — I don't know — peaceful, but with good manners. I think Michio felt many times that he was a samurai, and that his mission was the mission of a samurai, and certainly his life does reflect that in many ways.

But he did pursue his dream relentlessly. I did work a lot with him, and I met very few people with this drive and resilience. He was unstoppable. Often times the second shift at home would start at midnight when everyone was very tired. I remember working with him on proofreading some books. It was four in the morning. I was completely exhausted. I am much younger than him. I was exhausted, and Michio was reading. In my mind, I was thinking, "He cannot be doing this right. We are too tired. So, he is just pretending he is reading." And then he said, "Chico! We've got to change this, this is no good!" I said, "What do you mean, Michio?" It was just a little sentence, something not that important, and he was really awake. I would say, "Oh boy, this is amazing how he can do this! It's amazing how he could have this incredible drive."

He always wanted to change the world. He always had big plans for everything. He always targeted really high. He always aimed for the stars. Michio never wanted anything small. Never, that I know of anyway.

But he had, and I really miss this, an incredible sense of humor. Sometimes peculiar. Sometimes a little not so easy to grasp. But he had a very funny sense of humor that he could use in consultations very often. Not everyone understood what he meant sometimes. But I remember one time we were traveling together in Europe, after Aveline died, just visiting several countries. We had a dinner which — you know how these dinners go — took forever. Everyone was asking questions, and Michio would always say, "Yes," and there's a point when he says, "Chico! Let's go out."

So I find a good excuse. We come out. It's a very beautiful spring day, and it's very late. It's about one in the morning. We come out to the street. We want a bench to sit on, but there's no bench, so we both ended up sitting on the sidewalk dressed up in suits. And, we sit down, and Michio starts telling jokes. You know these jokes about, "There was this priest and a rabbit...." He started, and I have never heard him do anything like that. He makes up this joke and replaces the priest and the rabbi with macrobiotic people and Japanese. And I started playing the game, and I would add the Portuguese, and we were laughing like crazy.

Then we went to the hotel, and I said, "Gosh, I never heard Michio telling jokes! This was the first time." He actually knows jokes! He knew all these jokes about Japanese people, which I won't repeat here. But he could be really, really funny, and lately in these last few years, I would always call him on his birthday. I would say, "Happy birthday, Michio!" and he would reply back, "Happy birthday to you, too, Chico!" We were not born the same day, by the way, and I'll just have to stop at some point. He's really funny, and I will really miss his sense of humor.

Remembering Michio
Denny Waxman

On December 28th around 8 p.m., my wife Susan and I were in a restaurant having dinner with some friends. There was a call on my cell phone from Michio Kushi's son Norio. Norio and I have been close friends for many years. He wanted to let me know personally that his father had passed away that morning. He wanted to give me the details before the news went public. Knowing this day would come did not lessen the shock.

Michio and Aveline Kushi were my spiritual parents. They invited me into their family shortly after we met. Even though I am dedicating this memorial to Michio, it is difficult for me to think of and remember him without also appreciating and acknowledging Aveline.

I met Michio in February, 1969 when he came to lecture in Philadelphia before we opened our store, Essene. I got to the lecture early simply so I could ask him a question. I told him I was opening a macrobiotic store and asked him if he had any advice for me. His words were: "Keep it clean. If it isn't clean, it isn't macrobiotic." These words stuck with me forever, and I think his words were one of the keys to our success. The same effort we put into keeping the store spotless, we put into the quality of our food and the quality of service to our customers.

At nineteen, I was lost and confused, and had no idea about how I wanted to live my life. The one thing I knew for certain was that I didn't want to follow in the suggested path set by society. I had recently read George Ohsawa's books that talked about a brighter future and how we could create our health and happiness, but I needed more. At the lectures, Michio spoke of everything under the sun, from the meaning of life, to how to cure cancer, to world peace. One Peaceful World was the central theme to Michio's message. He taught that world peace can only be achieved through healthy people.

On the second day of Michio's lectures in Philadelphia, I was invited to the home of Rod and Peggy House with about twenty others. At this gathering, Michio said that he didn't want many friends. The statement startled me. Michio followed by saying he only wanted just a handful of friends who could really understand this way, and together we could change the world. At that moment, I knew I wanted to be one of those friends. Meeting Michio changed my life.

He had an amazing and indomitable spirit. In the early '70s, when I tried to expand the Essene distribution company too quickly, we ran into serious financial difficulties. As we were walking out the door on the way to a lecture, Michio paused and told me not to worry. He said that even if I lost everything, we would simply start again from my own home. This struck me deeply yet again, and demonstrated to me how clear and penetrating Michio's insight and advice was in all areas of life. Incidentally, we were able to reach a settlement, close the distribution company, and save the store.

No one could keep up with Michio; he was relentless in the pursuit of his dream to change this world. He often talked about lighting fires as he endlessly traveled the world to inspire people and ignite them into action. Michio taught me that anything was possible, and I always admired his vitality. His endless spirit continues to inspire my life and my own approach to healing. *The Book of Macrobiotics* largely sums up the heart of his teachings. I wanted to move to Boston to study with Michio, but Essene, being in Philadelphia, kept me there.

I went back and forth between Boston and Philadelphia to continue my studies and maintain my connection with Michio. Michio popularized study houses, which were houses run by individuals or couples where we could live, practice, and study together. The study houses made macrobiotic education both affordable and practical. I attended Michio's leadership seminar for two months in 1973. In addition, I stayed at different study houses for two weeks twice a year. I also attended every new seminar that Michio created and sponsored his visits to Philadelphia. Through these regular visits, my friendship and mentorship with Aveline began to grow and became a crucial part of my life. During this time, it became apparent to me how Aveline was both a powerful stabilizing factor for Michio as well as a driving force for the entire macrobiotic movement.

In 1981, during my twelfth year of practice, Michio asked me if I ever doubted macrobiotics. When I replied "No," he told me that now I could change the entire world. I was very blessed to have met Michio at such a young stage of my life. He told me on a few occasions that he was born too early to see the fruits of his labors, but that I would, and I took that to heart. He also told me that the macrobiotic movement would follow the development of this country, where the ideas started in Boston, but were enacted in Philadelphia. This is also part of the reason why I have chosen to remain in Philadelphia.

Michio had a powerful psychic ability that he used in his counseling. He had an amazing ability to see not only people's specific health, but even certain foods they had eaten on certain days. I was often self-conscious that he would be able to tell I had been eating something he may not have approved of. His long-term predictions were amazingly accurate. He painted a picture for society more than forty years ago that I would say that today is precise. He saw in the '60s that we would continue down a path towards increasing degenerative illness, social unrest, over medication, and the further destruction of the environment. The vast scope of his teachings demonstrated very clearly the relationships and connections between diet, health, environment, and spiritual development.

The last time I saw Michio was August 3, 2013 at the Kushi Institute Summer Conference in New Jersey. Michio scolded me among my peers for recommending sardines to a shared client. He asked me if I could help the client with plant-based recommendations alone, and if I was following up regularly to tell them to stop the sardines when they were no longer needed. The scolding was relentless and beyond intimidating, and I did my best to remain calm and stand by my recommendations. I finally said, "You know, Michio, that not everyone practices the way we like them to," and that changed the tone. There was a running joke among the teachers about sardines for the rest of the conference. It was an experience that I am sure I will ponder for the rest of my life.

The last time I spoke with Michio was this past October. I called him just before Susan and I left for the teachers' meeting in Lisbon to ask him if he had any messages for the group. He asked me to give his and Midori his wife's regards, and he hoped that everyone would study well together. These were the last words we exchanged. I always called on January 3 or 4 to wish him and his family a happy New Year, so I was very glad to have called him then. Otherwise, we would not have spoken.

There was no stone he left unturned regarding the education about all of health and all of life. Michio had a powerful presence and magnetism; people wanted to be around him. He had an amazing ability to inspire people and encourage them to pursue their dreams. People would travel great distances just to see him, and would also pay large sums of money for his counsel and guidance. He constantly tried to help people see and realize their full potential in both health and life.

It is my hope that the depth and scope of Michio's contributions will be more fully understood. Before Michio, there was no natural foods movement because there were practically no natural foods. He encouraged the development of local, natural food producers and processors, food stores, restaurants, educational, publishing, and distribution centers. High quality, natural foods as well as pickled and fermented foods are now widely available and sought after. He was largely responsible for introducing futons, the practice of acupuncture, Shiatsu massage and making the work of Masanobu Fukuoka (the author *One Straw Revolution*) known. His teachings have influenced people from all walks of life, across the entire range of professional and artistic fields.

We are on the cusp of a nutritional and biological revolution that is laying the groundwork for the age of macrobiotics. The future of macrobiotics is with those who can understand, reinterpret, and express the teachings of Michio, Aveline, and their associates for our times. Now that both Michio and Aveline have passed, I find it more important than ever to dedicate the next part of my life to mentoring the new generation of macrobiotic teachers and leaders. I want to align with those who are like-minded so that our combined expression conveys the attractiveness and timeliness of the spirit and teachings of macrobiotics.

It is hard to express the loss and sadness of Michio's passing. I find it unfortunate that his work is not more widely acknowledged and recognized today, despite how many lives have been transformed by his life. However, I feel that recognition of Michio's contributions to society will continue to grow, as will his memory. It is my hope that we, as his students and associates, can bring honor to the teachings that he and Aveline gave to us.

Remembering Michio
Melanie Brown Waxman

The first time I heard about Michio was in an old house in Bath that had slate floors and warm, stone walls. I was madly in love with my boyfriend, Patrick, who was the local macrobiotic guru. He had just cooked a delectable bowl of lentil soup with homemade tahini on wholesome bread and I was feeling totally satiated and rather high on life. It was then that I noticed Michio's *Book of Macrobiotics* sitting on the nearby table. I picked it up not really knowing that it would be the first step to an exciting, and at times, challenging journey into the world of macrobiotics. I was twenty at the time.

I remember feeling a deep surge of excitement when I realized that my health and destiny were in my hands. What a relief. Having heard many times about the bad luck of someone getting sick, those simple words were life changing.

I first met Michio at a lecture in London in 1982. He had the kind of energy that filled a room, not in an intense, knock you out way, but a quiet, embracing, power. He seemed to see things with a wry sense of humor, a chuckle about to burst forth, and a twinkle in his intelligent eyes.

The first lecture was mind blowing and not only because of Michio´s wisdom. During the question and answer session, a young girl with punky, purple spiked hair put her hand up and asked if sperm was a good source of protein. A number of people in the audience looked horrified and giggled nervously. Michio looked out the window in contemplation. He then turned and looked directly at her. "Maybe too yin. But OK for you." "And just one more question." she said. "You say that sex during menstruation is not advised, but is it okay if you really enjoy it?"

I think for once Michio was lost for words.

In my late teens, I had a lot of problems with my body image. I had an unhealthy dislike of how I looked and felt. Even though it improved when I started macrobiotics, I decided to ask Michio for some advice.

I explained to him that I felt fat and full even after eating a mouthful of food. Michio tilted his head one way and then the other as if he was looking at me from all angles.

"Like a pressure cooker?" He asked. I laughed and replied. "Very possibly." "Do you perspire?" "No." I admitted. Actually up until this point I was sort of glad that I didn't.

"Ah, so a pressure cooker with no way to let off steam." Said Michio. "Your skin is clogged." He explained. "And skin is the buffer between the inner and outer worlds. It allows Ki to flow back and forth. This is not happening smoothly for you."

One of Michio's suggestions was to scrub my skin daily with hot water. The results were astounding. My skin felt great, I began to perspire and soon felt the value of letting out the steam.

Over the years Michio gave me a lot of support, from advice on taking care of my children to adapting to living in a new country. It always amazed me that his suggestions were almost opposite to what I would have expected. Michio never told me to eat more strictly. In fact, he encouraged me to relax, enjoy, and eat more variety.

I was a very enthusiastic macrobiotic student and really threw myself into the philosophy, especially mastering the art of cooking. I developed an enormous zest for life and have since done things I never imagined possible. However, what I really did not master was natural birth control, and I somehow ended up with seven fabulous children. One time when we were driving to a seminar in Philadelphia, Michio turned to me and asked how many children I had. When I told him I had seven, he thought for a minute and said, "You are a millionaire." And no truer words were spoken as they have given me endless joy, excitement, and fun.

Michio had a tireless quality to him. He kept going under any circumstance. Michio always treated me with respect and in a gentle, caring manner. I feel incredibly lucky to have known him. He really is a wonderful example of how the thoughts, words, and actions of one person can make such a huge difference in the world. And just as from one candle, thousands more candles can sparkle, Michio's light continues to shine forth in the hearts of many, many people.

Remembering Michio
Ken Williamson

Meeting Michio in 1979 was both an end and a beginning. My life changed decisively in the years after as I dropped the vestiges of the past and set out in a new direction.

In early September of 1979 I was living in San Francisco and working in a natural food store, which at the time was the largest in the city but modest by today's standards. My curiosity about life's mysteries, coupled with a profound sense of disillusionment with modern societies, had led me to explore macrobiotics. My 21st birthday was close at hand.

My first sense of what we call macrobiotics had happened during the summer of 1977. Shortly after the death of both my father's parents within weeks of each other, after almost sixty years of marriage, my perspectives began to shift. My grandparents had come from deep Pennsylvania farming roots, and images of green fields, with abundant crops of soybeans and grain, occupied my mind all that summer. (I wish we still had their 120-acre farm today!) My way of eating drifted away from animal products and toward plant foods.

Later that year I traveled all throughout North America and landed in the Bay Area. Nominally I was on break from college! Finding a job in the natural foods store, I came to know and become friends over the next several years with people in the macrobiotic community there.

Joe Arseguel was a character beyond belief. A Basque refugee from the war torn Pyrenees of World War II, he had encountered George Ohsawa while in his twenties. (Joe was also quietly involved with the beatniks in the 1950s, and later in the 1960s, Bob Weir of the Grateful Dead would come over to eat dinner with Joe and his wife Miriam and their kids Benji and Ariege.) Joe acted as the medicine man for macrobiotics in the Bay Area during the 1970s. He had no aspirations to run a center and didn't want to be in charge of anything but everyone checked in with Joe. Just to get his blessing. He was also friends with Michio since the 1960s.

One September day in 1979 Joe called me and in his husky voice said, "Michio is coming to L.A. You should go."

"No," I said, "too busy with work. Besides how would I get there?"

"Oh. Well Robbie Swinnerton has a plane ticket he wants to give up. Paul Miksis and Frank and I are all going down on the same flight. You just take Robbie's ticket and come with us. Robbie is going to hitchhike so he can see the Pacific Coast." (Robbie was an English expatriate who had lived at the Kushi House for a while and then was staying in San Francisco for a few months.)

"Well Joe, let me think about it and I will let you know."

Days of pressure followed with pleas to just take a few days off from work all delivered in a rasping monotone usually accompanied by some intimation of doom if I did not travel to Los Angles that coming weekend.

On my 21st birthday, a Friday night, I decided to go. I called my boss and asked for a long weekend. She said OK. I called Joe and let him know I was in.

The next day, Saturday morning, was a gorgeous day for flying, clear blue skies and late summer warmth. I drank horribly strong airline coffee and had minor heart palpitations upon landing in the L.A. smog in the late morning. The older guys rented a ridiculously large black limousine to get us around L.A. for the weekend. For some reason they appointed me the driver, probably because they were paying for the car and decided my contribution was to chauffeur. Picture a lean kid with longish, dirty blond locks careening around L.A. in an absurd limo chauffeuring these salty macro guys. Then Joe announced he wanted to stay at the Chateau Marmont.

At the time the Marmont was a little, um, run down. The dive haunt of washed up actors and a selection of seedy characters, its desk staff laughed at us when we announced we wanted rooms. But the pool was great, I took a dip and then we were off to the L.A. Macro Center for three days of lectures with Michio.

Just turned twenty-one years old. Already feeling a little off center from muddy airline coffee, the surreal environs of L.A. and the very retro non-environmentalist quality of this macro expedition. Clouds of cigarette smoke in the car. The older guys arguing about directions to the Macro Center. And driving a very large gas-guzzling vehicle in the most intimidating car town in the United States. Then getting lost...

We finally found the Macro Center.

As best as I can recall, I walked in wearing a bathing suit and a cotton Indian shirt.

And we were late. Michio had already started speaking. About thirty to forty people were there.

He saw Joe and Paul and welcomed "San Francisco friends for gathering here." Michio was dressed in his usual formal attire, although I think he had taken off his jacket in deference to the heat.

Then he was talking about what hair meant on different areas of the body. Joe asked him what it meant if you had hair growing out your nose. Michio told him it means you are lazy.

Then Michio shifted and began talking about the Order of the Universe. I was sitting off to the side in what was a natural food store rearranged for the lectures. I was not in Michio's direct line of sight. He began tracing spirals on the blackboard and talking about the seven conditions of health. Something began to bother me. This was the wise Michio Kushi?

He seemed so assured with what he was saying. I tried but nothing really grabbed me until he said that the seventh condition of health was to never lie and that was difficult to do. The he grinned and went on to yin and yang.

Anger and doubt began to grow in me. How could this man be so self-assured? What could he really possibly know? Then I snapped inside…my thought was quite clear, "Who is this man and what does he know about the Order of the universe?"

As I heard my own thought, simultaneously Michio pivoted and turned to look at me. He stopped speaking, smiled, looked me right in the eyes and began to nod and nod. The grin grew larger and the nodding more accentuated. I looked right back at him and felt that somehow he had heard my question and sensed my anger at his presumptions. It was a bizarre moment. He had intuited I was upset and knew I did not fully trust what he was saying.

The crowd began to nervously laugh. They were all watching us. Michio was not distracted. I began to sense that he was seeing something more than maybe I knew about myself. I kept staring back at him. All of a sudden I liked him. He broke off and went back to his lecture.

The next day I asked him a question during his lecture, and he unexpectedly proceeded to tell me details of my relationship with a girlfriend and why that relationship was not good for me. The only thing I could say was "Which one?" And then a room full of people broke out laughing. More nodding and grins from Michio.

We became friends. So many more stories about Michio I could tell but the first day always stays in my mind.

The last time I spoke with him in depth was driving him to Newark airport after a lecture in Princeton, NJ. For some reason he began talking about what was the essence of his teaching. He said it was beginner's mind or non-credo. Which brought me right back to that Saturday afternoon in Los Angeles all those decades before.

Remembering Michio
Toyofumi Yoshida

I am Toyofumi Yoshida of Mitoku Co., Ltd. In Tokyo, Japan. I was very shocked and saddened to learn of Kushi-*sensei's* passing. I would like to offer my deepest condolences to his family. As you all—as you all know, Kushi-*sensei* left behind so many great accomplishments through his lifetime work. All of us gathered here today prove that. I am sure each one of us has special memories with Kushi-*sensei*. I would like to share a little piece of forty-seven years of history between Kushi-*sensei* and Mitoku Co., Ltd. Mr. Kazama who was founder of Mitoku, who was also my father-in-law, passed away three years ago.

Kushi-sensei and Kazama were introduced through a mutual friend. Kushi-*sensei* needed macrobiotic quality food in the United States. I was told that Kushi-*sensei* was very set in his mind and he needed macrobiotic quality food and that was that. Kazama was not so sure but he decided to believe Kushi-*sensei* and started to look for products that Kushi-*sensei* requested.

Back then in Japan, big new machines and mass production lines were everywhere. Everything was about making how many more you can make as fast as you can. Traditional food processing had all but disappeared. The Japanese yen was 360 yen against one dollar.

The dollar was worth three times more than today's rate. The yen was not traded freely. Export and import were very difficult. Against all that my father-in-law had traveled and researched all over Japan for long-fermented miso made in the traditional wooden keg; tamari and shoyu made from whole, rather than defatted soybeans; as well as wakame, kombu, and other seaweeds that were practically unknown in the U.S. at the time. Everything Kazama tried to put into shipping containers the Japanese government wanted to check.

Now traditional, natural, and organic Japanese foods are widely known all over the world. Tofu, sushi, tempura, and the other Japanese foods have become trendy. Who'd have thought non-Japanese would eat seaweed; having miso and shoyu in the regular household kitchen. Kushi-*sensei* did and believed almost fifty years ago. We have received so many ideas from Kushi-*sensei* for making good products to offer. Good products to make people happy and healthy.

I, on behalf of Mitoku, Co. Ltd., — and I think I can speak for Mr. Yuko Okada of Muso Co., Ltd., also and other companies like us, along with all the producers that are committed to make old and traditional products — will continue in our work to help Kushi-*sensei's* mission and the work he left behind.

Thank you. *Arigato Gozaimashita.*

Remembering Michio
Bettina Zumdick

Michio and Aveline Kushi taught the Macrobiotic Leadership Program in Germany in 1990. I had the privilege to attend along with sixteen fellow students. It was fascinating.

The daily schedule was full of activities: we would start the day with exercise class outside on the lawn, or taking a walk in the foothills of the mountains, or on rainy days meeting in one of the classrooms with one of our European instructors. Then breakfast, followed by a lecture until lunch. The interactive lecture would proceed like this: Michio would sit at the head of a long table—all the students gathered round. He would introduce the subject, for example, beginning with a brief explanation of yin and yang.

After the intro Michio took a book, which was positioned on the table in front of him, and handed it to the student sitting next to him. "Please describe a yin/yang complementary opposite pair that you discover in this book!" The first student elaborated: "The cover of the book versus the pages of the book," then the next: "The printed word versus blank pages or spaces." One by one, every student was asked to find another set of yin/yang pair. I happened to be sitting on the other side of Michio, which meant I was going to be the last student to find a complementary opposite pair, and I was becoming increasingly more stressed out as more and more of the pairs I could think of were voiced by my classmates. Would I manage to find a pair? I did, and perhaps this little bit of stress made us think faster and stay more concentrated.

Aveline taught cooking classes after lunch, which kept us busy almost until dinner. Michio presented the evening lectures.

The last evening Michio was with us, we were sitting in a circle in a cozy upstairs classroom. Michio gave a short talk on facial diagnosis. Then he addressed everyone present in the circle and made specific comments — about their constitution and answering individual questions. When it was my turn he pointed out that my constitution was more balanced and that I would become a brilliant teacher.

I am grateful I had the opportunity to study with Michio Kushi in person both in Europe and in the United States. Leaving the usual frame of reference of Western thinking allowed me to view both ends of the paradoxes we are faced with in life simultaneously, integrating both and rising to a third position, which allows us to stretch our consciousness further and have more fun in our life.

Michio lecturing at Kushi Institute in London in 1977

The Kushi Institute

Founded by Michio and Aveline Kushi in 1978, Kushi Institute in America has offered classes in macrobiotic education to the general public, trained several generations of teachers, counselors, and chefs, and engaged in pioneer scientific and medical research.

Located in the beautiful Berkshire mountains of western Massachusetts on 600 acres of woodland, meadows, and streams, Kushi Institute hosts year round programs, including the one-week residential Way to Health Program, the four-level Leadership Training Program, the Macrobiotic Breast Cancer Seminar and other special seminars and workshops, and holiday events and activities. The highlight of the year is the annual Macrobiotic Summer Conference featuring over 100 theory and cooking classes given by forty or more teachers from around the world.

Like many schools and nonprofit organizations, Kushi Institute (K.I.) is dependent on the goodwill and donations of its alumni, students, and friends and has started an Annual Fund to supplement revenues from tuition, rooms, and meals. Donations go

Senior Teacher Lino Stanchich (with hat) leads a class at Kushi Institute Summer Conference
Photo by Sachi Kato

toward meeting yearly expenses for operations, educational programing, and outreach. In 2014, we raised over $100,000 in donations and gifts. You can make a tax-deductible contribution to Kushi Foundation by calling (413) 623-5741, sending your check to Kushi Foundation, 198 Leland Road, Becket MA 01223, or visiting our website and donating online via PayPal or KushiInstitute.org. Help preserve the legacy and further the dream. Please donate now. Thank you for your kind consideration.

Strawberry Amazake Pudding
Photo by Sachi Kato

One Peaceful World Day

After Michio Kushi passed away on December 28, 2014, Kushi Institute honored his life and teachings by declaring his birthday, May 17, One Peaceful World Day. The first OPW Day festivities were held in Becket on the weekend of May 16 and 17, 2015 and included a special fundraising dinner for macrobiotic education and the award of the first annual Kushi Peace Prize for outstanding contribution to planetary health, peace, and sustainability.

Shizuko Yamamoto, a Shiatsu teacher and longtime associate of Michio and Aveline Kushi, received the first award posthumously. She died in Japan several weeks earlier. A delicious brunch, prayers and meditation at the Aveline Kushi Memorial Peace Park, and remembrances of Michio and Aveline by K.I. teachers and guests followed the next day.

Around the world, individuals, families, and centers celebrated OPW Day in various ways. The K.I. hopes this occasion will become a global macrobiotic holiday.

Nominations for the annual Peace Prize are welcomed. Members of the OPW Prize Committee include Edward Esko, Alex Jack, Patricio Garcia de Parades, Christina Pirello, Jane Stanchich, Bill Tara, Chico Varatojo, and Denny Waxman.

Please send your nominations to: Kushi Institute, 198 Leland Road, Becket MA 01223, 413-623-6457, www.kushiinstitute.org.

ABOUT THE CONTRIBUTORS

Cathy Albanese has been practicing macrobiotics for nearly twenty-eight years and is a Kushi Institute certified teacher, counselor, and cook. She is J.F. Rowny Professor Emerita and Research Professor at the University of California, Santa Barbara, former chair of the Department of Religious Studies there, former president of the American Academy of Religion, and author of numerous books and articles in American religious history.

Carlos Aponte, a longtime macrobiotic educator and organization development coach, is executive director of AllCare Provider Services in the Bronx. He has also held leadership positions with the Global Community Charter School, Kushi Institute, Center for Natural Healing, and New Visions for Public Schools.

Andrea Beaman is a macrobiotic teacher, holistic health coach, and natural foods chef based in New York City. She is the author of *The Whole Truth – How I Naturally Reclaimed My Health, and You Can Too!*

Jan and John Belleme studied miso making in Japan and helped found the American Miso Company. They have been writing about the culinary and medicinal qualities of miso and other Japanese foods for over twenty-five years. Their books include: *Culinary Treasures of Japan, Cooking with Japanese Foods*, and *Japanese Foods that Heal*. In recent years, John has been an organizer for Holistic Health at Sea. They live in Saluda, NC.

David Briscoe has been teaching macrobiotics and providing macrobiotic counseling for over 35 years with his wife Cindy. He is the author of *A Personal Peace: Macrobiotic Reflections on Mental and Emotional Recovery* and resides in Oroville, CA.

Simon Brown directed London's Community Health Foundation in the U.K. from 1986 to 1993. He is the author of *Practical Feng Shui, Macrobiotics for Life, Feng Shui Life Coach,* and *The Secrets of Face Reading.*

Bob Carr directed the East West Center in Cleveland for many years. He is currently farming organically in the Czech Republic.

Martha C. Cottrell, M.D. served as medical director for the Fashion Institute of Technology in New York City. She co-authored *AIDS, Macrobiotics, and Natural Immunity* with Michio Kushi. She lives in Asheville, NC.

Christian Elwell is the founder of South River Miso. He and his wife Gaella have introduced many new types of miso and also grow rice on their farm in Conway, MA.

Edward Esko studied with the Kushis from the early 1970s, served as vice president of the East West Foundation, and currently serves as associate director of Kushi Institute. He wrote *Holistic Health through Macrobiotics* and other books with Michio and is the author of *Contemporary Macrobiotics* and *Rice Field Essays.*

Wendy Esko is director of marketing research for Eden Foods in Clinton, MI. She taught cooking at Kushi Institute for many years and is the author or coauthor of many books including *Introducing Macrobiotic Cooking* with Aveline Kushi and *The Beautiful Big Brown Rice Cookbook.*

Bernard Faber is a writer and photographer based in Amsterdam. He served as associate director of the Kushi Institute of Europe.

Alice Fava practices law in Toronto. She hosted the Kushi Institute Extension Program in Toronto and is completing Level IV at the K.I. in Becket. She directs the Macrobiotic Centre of Toronto.

Olaf Fischer served as director of Kushi Institute for ten years. He gives motivational seminars and lives in the Berkshires.

Drusilla Graham is a longtime student and associate of Michio and Aveline Kushi. She lives in Connecticut.

Virginia M. Harper healed herself of Crohn's disease and is the author of *Controlling Crohn's Disease the Natural Way*. She is founder and director of You Can Heal You…One Meal at a Time, which teaches people how they can heal themselves from any digestive distress. She divides her time working from her home base in Franklin, TN and Alicante, Spain where she is a macrobiotic counselor for Sha Wellness Clinic.

Rod House, an artist and poet, has been macrobiotic for nearly a half century. He taught art at the New England College of Art, managed Gingha Japanese Macrobiotic Restaurant, and is currently a visiting faculty member of the Kushi Institute. He lives in Lee, MA.

Naomi Ichikawa is a macrobiotic teacher, counselor, and cook and founder of macrobiotics-japan.com. She divides her time between Tokyo and the Berkshires.

Alex Jack, a macrobiotic teacher, counselor, and author, served as editor-in-chief of *East West Journal*, director of the One Peaceful World Society, and founder of Amberwaves. He is executive director of Kushi Institute and co-author with Michio Kushi of *The Cancer Prevention Diet, Diet for a Strong Heart,* and *One Peaceful World* and with Aveline Kushi of *Aveline Kushi's Complete Guide to Macrobiotic Cooking*. He lives in Becket, MA.

Gale Jack is a macrobiotic teacher, counselor, and cook. She is author of *Promenade Home: Macrobiotics and Women's Health* and editor of *Women's Health Guide*. She lives in Lenox, MA.

Phil Jannetta is a macrobiotic teacher, counselor, and author living in the Pittsburgh area. He served as editor of *Order of the Universe* magazine, directed a macrobiotic center in Tokyo, and taught regularly at the Kushi Institute of Europe. He is coauthor with Michio of *Macrobiotics and Oriental Medicine*.

Woody Johnson is the founder of Woodland Energy, inventor of the HUBERT® solar energy generator, and vice president of Quantum Rabbit, LLC, a macrobiotic company doing pioneer work in transmutation. He lives in Ashburnham, MA.

Sachi Kato was born in Gifu, Japan and moved to California where she studied and worked in the field of photography. She studied at Kushi Institutes in the U.S., Europe, and Japan and taught and served as a head chef at the K.I. in Becket. Her work as a macrobiotic teacher, counselor, and author fulfills her passion for sharing nurturing food.

Bill Kaufman, a student of philosophy, was one of Michio's early students. Together with his wife, Andrea, he managed several Boston-area macrobiotic student houses where he lectured frequently along with lecturing at the East West Foundation.

Kit Kitatani healed himself of stomach cancer with the help of macrobiotics. He served as deputy secretary-general of the United Nations and founder and chairman of 2050, a nonprofit in Japan assisting development in emerging countries.

Ronald Koetzsch studied with the Kushis in the late 1960s, taught at the Kushi Institute, and authored *Macrobiotics: Yesterday and Today* and other books. He is an executive with the Rudolf Steiner schools in California.

Susan Krieger is a teacher and counselor of macrobiotics, Chinese medicine, and acupuncture. She lives in New York City.

Dennis Kucinich, a six-term Congressman from Ohio, led opposition to the wars in Iraq and Afghanistan in Congress. He also sponsored legislation to create a Department of Peace and for mandatory labeling of GMOs. He is currently an author, public speaker, and commentator for Fox TV News.

Angelica Kushi is a performer, aerialist, yoga teacher, personal chef, health coach and hang gliding pilot. She is based in NYC.

Gabriele Kushi is the founder and director of Kushi's Kitchen. She is the author of *Embracing Menopause Naturally, Eleven Macrobiotic Natural Foods Cooking DVDs,* and *The Macrobiotic Kitchen in Ten Easy Steps* with Michio Kushi. She lives in Minneapolis.

Hisao Kushi is the youngest child of Michio and Aveline Kushi and grew up in Brookline, MA. He practices law and lives in Santa Monica, CA.

Lawrence H. Kushi, Sc.D., the Kushis' second son, is the associate director for etiology and prevention research, division of research, Kaiser Permanente. His research has focused on the role of food and nutrition in the development and prevention of coronary artery disease and breast and other cancers.

Lianna Kushi, the oldest daughter of Norio and JoAnne Kushi, is marketing manager for FamilyID, a technology startup that connects families and programs online. She is active in arts and community activities and lives in Lowell, MA.

Norio Kushi, Michio and Aveline Kushi's oldest son, has a passion for wheels. He bicycled up to 90 miles a day as a child, drove a taxi, and drove a big rig throughout North America. He lives in Asheville, NC.

Phiya Kushi, the Kushis's third son, served as director of the Kushi Institute. He currently lives in Alaska at the Ionia Macrobiotic Community and travels and teachers internationally.

Sean Kushi, the oldest son of Norio and JoAnne Kushi, grew up in New England and North Carolina. He leads a life surrounded by homemade foods, arts, bicycling, and adventures to new destinations and experiences.

Janet M. Lacey, DrPH, RD, LDN, began studies of macrobiotic philosophy, integrative medicine, and cooking with Michio and Aveline Kushi in the mid-1970s. She is a professor of nutrition at West Chester University in Pennsylvania, past-chair of the Vegetarian Nutrition Dietetic Practice Group of the Academy of

Nutrition and Dietetics, and author of *Fields of Nourishment: Plant-Based Recipes with their Nutrient Profiles*.

Carol Louro is founder and director of the East West Center in New Bedford, MA and worked with Michio and Aveline for many years.

Judy and Larry MacKenney are macrobiotic teachers, counselors, and cooks. They co-directed the Way to Health program at Kushi Institute and founded Harmony Haven Healing Arts that offers hands-on health and wellness workshops. Judy healed herself of Stage IV non-Hodgkin's lymphoma with macrobiotics. They live in Nokomis, FL.

Bob Mattson is editor of *The Macrobiotic Directory* and other compilations. He lives in the Boston area.

Tom Monte served as associate editor of *East West Journal*, co-author of *Recalled by Life* with Dr. Anthony Sattilaro, and author of nearly 35 books on macrobiotics and holistic health. He teaches worldwide and lives in Amherst, MA.

Rich Myers was the head of Citizens for Dietary Choice, a 1990s advocacy group promoting nutritional freedom and choice throughout the U.S. He lives in Washington, D.C.

Gideon Nelissen, the elder son of Adelbert and Wieke Nelissen, grew up in a macrobiotic household. He is a symphony violinist in Amsterdam.

Horriah Nelissen, the eldest daughter of Adelbert and Wieke Nelissen, teaches at a Waldorf School and teaches cooking and healthcare at the Kushi Institute of Europe.

Wieke Nelissen is the co-founder and director of the Kushi Institute of Europe with her late husband Adelbert. She has taught macrobiotic cooking, women's health, and family health all over Europe for over 30 years. She has written many articles on cooking and authored the *Summer Conference 2004 Cookbook*.

Mayumi Niimi Nishimura is an international macrobiotic cooking teacher and counselor who divides her time between Japan and the United States. She taught at Kushi Institute, cooked for Madonna, and is the author of *Mayumi's Kitchen.*

Patricio Garcia de Parades was introduced to macrobiotics at the age of five by his mother, Luisa Baranda, in his native Spain. After completing studies at the Kushi Institute, he began to give cooking classes and teach in Southeast Asia, South America, and Spain. In 1998 he moved to Japan and has served as executive chef at Kushi Garden and Chaya Macrobiotic Restaurant and Education Director at the Kushi Institute of Japan.

Christina Pirello healed herself of leukemia at age twenty-six and for the last twenty-two years has been teaching cooking classes and lecturing on the power of whole, natural foods. She is the Emmy Award winning host of the PBS series *Christina Cooks* and author of six cookbooks.

Jessica Porter graduated from Kushi Institute and teaches macrobiotic cooking in Santa Monica, CA. She is the author of *The Hip Chick's Guide to Macrobiotics* and co-wrote *The Kind Diet* with Alicia Silverstone.

Michael J. Potter co-founded Eden Foods in Ann Arbor where he has served as President and Chairman since 1972. He also help found American Soy Products, Inc., America's first soymilk manufacturing facilities and the largest processor of organically grown soybeans in the world.

Sandy Pukel founded the Macrobiotic Foundation of Florida, Oakfeed Natural Foods Store, and Holistic Health at Sea. He lives in Coconut Grove, FL.

Arthur H. Robbins studied macrobiotics at the Kushi Institute and with Michio personally in the 1980s. He is a professional macrobiotic chef and a native of Quebec.

Evan Root has been active in the macrobiotic community since 1964, including working at Erewhon, the Kushis' pioneer natural foods store in Boston. Since 1981, he has worked with large groups, individuals, prison inmates, people with spiritual goals and businesses interested in productive, collaborative working relationships in a non-dualistic perspective. In 1993 he founded Kindling Point, an educational forum. He lives in Ashland, MA.

Michael Rossoff studied with Michio in the 60s and 70s, directed macrobiotic center in the Washington D.C. area for twenty years, and published *MacroMuse*. As an acupuncturist, he teaches internationally and served as dean at Atlantic University of Chinese Medicine near Asheville, NC where he lives.

Naoki Sakaguchi served as a head chef and cooking teacher at the Kushi Institute in Becket. He is currently living and teaching in Japan.

David Sergel, a native of Australia, taught at Kushi Institute for 15 years, authored The *Natural Way of Zen Shiatsu*, and offers macrobiotic services in Fairfield, CT.

Rudy Shur is founder of Avery Publications and Square One Publishers in New York. He has published many of Michio's books, including *The Macrobiotic Way, The Book of Macrobiotics,* and *Macrobiotic Home Remedies.*

Kezia Snyder, a longtime student of Michio and Aveline, is a macrobiotic cook, teacher, and counselor living in New York City.

Bill Spear, an international macrobiotic teacher, counselor, and author, is founder of The Passage, Vital Design, and Fortunate Blessings Foundation which works with refugees around the world. He is also author of *Feng Shui Made Easy* and other books and lives in Litchfield, CT.

Jane Quincannon Stanchich, licensed nutritionist, certified macrobiotic teacher, counselor, author, and chef, is an international teacher of macrobiotic natural health principles for over thirty years. She lives in Asheville, NC.

Lino Stanchich is a licensed nutritionist, author, international macrobiotic educator, and counselor with over forty-five years' experience. He is the author of *Power Eating Program, You Are How You Eat, Macrobiotic Healing Secrets,* and *Natural Kidney Health Program*, as well as a variety of tapes and videos. He lives in Asheville, NC.

Sanae Suzuki graduated from Kushi Institute, coauthored *Love, Sanae* and other books with her husband Eric, and runs the Seed restaurant in Southern California.

Bill Tara has been an advocate for macrobiotics and natural heath care since 1967. He served as vice president of Erewhon Trading Company in America and Sunwheel Natural Foods in the U.K. He founded the Community Health Foundation in London, England and directed K.I. activities in London and Boston. He edited and published *Your Face Never Lies*, based on the teachings of Michio Kushi, *Macrobiotics and Human Behavior*, and *Natural Body/Natural Mind*. He lives in Glasgow, Scotland with his wife Marlene Watson Tara, author of several macrobiotic cookbooks.

Eric Utne is the founder of *Utne Reader*. He was a student of Michio Kushi from 1969-1974. His remarks are adapted from his forthcoming memoir, to be published by Random House in 2016.

Francisco "Chico" Varatojo studied macrobiotics in Boston with Michio and is director of the Macrobiotic Institute in Lisbon. He teaches macrobiotics in many countries in Europe and was for six years chairman of the International Macrobiotic Assembly. Chico is known for his work in Portuguese prisons, teaching inmates macrobiotics, and from his attributions to TV programs, magazines and daily papers.

Denny Waxman founded Essene Market & Cafe, the first natural foods store in Philadelphia, and is a longtime macrobiotic teacher and counselor. He is the founder of the Strengthening Health Institute in Philadelphia and author of *Ten Steps To Strengthening Health* with Ruth Ann Flynn, *The Great Life Diet,* and *The Complete Macrobiotic Diet.*

Melanie Brown Waxman has worked with clients and students from all over the world. Her studies in the healing arts began in the 1980's and she went on to specialize in health education, macrobiotic cooking, coaching, writing and massage. She has lived in several countries, written six books, and is the mother of seven children.

Ken Williamson started the Macrobiotic Center of Princeton in 1982 and has since run several natural foods businesses and a macrobiotic café.

Toyufumi Yoshida is the president of Mitoku, the macrobiotic food company in Tokyo that distributes worldwide.

Bettina Zumdick, a native of Germany, is a faculty member of Kushi Institute, teaches internationally and is the author of *Authentic Foods.* She lives in Lee, MA.

Michio at his home in Brookline, Massachusetts with Shizuko Yamamoto, Aveline Kushi, William Dufty, and Cecile Levin. Photo of George Ohsawa at center.

Michio Kushi

Michio Kushi, leader of the international macrobiotic community for over a half-century, introduced natural and organic foods, alternative and complementary medicine, and novel approaches to war and peace, energy and the environment, and other planetary issues.

Born in Japan on May 17, 1926, he studied international law at Tokyo University and came to the United States in 1949. Influenced by the macrobiotic teaching of George Ohsawa, with whom he studied in Japan and later on his visits to America, Michio and his wife Aveline (1923-2001) settled in the Boston area. In the 1960s, the Kushis founded Erewhon, the pioneer natural foods company, and in the 1970s and 1980s founded the East West Foundation, *East West Journal,* Kushi Foundation, and the One Peaceful World Society. In 1985 he became General President of the World Federation of Natural Alternative Medicine, an association of 300 organizations.

Michio and Aveline traveled around the world, spreading macrobiotics and a natural way of life. They gave hundreds of seminars in Europe and Japan, and Michio led a seminar for medical experts convened by WHO (World Health Organization) on AIDS and diet in Central Africa.

Michio inspired research on the macrobiotic approach to heart disease, cancer, diabetes, and other chronic disorders at Harvard Medical School, the Framingham Heart Study, the National Institutes of Health, Center for Disease Control and Prevention, and other universities, medical associations, and government agencies. The Smithsonian Institution created a permanent Kushi Family Collection on Macrobiotics and Alternative Health Care at the National Museum of American History in Washington, D.C. in 1999 and held a gala celebration in honor of him, his wife, and the macrobiotic community. The U.S. House of Representatives unanimously passed a resolution praising his contribution to the health and well being of modern society.

Over the years, Michio authored more than fifty books on personal and planetary health, including *The Book of Macrobiotics, The Cancer Prevention Diet, The Macrobiotic Way,* and *One Peaceful World.* He received the Award of Excellence from the United Nation's Writer's Society.

Michio continued to teach and counsel actively until his death at age eighty-eight. He leaves his wife Midori, four children, fourteen grandchildren, and thousands of grateful students, families, and communities that benefited from his teachings.

We are indeed fortunate to have known Michio and Aveline Kushi. Their legacy lives on.

Made in the USA
Middletown, DE
16 July 2015